Anton von Werner.

Photogravure Berlin Photographic Co.

PRINTED ON THE HESS PRESS.

GREAT MEN AND FAMOUS WOMEN

A Series
of
Pen and Pencil Sketches
of
THE · LIVES · OF · MORE · THAN · 200
OF · THE · MOST · PROMINENT · PER-
SONAGES · IN · HISTORY

VOL. IV.

EDITED BY
CHARLES F. HORNE

NEW-YORK: SELMAR HESS · PUBLISHER

CONTENTS OF VOLUME IV.

LIST OF ILLUSTRATIONS

VOLUME IV.

PHOTOGRAVURES

WOOD-ENGRAVINGS AND TYPOGRAVURES

WILLIAM III. OF ENGLAND

(1650–1702)

WILLIAM, Prince of Orange, the third king of England of that name, born November 14, 1650, was the posthumous son of William II., Prince of Orange, and Mary Stuart, daughter of Charles I. of England. The fortunes of his childhood did not promise that greatness which he attained. His father had been thought to entertain designs hostile to the liberties of the United Provinces, and the suspicions of the father produced distrust of the son. When Cromwell dictated terms of peace to the Dutch in 1654, one of the articles insisted on the perpetual exclusion of the Prince of Orange from all the great offices formerly held by his family ; and this sentence of exclusion was confirmed, so far as Holland was concerned, thirteen years after, by the enactment of the Perpetual Edict, by which the office of Stadtholder of Holland was forever abolished. The restoration of the Stuarts, however, was so far favorable to the interests of the House of Orange, as to induce the princess-royal to petition, on her son's behalf, that he might be invested with the offices and dignities possessed by his ancestors. The provinces of Zealand, Friesland, and Guelderland warmly espoused her cause : even the States of Holland engaged to watch over his education, "that he might be rendered capable of filling the posts held by his forefathers." They formally adopted him as "a child of the state," and surrounded him with such persons as were thought likely to educate him in a manner suited to his station in a free government.

A storm broke upon Holland just as William was ripening into manhood ;

and discord at home threatened to aggravate the misfortunes of the country. The House of Orange had again become popular; and a loud cry was raised for the instant abolition of the Perpetual Edict, and for installing the young prince in all the offices enjoyed by his ancestors. The Republican party, headed by the De Witts, prevented this; but they were forced to yield to his being chosen captain-general and high-admiral. Many persons hoped that William's military rank and prospects would incline his uncle Charles II. to make common cause with the friends of liberty and independence; but the English monarch was the pensioner of the French king, and France and England jointly declared war against the States, April 7, 1672. The Dutch made large preparations; but new troops could not suddenly acquire discipline and experience. The enemy meditated, and had nearly effected, the entire conquest of the country; the populace became desperate; a total change of government was demanded; the De Witts were brutally massacred, and William was invested with the full powers of stadtholder. His fitness for this high office was soon demonstrated by the vigor and the wisdom of his measures. Maestricht was strongly garrisoned; the prince of Orange, with a large army, advanced to the banks of the Issel; the Dutch fleet cruised off the mouth of the Thames, to prevent the naval forces of England and France from joining. The following year, 1763, Louis XIV. took Maestricht; while the Prince of Orange, not having forces sufficient to oppose the French army, employed himself in retaking other towns from the enemy. New alliances were formed; and the prince's masterly conduct not only stopped the progress of the French, but forced them to evacuate the province of Utrecht. In 1674 the English Parliament compelled Charles II. to make peace with Holland. The Dutch signed separate treaties with the Bishop of Munster and the Elector of Cologne. The gallantry of the prince had so endeared him to the States of Holland, that the offices of stadtholder and captain-general were declared hereditary in his male descendants. Meanwhile he continued to display both courage and conduct in various military operations against the French. The battle of Seneffe was desperately fought. After sunset, the conflict was continued by the light of the moon; and darkness, rather than the exhaustion of the combatants, put an end to the contest, and left the victory undecided. The veteran Prince of Condé gave a candid and generous testimonial to the merit of his young antagonist: "The Prince of Orange," said he, "has in every point acted like an old captain, except in venturing his life too much like a young soldier."

In 1675 the sovereignty of Guelderland and of the county of Zutphen was offered to William, with the title of duke, which was asserted to have been formerly vested in his family. Those who entertained a bad opinion of him, and attributed whatever looked like greatness in his character to ambition rather than patriotism, insinuated that he was himself the main-spring of this manifest intrigue. He had at least prudence enough to deliberate on the offer, and to submit it to the judgment of the States of Holland, Zealand, and Utrecht. They viewed with jealousy the aristocratic dignity, and he wisely refused it. This forbearance was rewarded by the province of Utrecht, which adopted the precedent of Holland, in voting the stadtholdership hereditary in the heirs-male of his body.

The campaign of 1675 passed without any memorable event in the Low Countries. In the following year hopes of peace were held out from the meeting of a congress at Nimeguen ; but the articles of peace were to be determined rather by the events of the campaign than by the deliberations of the negotiators. The French took Condé and several other places ; the Prince of Orange, bent on retaliation, sat down before Maestricht, the siege of which he urged impetuously ; but the masterly movements of the enemy, and a scarcity of forage, frustrated his plans. Aire had already been taken ; the Duke of Orleans had made himself master of Bouchain ; Marshal Schomberg, to whom Louis had intrusted his army on retiring to Versailles, was on the advance ; and it was found expedient to raise the siege of Maestricht. It was now predicted that the war in Flanders would be unfortunate in its issue ; but the Prince of Orange, influenced by the mixed motives of honor, ambition, and animosity, kept the Dutch Republic steady to the cause of its allies, and refused to negotiate a separate peace with France. In October, 1677, he came to England, and was graciously received by the king, his uncle. His marriage with Mary, eldest daughter of the Duke of York, was the object of his visit. That event gave general satisfaction at the time ; the consequences which arose from it were unsuspected by the most far-sighted. At first the king was disinclined to the match ; then neutral ; and at last favorable, in the hope of engaging William to fall in with his designs, and listen to the separate proposals of the French monarch. The prince, on his part, was pleased with the prospect, because he expected that the King of England would, at length, find himself obliged to declare against Louis, and because he imagined that the English nation would be more strongly engaged in his interest, and would adopt his views with respect to the war. In this he was disappointed, though the Parliament was determined on forcing the king to renounce his alliance with Louis. But the States had gained no advantage commensurate with the expense and danger of the contest in which they were engaged, and were inclined to conclude a separate treaty. Mutual discontent among the allies led to the dissolution of the confederacy, and a peace advantageous to France was concluded at Nimeguen in 1678 ; but causes of animosity still subsisted. The Prince of Orange, independent of political enmity, had now personal grounds of complaint against Louis, who deeply resented the zeal with which William had espoused the liberties of Europe and resisted his aggressions. He could neither bend so haughty a spirit to concessions, nor warp his integrity even by the suggestions of his dominant passion, ambition. But it was in the power of the French monarch to punish this obstinacy, and by oppressing the inhabitants of the principality of Orange, to take a mean revenge on an innocent people for the imputed offences of their sovereign. In addition to other injuries, when the Duchy of Luxembourg was invaded by the French troops, the commanding officer had orders to expose to sale all the lands, furniture, and effects of the Prince of Orange, although they had been conferred on him by a formal decree of the

States of the country. Whether to preserve the appearance of justice, or merely as an insult, Louis summoned the Prince to appear before his Privy Council in 1682, by the title of *Messire Guillaume Comte de Nassau*, living at The Hague in Holland. In the emergency occasioned by the probability of the Dutch frontier being attacked in 1683, the Prince of Orange exerted all his influence to procure an augmentation of the troops of the republic; but he had the mortification to experience an obstinate resistance in several of the States, especially in that of Holland, headed by the city of Amsterdam. His coolness and steadiness, qualities invaluable in a statesman, at length prevailed, and he was enabled to carry his measures with a high hand.

The accession of James II. to the throne of Great Britain, in 1685, was hailed as an opportunity for drawing closer both the personal friendship and the political alliance between the stadtholder of the one country and the king of the other; but a totally different result took place. The headstrong violence of James brought about a coalition of parties to resist him; and many of the English nobility and gentry concurred in an application to the Prince of Orange for assistance. At this crisis, William acted with such circumspection as befitted his calculating character. The nation was looking forward to the prince and princess as its only resource against tyranny, civil and ecclesiastical. Were the presumptive heir to concur in the offensive measures, he must partake with the king of the popular hatred. Even the continental alliances, which William was setting his whole soul to establish and improve, would become objects of suspicion to the English, and Parliament might refuse to furnish the necessary funds. Thus by one course he might risk the loss of a succession which was awaiting him; by an opposite conduct, he might profit by the king's indiscretion, and even forestall the time when the throne was to be his in the course of nature. The birth of a son and heir, in June, 1688, seemed to turn the scale in favor of James; but the affections of his people were not to be recovered; it was even asserted that the child was supposititious. This event, therefore, confirmed William's previous choice of the side which he was to take; and his measures were well and promptly concerted. A declaration was dispersed throughout Great Britain, setting forth the grievances of the kingdom, and announcing the immediate introduction of an armed force from abroad, for the purpose of procuring the convocation of a free parliament. In a short time, full four hundred transports were hired; the army rapidly fell down the rivers and canals from Nimeguen; the artillery, arms, stores, and horses were embarked; and, on October 21, 1668, the prince set sail from Helvoetsluys, with a fleet of near five hundred vessels, and an army of more than fourteen thousand men. He was compelled to put back by a storm; but, on a second attempt, he had a prosperous voyage, while the king's fleet was wind-bound. He arrived at Torbay on November 4th, and disembarked on the 5th, the anniversary of the gunpowder treason. The remembrance of Monmouth's ill-fated rebellion prevented the western people from joining him; but at length several persons of consideration took up the cause, and an association was formed for its support. At this

GLINDONI PINXIT.

COUNCIL OF WAR AFTER THE LANDING OF WILLIAM OF ORANGE.

last hour James expressed his readiness to make concessions; but it was too late; they were looked on only as tokens of fear; the confidence of the people in the king's sincerity was gone forever. But, how much soever his conduct deserved censure, his distresses entitled him to pity. One daughter was the wife of his opponent; the other threw herself into the hands of the insurgents. In the agony of his heart the father exclaimed, "God help me! my own children have forsaken me!" He sent the queen and infant prince to France. Public affairs were in the utmost confusion, and seemed likely to remain so while he stayed in the island. After many of those perplexing adventures and narrow escapes which generally befall dethroned royalty, he at length succeeded in embarking for the continent.

The prince issued circular letters for the election of members to a convention, which met January 22, 1689. It appeared at once that the House of Commons, agreeably to the prevailing sentiments both of the nation and of those in present authority, was chiefly chosen from among the Whig party. The throne was declared vacant by the following vote: "That King James the Second, having endeavored to subvert the constitution of the kingdom by breaking the original contract between king and people; and having, by the advice of Jesuits and other wicked persons, violated the fundamental laws, and withdrawn himself out of the kingdom, has abdicated the government, and that the throne is thereby vacant." By the national consent, the vacancy was supplied by his daughter Mary and her husband William jointly.

The Prince of Orange lost no time in apprising the States-General of his accession to the British throne. He assured them of his persevering endeavors to promote the well-being of his native country, which he was so far from abandoning, that he intended to retain his high offices in it. War with France was renewed early in 1689 by the States, supported by the house of Austria and some of the German princes; nor was it difficult for William to procure the concurrence of the English Parliament, when the object was the humiliation of France and her arbitrary sovereign. In the spring of 1689, James landed in Ireland with a French force, and was received by the Catholics with marks of strong attachment. Marshal Schomberg was sent to oppose him, but was able to effect little during the campaign of that year. William, in the meantime, had been successful in suppressing a Jacobite insurrection in Scotland, and embarked for Ireland with a reinforcement in the summer of 1690. He immediately marched against James, who was strongly posted on the River Boyne. Schomberg passed the river in person, and put himself at the head of a corps of French Protestants. Pointing to the enemy, he said, "Gentlemen, behold your persecutors!" With these words he advanced to the attack, but was killed by a random shot from the French regiments. The death of this general was near proving fatal to the English army; but William retrieved the fortune of the day, and totally dispersed the opposite force. In this engagement the Irish lost 1,500 men, and the English about one-third of that number.

Disturbances again took place among the Jacobites in the Scotch Highlands.

14

A simultaneous insurrection was planned in both kingdoms, while a descent from the French coast was to have divided the attention of the friends of government ; but the defeat of the French fleet near Cape La Hogue, in 1692, frustrated this combined attempt, and relieved the nation from the dread of civil war. In 1691 the king had placed himself at the head of the Grand Alliance against France, of which he had been the prime mover ; he was, therefore, absent on the continent during the dangers to which his new kingdom was exposed. His repeated losses in the following campaigns rather impaired than enhanced his military renown, though they increased his already high reputation for personal courage. The death of Queen Mary, which took place early in 1695, proved a severe calamity, both to the king and the nation. She had been a vigilant guardian of her husband's interests, which were constantly exposed to hazard by the conflicts of party and by the disadvantages under which he labored as a foreigner. In 1696 a congress was opened at Ryswick, to negotiate a general peace ; and William did not interpose any obstacles. In the following year the treaty was concluded.

The King of Spain's death led to the last event of great importance in William's reign. The powers of Europe had arranged plans to prevent the accumulation of the Spanish possessions in the houses of Bourbon and Austria ; but the French king violated all his solemn pledges, by accepting the deceased monarch's will in favor of his own grandson, the Duke of Anjou. In consequence of this breach of faith, preparations were made by England and Holland for a renewal of war with France ; but a fall from his horse prevented William from further pursuing his military career, and the glory of reducing Louis XIV. within the bounds of his own kingdom was left to be earned by the generals of Queen Anne. The king was nearly recovered from the lameness consequent on his fall, when fever supervened ; and he died March 8, 1702, in the fifty-second year of his age and thirteenth of his reign.

The character of King William has been drawn with all the exaggeration of panegyric and obloquy by opposing partisans. His native country owes him a lasting debt of gratitude, as the second founder of its liberty and independence ; and his adopted country is bound to uphold his memory, as its champion and deliverer from civil and religious thraldom. In short, the attachment of the English nation to constitutional rights and liberal government may be measured by its adherence to the principles established at the Revolution of 1688 and its just estimate of that sovereign and those statesmen who placed the liberties of Great Britain on a solid and lasting foundation.

ISAAC NEWTON

By John Stoughton, D.D.

(1642–1727)

As a literary philosopher, Bacon surpasses Newton; as an experimental philosopher, Newton surpasses Bacon. Newton's works contain nothing in point of style and illustration comparable to Bacon's essays; Bacon's works contain nothing in point of scientific discovery and mathematical calculation comparable to Newton's "Optics" and "Principia."

Newton has been the great glory of the Royal Society; and the Royal Society is justly proud of its most illustrious ornament. He joined it in January, 1674, when he was excused the ordinary payment of a shilling a week, "on account of his low circumstances as he represented." In 1703 he was elected to the presidential chair, which he continued to occupy until his death, in 1727. Characteristic mementoes of him are preserved among the Royal Society's treasures. There is a solar dial made by the boy Isaac, when, instead of studying his grammar and learning Virgil and Horace, he was busy making windmills and water-clocks. We fancy we see him going along the road to Grantham on a market day with the old servant whom his mother sent to take care of him, and then stopping by the wayside to watch the motions of a water-wheel, reflecting upon the mechanical principles involved in the simplest contrivances. It is pleasant, with our knowledge of what he afterward became, to sit down on the green bank by the river side, and to speculate upon the ignorance of the old servant who accompanied him, and of the farmers they saluted by the way, as to the illustrious destiny which awaited the widow's son who lived in the manor house of Woolsthorpe. The reflecting telescope, preserved along with the dial, was made by Newton in his thirtieth year, and reminds us of the deep mathematical studies he was then pursuing at Cambridge. The autograph MS. of the "Principia," also in the possession of the Royal Society, gives increased vividness to the picture of this extraordinary person in his study, solving mysterious problems, and suggesting others still more mysterious; and then the lock of silvery hair adds the last touch to fancy's picture—like a stroke of the pencil which, when a portrait is nearly complete, gives life and expression to the whole.

Newton was portly but not tall, his silvery locks were abundant without any baldness, and his eyes were sparkling and piercing, though perhaps they failed to indicate the profound genius which through them looked into the secrets of the universe.   Wonderful humility blended with his intellectual greatness.   To other men he seemed a spirit of higher rank, having almost superhuman faculties of mental vision, wont to soar into regions which the vulture's eye hath never seen ; to himself he was but a boy playing with the shells on the seashore, while the ocean lay undiscovered before him.   Others were taken up with what Newton accomplished, Newton was taken up with what remained to be done.   So it is ever with the highest genius ; the broader the range of view, the wider the horizon of mystery.   He who understands more than others is conscious beyond others of what still remains to be understood.

Isaac Newton was born at Woolsthorpe, in Lincolnshire, on December 25, 1642, one year after the death of Galileo, and just as England was being plunged into the confusion and miseries of civil war.   Strange to say, as a lad, at first he was inattentive to study ; but being struck a severe blow by a school-fellow, he strangely retaliated by determining to get above him in the class, which he accomplished, and ere long became head of the school.   His play hours were employed in mechanical contrivances, and a windmill in the course of erection on the Grantham road was an object of intense curiosity and a source of immense instruction.   He soon had a windmill of his own, at the top of the house in which he lived.   He had also a water-clock in his bedroom, and a mechanical carriage in the parlor, in which he could wheel himself.   Paper kites and paper lanterns were his favorite toys.   In the yard of the house he traced on a wall the movements of the sun by means of fixed pins ; the contrivance received the name of " Isaac's dial," and was a standard of time to the country people in the neighborhood.

He entered Trinity College, Cambridge, June 5, 1660, just as England was astir with restoration festivities, and he soon devoted himself to mathematical studies.   Euclid he took in at a glance, and afterward proceeded to master Descartes's geometry.   Isaac Barrow, then Lucasian Professor of Mathematics, became his friend and tutor ; and the pupil repaid the master's kind attention by services rendered to him in connection with his optical lectures.   In 1669, Newton succeeded Barrow in his professorship.   He rose to eminence in the university, and in 1688 was chosen its representative in the Convention parliament.   In 1695 he was appointed Warden of the Mint, and was promoted to the Mastership in 1699.   After his appointment to a government office he left Cambridge to reside in London, and occupied for a time a house in Jermyn Street.   From 1710 till two years before his death he lived close to Leicester Square.   Next door to Orange Street Chapel there stands an old house which has seen a good many changes, and is identified as the abode of Sir Isaac, who had been knighted by Queen Anne in 1705.   We visited it many years ago.   The part of the house most intimately associated with his name is the little observatory perched on the roof.   We were permitted to ascend into that spot, to see it desecrated by its present use, for there we found a shoemaker busy at his toil.   A glass cupola

LOUDAN, FECIT.

NEWTON ANALYSING THE RAY OF LIGHT.

probably crowned the observatory in Newton's time, and evidently there was a window in each of the four walls. So here he looked out on the London of nearly a century and a half ago, hardly less crowded and smoky about the neighborhood than now. Overhead, where Newton turned his eyes with most interest, we know it was just the same ; the same beautiful stars shining out on a cold winter's night, the same planets sailing along the same blue ocean, the same moon throwing its light over the same old city. What observations, keen and searching, what calculations, intricate and profound, what speculations, far-reaching and sublime, must there have been, when one of the most gifted of mortals from that spot looked out upon the heavens, and in thought went forth on voyages of discovery into the distant regions of the universe ! At the calm, still hour of midnight, Sirius watching over the city of sleepers, Jupiter carrying his brilliant lamp along his ancient pathway, every one of the luminaries in the place appointed by Him who calleth them all by their names—there stood the thoughtful man, with his reflecting telescope, occupied with thoughts which we common mortals in vain endeavor to conjecture.

The first department in the field which Newton explored with characteristic success was the study of optics. Philosophers were busy with inquiries into the nature of light. It had been long believed that every colored ray is equally refracted when passing through a lens. Newton determined to analyze the prismatic hues. He made a hole in a window-shutter, and darkening the room, let in a portion of light, which he passed through a prism. The *white* sunbeam formed a circular image on the opposite wall, but the *prismatic colors* formed an image five times as long as it was broad. He was curious to know how this came to pass. Satisfied that the length of the image in the latter case did not arise from any irregularity in his glass, or from any differences in the incidence of light from different parts of the sun's disk, or from any curvature in the direction of the rays, he concluded, after thorough reflection, that light is not *homogeneous*, but that it consists of rays of diverse refrangibility. The red hue he saw was less refracted than the orange, the orange less refracted than the yellow, and the violet more than any of the rest. These important conclusions he applied in the construction of the first reflecting telescope ever used in the survey of the heavens, and an instrument is preserved in Trinity College Library bearing the inscription, "Invented by Sir Isaac Newton, and made with his own hands, 1671."

At the request of the Royal Society, he published in the "Transactions" an account of his optical discoveries, and proved that white light is a compound of seven prismatic colors.

Everybody is familiar with the story of Newton's watching the apple fall from the tree. The tradition is fondly cherished on the spot where the philosopher is said to have been struck by the fact. The *law* by which the apple falls, not the *reason* which underlies the law, formed the subject of Newton's reflections, and led to the grandest of modern discoveries. The unknown cause of the apple's descent is the unknown cause of the planet's motion. That was the truth, simple and grand, which he brought to light and inculcated on the world. He undertook long calculations which he expected would prove this theory, but they failed to give the desired result. He consequently for a time desisted from the inquiry and turned his attention to other subjects. The error in Newton's first calculation arose from his taking the radius of the earth according to the received notion that a degree measured sixty miles, whereas Picard had determined it to be sixty-nine and a half miles. This was mentioned at a meeting of the Royal Society in 1682, at which Newton was present. "It immediately struck him that the value of the earth's radius was the erroneous element in his first calculation. With a feverish interest in this result, little imagined by those present, he hurried home, resumed his calculation with the new value, and having proceeded some way in it, was so overpowered by nervous agitation at its anticipated result, that he was unable to go on, and requested a friend to finish it for him, when it came out, *exactly establishing the inverse square* as the true measure of the moon's gravitation, and thus furnishing the key to the whole system." Hence proceeded Newton's immortal work, the "Principia."

The sublimest conclusion which Newton drew from his cautious and successful investigations of the laws of nature is put, with his characteristic humility, in the form of a query : "These things being rightly described, does it not appear from the phenomena that there is a Being incorporeal, living, intelligent, omnipresent, who, in infinite space (as it were in His sensory), sees the things themselves intimately, and thoroughly perceives them, and comprehends them wholly by their immediate presence to Himself ? "

Newton spent his last days in Kensington. "I was, Sunday night," says his nephew, "March 7, 1725, at Kensington, with Sir Isaac Newton in his lodgings, just after he was come out of a fit of the gout, which he had in both of his feet for the first time, in the eighty-third year of his age. He was better after it, and had his health clearer and memory stronger than I had known them for some years." A year later the same diarist says : "April 15, 1726. I passed the whole day with Sir Isaac Newton, at his lodgings, Orbell's Buildings, Kensington, which was the last time I saw him." The house was lately in existence, situated in what is called Bullingham Place, retaining, when we visited it, a mansion-like aspect, with a large garden and tall trees. There he died, March 20, 1727, having on the previous day been able to read the newspaper and to hold a long conversation with Dr. Mead.

His body was laid in state in the Jerusalem Chamber, and then buried in Westminster Abbey.

PETER THE GREAT

(1672–1725)

At the close of the sixteenth century, the dominions of Russia, or Muscovy, as it was then more generally called, were far thrown back from the more civilized nations of southern Europe, by the intervention of Lithuania, Livonia, and other provinces now incorporated in the Russian empire, but then belonging either to Sweden or Poland. The Czar of Muscovy, therefore, possessed no political weight in the affairs of Europe, and little intercourse existed between the court of Moscow and the more polished potentates whom it affected to despise as barbarians, even for some time after the accession of the reigning dynasty, the house of Romanoff, in 1613, and the establishment of a more regular government than had previously been known. We only read occasionally of embassies being sent to Moscow, in general for the purpose of arranging commercial relations. From this state of insignificance, Peter, the first Emperor of Russia, raised his country, by introducing into it the arts of peace, by establishing a well-organized and disciplined army in the place of a lawless body of tumultuous mutineers, by creating a navy, where scarce a merchant vessel existed before, and, as the natural result of these changes, by important conquests on both the Asiatic and European frontiers of his hereditary dominions. For these services his countrymen bestowed on him, yet living, the title of Great; and it is well deserved, whether we look to the magnitude of those services, the difficulty of carrying into effect his benevolent designs, which included nothing less than the remodelling a whole people, or the grasp of mind and the iron energy of will, which were necessary to conceive such projects and to overcome the difficulties which beset them. It will not vitiate his claim to the epithet that his manners were coarse and boisterous, his amusements often ludicrous and revolting to a polished taste; if that claim be questionable, it is because he who aspired to be the reformer of others was unable to control the violence of his own passions.

The Czar Alexis, Peter's father, was actuated by somewhat of the spirit which so distinguished the son. He endeavored to introduce the European discipline into his armies ; he had it much at heart to turn the attention of the Russians to maritime pursuits ; and he added the fine provinces of Plescow and Smolensko to his paternal dominions.   At the death of Alexis, in 1677, Peter was but five years old.   His eldest brother Theodore succeeded to the throne.   Theodore died after a reign of five years, and named Peter his successor, passing over the second brother, Ivan, who was weak-minded.   Their ambitious sister, Sophia, stirred the strelitzi, or native militia, to revolt in favor of Ivan, and Peter and his mother had to take refuge in the Troitski convent.   This retreat being discovered, they were driven for protection to the church altar itself, where the religion or superstition of the wild soldiery saved the intended victims.   We pass in silence over the remaining intrigues and insurrections which troubled the young czar's minority.   It was not until the close of the year 1689, in the eighteenth year of his age, that he finally shook off the trammels of his ambitious sister, and assumed in reality, as well as in name, the direction of the state.   How he had been qualified for this task by education does not clearly appear ; but even setting aside the stories which attribute to his sister the detestable design of leading him into all sorts of excess, and especially drunkenness, with the hope of ruining both his constitution and intellect, it is probable that no pains whatever had been taken to form his intellect or manners for the station which he was to occupy. One of the few anecdotes told of his early life is, that being struck by the appearance of a boat on the river Yausa, which runs through Moscow, and noticing it to be of different construction from the flat-bottomed vessels commonly in use, he was led to inquire into the method of navigating it.   It had been built for the Czar Alexis by a Dutchman, who was still in Moscow.   He was immediately sent for ; he rigged and repaired the boat, and under his guidance the young prince learned how to sail her, and soon grew passionately fond of his new amusement. He had five small vessels built at Plescow, on the lake Peipus ; and not satisfied with this fresh-water navigation, hired a ship at Archangel, in which he made a voyage to the coast of Lapland.   In these expeditions his love of sailing was nourished into a passion which lasted through life.   He prided himself upon his practical skill as a seaman ; and both at this time and afterward exposed himself and his friends to no small hazard by his rashness in following this favorite pursuit.

The first serious object of Peter's attention was to reform the army.   In this he was materially assisted by a Swiss gentleman named Lefort ; at whose suggestion he raised a company of fifty men, who were clothed and disciplined in the European manner, the Russian army at that time being little better than a tribe of Tartars.   As soon as the little corps was formed, Peter caused himself to be enrolled in it as a private soldier.   It is a remarkable trait in the character of the man, that he thought no condescension degrading which forwarded any of his ends.   In the army he entered himself in the lowest rank, and performed successively the duties of every other ; in the navy he went still further, for he insisted on performing the menial duties of the lowest cabin-boy, rising step by step, till he was qualified to rate as an able seaman.   Nor was this done merely

STEUBEN PINXIT.

THE LIFE OF PETER THE GREAT SAVED AT THE FOOT OF THE ALTAR.

for the sake of singularity; he had resolved that every officer of the sea or land service should enter in the lowest rank of his profession, that he might obtain a practical knowledge of every task or manœuvre which it was his duty to see properly executed; and he felt that his nobility might scarcely be brought to submit to what in their eyes would be a degradation, except by the personal example of the czar himself. Meanwhile he had not been negligent of the other arm of war; for a number of Dutch and Venetian workmen were employed in building gunboats and small ships of war at Voronitz, on the river Don, intended to secure the command of the Sea of Azof, and to assist in capturing the strong town of Azof, then held by the Turks. The possession of this place was of great importance, from its situation at the mouth of the Don, commanding access to the Mediterranean Sea. His first military attempts were accordingly directed against it, and he succeeded in taking it in 1696.

In the spring of the ensuing year, the empire being tranquil and the young czar's authority apparently established on a safe footing, he determined to travel into foreign countries, to view with his own eyes, and become personally and practically familiar with the arts and institutions of refined nations. There was a grotesqueness in his manner of executing this design, which has tended, more probably than even its real merit, to make it one of the common-places of history. Every child knows how the Czar of Muscovy worked in the dock-yard of Saardam in Holland, as a common carpenter. In most men this would have been affectation; and perhaps there was some tinge of that weakness in the earnestness with which Peter handled the axe, obeyed the officers of the dock-yard, and in all points of outward manners and appearance, put himself on a level with the shipwrights who were earning their daily bread. It seems, however, to have been the turn of Peter's mind always to begin at the beginning; a sound maxim, though here, perhaps, pushed beyond reasonable bounds. And his abode and occupations in Holland formed only part of an extensive plan. On quitting Russia he sent sixty young Russians to Venice and Leghorn to learn ship-building and navigation, and especially the construction and management of galleys moved by oars, which were so much used by the Venetian republic. Others he sent into Holland, with similar instructions; others into Germany, to study the art of war, and make themselves well acquainted with the discipline and tactics of the German troops. So that while his personal labor at Saardam may have been stimulated in part by affectation of singularity, in part, perhaps, by a love of bodily exertion common in men of his busy and ardent temper, it would be unjust not to give him credit for higher motives; such as the desire to become thoroughly acquainted with the art of ship-building, which he thought so important, and to set a good example of diligence to those whom he had sent out on a similar voyage of education.

Peter remained nine months in Holland, the greatest part of which he spent in the dock-yard of Saardam. He displayed unwearied zeal in seeking out and endeavoring to comprehend everything of interest in science and art, especially in visiting manufactories. In January, 1698, he sailed for London in an English man-of-war, sent out expressly to bring him over. His chief object was to perfect himself in the higher branches of ship-building. With this view he occupied Mr. Evelyn's house, adjoining the dock-yard of Deptford; and there remain in that gentleman's journal some curious notices of the manners of the czar and his household, which were of the least refined description. During his stay he showed the same earnestness in inquiring into all things connected with the maritime and commercial greatness of the country, as before in Holland; and he took away nearly five hundred persons in his suite, consisting of naval captains, pilots, gunners, surgeons, and workmen in various trades, especially those connected with the naval service. In England, without assuming his rank, he ceased to wear the attire and adopt the habits of a common workman; and he had frequent intercourse with William III., who is said to have conceived a strong liking for him, notwithstanding the uncouthness of his manners. Kneller painted a portrait of him for the king, which is said to have been a good likeness.

He left London in April, 1698, and proceeded to Vienna, principally to inspect the Austrian troops, then esteemed among the best in Europe. He had intended to visit Italy; but his return was hastened by the tidings of a dangerous insurrection having broken out, which, though suppressed, seemed to render a longer absence from the seat of government inexpedient. The insurgents were chiefly composed of the Russian soldiery, abetted by a large party who thought everything Russian good, and hated and dreaded the czar's innovating temper. Of those who had taken up arms, many were slain in battle; the rest, with many persons of more rank and consequence, suspected of being implicated in the revolt, were retained in prison until the czar himself should decide their fate. Numerous stories of his extravagant cruelties on this occasion have been told, which may safely be passed over as unworthy of credit. It is certain, however, that considerable severity was shown. This insurrection led to the complete remodelling of the Russian army, on the same plan which had already been partially adopted.

During the year 1699 the czar was chiefly occupied by civil reforms. According to his own account, as published in his journal, he regulated the press, caused translations to be published of various treatises on military and mechanical science and history; he founded a school for the navy; others for the study of the Latin, German, and other languages; he encouraged his subjects to cultivate foreign trade, which before they had absolutely been forbidden to do under pain of death; he altered the Russian calendar, in which the year began on September 1st, to agree in that point with the practice of other nations; he broke through the Oriental custom of not suffering women to mix in general society; and he paid sedulous attention to the improvement of his navy on the river Don. We have the testimony of Mr. Deane, an English ship-builder, that the czar had turned his manual labors to good account, who states in a letter to England, that "the czar has set up a ship of sixty guns, where he is both foreman and master-builder; and, not to flatter him, I'll assure your lordship it will be the best ship among them, and it is all from his own draught : how he framed her together, and how he made the moulds, and in so short a time as he did, is really wonderful."

He introduced an improved breed of sheep from Saxony and Silesia ; despatched engineers to survey the different provinces of his extensive empire ; sent persons skilled in metallurgy to the various districts in which mines were to be found ; established manufactories of arms, tools, stuffs ; and encouraged foreigners skilled in the useful arts to settle in Russia, and enrich it by the produce of their industry.

We cannot trace the progress of that protracted contest between Sweden and Russia, in which the short-lived greatness of Sweden was broken : we can only state the causes of the war and the important results to which it led. Peter's principal motive for engaging in it was his leading wish to make Russia a maritime and commercial nation. To this end it was necessary that she should be possessed of ports, of which, however, she had none but Archangel and Azof, both most inconveniently situated, as well in respect of the Russian empire itself, as of the chief commercial nations of Europe. On the waters of the Baltic Russia did not possess a foot of coast. Both sides of the Baltic, both sides of the Gulf of Finland, the country between the head of that gulf and the Lake Ladoga, including both sides of the River Neva, and the western side of Lake Ladoga itself, and the northern end of Lake Peipus, belonged to Sweden. In the year 1700, Charles XII. being but eighteen years of age, Denmark, Poland, and Russia, which had all of them suffered from the ambition of Sweden, formed a league to repair their losses, presuming on the weakness usually inherent in a minority. The object of Russia was the restoration of the provinces of Ingria, Carelia, and Wiborg, the country round the head of the Gulf of Finland, which formerly had belonged to her ; that of Poland, was the recovery of Livonia and Esthonia, the greater part of which had been ceded by her to Charles XI. of Sweden. Denmark was to obtain Holstein and Sleswick. But Denmark and Poland very soon withdrew, and left Russia to encounter Sweden single-handed. To this she was entirely unequal ; her army, the bulk of it undisciplined, and even the disciplined part unpractised in the field, was no match for the veteran troops of Sweden, the terror of Germany. In the battle of Narva, a town on the river which runs out of the Peipus Lake, fought November 30, 1700, 9,000 Swedes defeated signally near forty thousand Russians, strongly intrenched and with a numerous artillery. Had Charles prosecuted his success with vigor, he might probably have delayed for many years the rise of Russia ; but whether from contempt or mistake he devoted his whole attention to the war in Poland, and left the czar at liberty to recruit and discipline his army, and improve the resources of his kingdom. In these labors he was most diligent. His troops, practised in frequent skirmishes with the Swedes quartered in Ingria and Livonia, rapidly improved, and on the celebrated field of Pultowa broke forever the power of Charles XII. This decisive action did not take place until July 8, 1709. The interval was occupied by a series of small, but important additions to the Russian territory. In 1701–2, great part of Livonia and Ingria were subdued, including the banks of the Neva, where on May 27, 1703, the city of St. Petersburg was founded. It was not till 1710 that the conquest of Courland, with the remainder of Livonia, including the important harbors of Riga and Revel, gave to Russia that free navigation of the Baltic Sea which Peter had longed for as the greatest benefit which he could confer upon his country.

After the battle of Pultowa Charles fled to Turkey, where he continued for some years, shut out from his own dominions, and intent chiefly on spiriting the Porte to make war on Russia. In this he succeeded; but hostilities were terminated almost at their beginning by the battle of the Pruth, fought July 20, 1711, in which the Russian army, not mustering more than forty thousand men, and surrounded by five times that number of Turks, owed its preservation to Catherine, first the mistress, at this time the wife, and finally the acknowledged partner and successor of Peter on the throne of Russia. By her coolness and prudence, while the czar, exhausted by fatigue, anxiety, and self-reproach, was laboring under nervous convulsions, to which he was liable throughout life, a treaty was concluded with the vizier in command of the Turkish army, by which the Russians preserved indeed life, liberty, and honor, but were obliged to resign Azof, to give up the forts and burn the vessels built to command the sea bearing that name, and to consent to other stipulations, which must have been very bitter to the hitherto successful conqueror. Returning to the seat of government, his foreign policy for the next few years was directed to breaking down the power of Sweden, and securing his new metropolis by prosecuting his conquests on the northern side of the Gulf of Finland. Here he was entirely successful; and the whole of Finland itself, and of the gulf, fell into his hands. These provinces were secured to Russia by the peace of Nieustadt, in 1721. Upon this occasion the senate or state assembly of Russia requested him to assume the title of Emperor of all the Russias, with the adjunct of Great, and Father of his Country.

If our sketch of the latter years of Peter's life appears meagre and unsatisfactory, it is to be recollected that the history of that life is the history of a great empire, which it would be vain to condense within our limits, were they greater than they are. Results are all that we are competent to deal with. From the peace of Nieustadt, the exertions of Peter, still unremitting, were directed more to consolidate and improve the internal condition of the empire, by watching over the changes which he had already made, than to effect farther conquests, or new revolutions in policy or manners. He died February 8, 1725, leaving no surviving male issue. Some time before he had caused the Empress Catherine to be solemnly crowned and associated with him on the throne, and to her he left the charge of fostering those schemes of civilization which he had originated.

MARIA THERESA*

By Anna C. Brackett

(1717–1780)

MARIA THERESA, Archduchess of Austria, was born May 13, 1717, daughter of Charles VI. of the house of Hapsburg—ruling Austria for more than four hundred years—and of Elizabeth of Brunswick. From her father she inherited the "deadly Hapsburg tenacity," and from her mother much good sense and capacity for managing affairs, all of which stood her in good stead. She was especially fortunate in three things : that she lived in the time of Frederick the Great of Prussia, for thus she had given to her a chance to know of what stuff she was made ; that she did not marry him, as was proposed by the great Eugene ; and that she did not live to see the beautiful head of her daughter, Marie Antoinette, fall under the guillotine. Though the court of Charles VI. rivalled in ceremonial observance that of Spain, the little archduchess was reared in almost Spartan simplicity of dress and food. From Jesuit text-books she learned her history and geography, and she spoke several languages, none of which, however, could she ever write or spell quite correctly. But chiefly she was taught the pre-eminent dignity and power of the Hapsburgs, and the necessary indivisibility of the Austrian state. She learned to hunt, to shoot, and to dance, and at suppers of state she and her little sister were sometimes allowed to present to their stately mother her gloves and fan when the emperor rose. She had an aversion to business and great diffidence of her own capacity, and though the emperor took her to the council of state at the time of the Polish election, when she was only sixteen, he yet failed to give her any real knowledge of the commonest forms of business. In this austere court, never seeing a smile on her father's face, she grew up, "the prettiest little maiden in the world," to a radiant woman, heir-expectant to the throne by virtue of the Pragmatic Sanction, an order of state by means of which the Emperor Charles VI. had undertaken to settle the Austrian succession.

At nineteen she was "beautiful to soul and eye," tall and slight, with brilliant complexion, sparkling gray eyes, and a profusion of golden wavy hair. She had an aquiline nose,—strange to say for a Hapsburg, an exceedingly lovely mouth,—and very beautiful hands and arms. Her voice was sharp but musical, and her quick speech and animated gestures betrayed an ardent and impetuous nature, though she never lost her high and dignified bearing. Her anger was easily roused, but never lasted long, especially when a fault had been committed against herself, and when she knew that she had been too angry she tried to atone by overflowing kindness. She needed only to be convinced that a thing was wrong, to give it up. Whatever she did she did with her whole heart, and gratitude was one of her strongest characteristics. Withal she kept a constant and steadfast soul, and her nature was delicate and refined ; she was a worthy sister of Isabella of Castile. At nineteen, largely through her own persistence, she escaped being made a sacrifice to the political needs of Austria in being given to the heir of Philip V. of Spain, and married the man of her choice, Francis Stephen, the grandson of that Duke of Lorraine who, in 1683, together with John Sobieski, King of Poland, had saved Vienna from the Turks. Her husband was of comely person and suave manners, kind-hearted, though not strong nor brilliant. To him she bore five sons and eleven daughters. She was looking forward to the birth of her eldest son, when, at the age of twenty-three, October 20, 1740, she was proclaimed by the heralds Sovereign Archduchess of Austria, Queen of Hungary and Bohemia, for her father lay dead in Vienna, and all the cares and anxieties of government had fallen upon her shoulders. Austria was not one nation, but composed of many differing and scattered peoples jealous of their ancient rights, among whom there could be no sense of unity, and in his many disastrous wars her father had lost several of its possessions. There was the depression of defeat and mismanagement among the state-counsellors, there were only $65,000 in the treasury, and an army of but 68,000 soldiers. The powers that had given in their adhesion to the Pragmatic Sanction were tardily and but half acknowledging her succession, and from France she could get nothing but dissimulation and uncertainty. On November 1st the young royal wife was joyfully and peacefully creating her husband Grand Master of the Order of the Golden Fleece, and co-regent, and conferring upon him the Bohemian electoral vote. In less than six weeks from that day the Elector of Bavaria had laid formal claim to her throne, Frederick of Prussia had marched his troops into Silesia, one of her finest provinces, calling it his own, and the war of the Austrian Succession was on for seven long years ; for the high, heroic heart would not yield one inch, and the sovereign ruler of Austria had met with fine Hapsburg scorn the insulting proposition of the King of Prussia that he would gladly support her right to the throne of her ancestors, provided she would resign to his obliging majesty the whole of Silesia.

The aged counsellors who took it upon themselves to dictate to the young and inexperienced ruler soon found out their mistake. The little girl who had displayed an aversion for business was now a woman with talent for its details, only eager for instruction in order to make up her own mind. The army must be increased and improved, and the people aroused to enthusiasm, if Frederick was to be checked. And it was not Frederick alone that was to be feared, for a great coalition of European powers was formed against her, and she had but

England and Saxony to depend on for help, while the enemy was already within her dominions. March 13, 1741, her son Joseph was born, and by September 11th the young mother was in Hungary to urge its people to come to the aid of the threatened country in its extremity. In deep mourning and still pale and delicate, holding the little archduke in her arms, her appeal to the Hungarian nobles roused them to lofty enthusiasm and gained their unswerving devotion. She never forgot this, and when she lay dying, spoke of them with grateful affection. The war went on with varying fortunes, but she kept heart and hope, though by the end of 1741 the powers were plotting the partition of Austria as a probable event. By 1743 the luck had changed; the Austrian army had redeemed itself, and Maria Theresa was fancying that she should be able to conquer Prussia. It was about this time that she began greatly to rely on Kaunitz, who afterward became Prime Minister, and who shaped for all the after-years of her reign the policy of her rule. The old ministers left her by her father were not able to meet the new difficulties, and the sovereign was often in great anxiety amid conflicting and hesitating counsels, for it was nothing less than the very existence of the country that was at stake. She was thirty-one years old when the war came to an end by the peace of Aix-la-Chapelle, the particulars of which were entrusted to Kaunitz while he was ambassador at London. By that treaty Maria Theresa gained the final guarantee of the Pragmatic Sanction, though she had to cede two of her Italian duchies to the Spanish Bourbons, and Glatz and the much-desired Silesia to the "bad neighbor," as she always called Frederick. She was twenty-eight when she had the pleasure of seeing her husband elected Emperor of the Holy Roman Empire, gaining as his wife the title of empress, and being thus often spoken of as the empress-queen.

The war was over, but she knew full well that it was only for a short time, and she spent the eight years of restless peace that followed, in the most unremitting efforts to enable her country to endure the next attack. She had proved that she could create heroes out of common men ; she was now to extort praise even from Frederick of Prussia for "accomplishing designs worthy of a great man." A military academy was created at Vienna ; order and economy were brought into the treasury and the army ; she established camps of instruction and went herself to visit them, recompensing brave officers, calling forth abilities and emulation. The Department of Justice was disjoined from that of the Police, a superior court was established, and the direction of the finances given to a special council, reporting every week to the empress. She often consulted men who were not in office upon matters of policy, and thus got many valuable suggestions. Meantime Kaunitz was ambassador at Paris, and had been bending all his efforts to secure a French alliance, which seemed to him of so much importance that he even induced his royal mistress to write to the Pompadour with a view to securing the influence of Louis XV. in the impending war. This was not the only time that Maria Theresa sacrificed the woman in her to the ruler, for though above all breath of scandal, and devotedly attached to husband and children, she never forgot that she was Austria, and must maintain

her inheritance.   Then came on the Seven Years' War, in which she had as
allies almost all Europe, though at its close she had to give up the last hope of
ever regaining Silesia, which was as dear to her as Calais to Mary of England, Frederick agreeing to vote for Joseph as successor to his father as
emperor.   It was in this war, after the victory of Kolin, that she founded
the military order of Maria Theresa, the beautiful cross of which is still the
highest and most coveted Austrian decoration.   At the end of the war she was
forty-six years old, and it was only two years after, August 18, 1765, that she
herself made the shroud for her husband, and put on the mourning which was to
last for fifteen years.   Ever after that she spent in seclusion the whole month of
August and the 18th of every other month, thus breaking the routine of her
busy days.   I give in brief the account of one of these : Rising at five or six,
according to the season, prayer, dressing, hearing mass, breakfast, work till nine
on petitions and reports, a second mass, a visit to her children, more work till
dinner at one, and again work.   This she was apt to do in a sentinel-guarded
arbor to which she would go from the palace, carrying despatches and papers in
a tray slung by a cord round her neck.   Vespers at six, an evening card-party,
supper, a walk at eight, and then sleep.   After the death of Francis she made her
son Joseph joint-ruler, but soon found herself obliged to limit his authority to
the care of the army.   At fifty the small-pox greatly marred her beauty, though
she was now at the age when the constant beauty of soul of her life shone fair
on the lofty face.   When she was fifty-three she bade good-by to the little fif-
teen-years-old Marie Antoinette, going, as she hoped, to assure the alliance of
France, never to see her again.   To her for the rest of Maria Theresa's life, as
to the other married daughters, went a courier every three weeks with letters,
which have been preserved, and may still be read for knowledge of the mother
and empress.   At fifty-five Maria Theresa became a party to the partition of
Poland, and because this transaction is regarded as a blot upon her character, I
give in full the words which she sent to Kaunitz when she returned to him the
signed agreement.   She was then fifty-five years old, and keen memories of 1741
and of her young life must have stirred the trembling pen as she wrote on it :
"*Placet*, because so many great and learned men wish it ; but when I have been
long dead, people will see what must come from the violation of everything that
until now has been deemed holy and right."   And then on a slip of paper sent
with the document stood these words : "When all my countries were attacked,
and I no longer knew where I might go quietly to lie in, I stood stiff on my
good right and the help of God.   But in this affair, when not only clear justice
cries to Heaven against us, but also all fairness and common-sense condemn us,
I must confess that all the days of my life I have never felt so troubled, and I
am ashamed to show myself before the people.   Let the prince consider what an
example we give to the world, when, for a miserable slice of Poland or of Mol-
davia and Wallachia, we risk the loss of our honor and reputation.   I feel that I
am alone, and no longer in health and strength ; and therefore, although not
without my greatest sorrow. I allow matters to take their own course."

The heaviest burdens and greatest trials of her life were now over. The fruit of her careful plans was beginning to be reaped in prosperity, and a long period of tranquillity had come. She turned all her attention to reforms : academies were established, among others one for the education of the Magyar noble youth in Vienna, that these might become the more surely incorporated with the Austrian system. The public schools were reconstituted, the monasteries reformed, and no longer allowed to furnish asylums for criminals. Priests were forbidden to be present at the making of wills, and the Inquisition was suppressed. Through most convincing efforts on the part of Kaunitz, the Jesuits had been finally expelled from the country. Agriculture, trade, and commerce were encouraged, though by the advice of England the navy was given up. Inoculation for the small-pox was introduced, and a hospital for its treatment, as well as a home for veteran soldiers, built in Vienna. When she was sixty, the war of the Bavarian Succession was happily ended, in opposition to the will of Joseph, by her most untiring efforts. Servitude and the torture had been abolished ; the taxes, on a better basis, were bringing in large returns ; a standing army had been created, the monarchy lifted and strengthened, and the court and the people stood together against oppression from the aristocracy. Austria had been carried from the Middle Ages into modern times, and was no longer a conglomeration but a nation.

Maria Theresa had reached the age of sixty-three when the brave religious spirit, over which flattery had had no power, was waiting in pain and anguish but not in fear the hour of its release. The generous and open hand could no longer give ; the heart so keenly sensitive to criticism was to dread it no more ; the eyes that, as she had written to Marie Antoinette, had shed so many relieving tears were nevermore to need that relief. " You are all so timid," she said, " I am not afraid of death. I only pray to God to give me strength to the end." She did not forget Poland, she gratefully remembered Hungary, and then, with the cry, " To Thee ! I am coming !" she sank back dead, in the arms of the son whom, as a little baby, she had held up in her brave arms to plead for the loyalty of the Hungarian nobles. The high imperial heart had ceased to beat, the house of Hapsburg had come to an end, and Joseph II., of the house of Hapsburg-Lorraine, was the sovereign ruler of Austria.

Anna C. Brackett

15

EDMUND BURKE*

BY DR. HEINRICH GEFFCKEN

(1730–1797)

EDMUND BURKE, the great British politician, and one of the greatest political philosophers that ever lived, was born at Dublin, January 1, 1730, as son of a petty attorney. Conformably to the wishes of his father, he began to study law in London, but found it so little attractive that, encouraged by eminent men, particularly by Johnson, he turned to literary pursuits. His first work, "Vindication of Natural Society" (1756), which at once won him fame, is a keen satire on Bolingbroke, showing that the attacks of that writer upon revealed religion might as well be turned against all social and political institutions. His reputation was still enhanced by the "Philosophical Inquiry into the Origin of our Ideas on the Sublime and Beautiful" (1757); and at the same time he showed, by publishing "Dodd's Annual Register," that he was equally gifted for politics. As a preliminary for practical activity in that domain, he became private secretary of Gerard Hamilton, the lieutenant-general's assistant for Ireland, but soon found that his chief's smart mediocrity only wanted to turn to advantage the secretary's scantily rewarded talent. He returned to London (1764), and at once entered upon the political career in which he was to play so eminent a part.

The Grenville ministry was dismissed and replaced by an administration ·of rather heterogeneous elements, under Lord Rockingham, not a great statesman, but combining unblemished character and solid gifts with rank and wealth. Burke became his private secretary and influential adviser, being at the same time elected a member for Wendover. Matters then were in a very critical state : while discontent was fast rising in America and commerce trembling for its colonial trade, two parties were fiercely opposed in Parliament. Pitt deemed it treason against the Constitution and to the colonies to tax America without its consent. Grenville declared it treason to crown and legislature to abandon that right. Burke, though in principle more inclining to Pitt, advised a middle course by redressing the grievances of the colonies, while maintaining the dignity of the crown. The government proposed (January, 1766) to repeal Grenville's Stamp Act, but to guard the constitutional rights of the mother-country by a "Declaratory Act." In the debate on these bills Burke made his maiden speech, which called forth universal admiration; a friend wrote to him, "You have made us hear a new eloquence." The bills passed, but the ministry, mined by both parties, soon afterward was obliged to resign. Burke summed up its activity in an excellent pamphlet, "A Short Account of a Late Short Administration," and now entered into opposition against Lord Chatham's ministry, which he called "a tessellated pavement without cement." On the other hand, he victoriously refuted the attacks of the Grenvilles against Rockingham, in his "Observations on the Present State of the Nation," exhibiting the emptiness of his opponents' declamations on the declining wealth of the country, and proving that its resources were fast increasing.

Burke rises still higher in the "Thoughts on the Causes of the Present Discontents" (1770), a powerful plea for the British Constitution in its development from 1688, and exhibiting the full maturity of his talent. He denies that the prevailing discontents are due to some factious libellers exciting the people, who have no interest in disorder, but are only roused by the impatience of suffering. The discontents were real, and their cause was a perversion of the true principles on which the Constitution rested. As hitherto, business had gone alternately through the hands of Whigs and Tories, the opposition controlling the government; but now a court faction had sprung up called "the king's friends," a double cabinet, acting as irresponsible wire-pullers behind the scenes. These men deriving, like Janissaries, a kind of freedom from the very condition of their servitude, were sitting in secondary, but efficient, departments of office and in the household of the royal family, so as to occupy the avenues to the throne and to forward or frustrate the execution of any measure according to their own interests; they endeavored to separate the crown from the administration, and to divide the latter within itself. To this cabal it was owing that British policy was brought into derision in those foreign countries which, a while ago, trembled at the power of England's arms. Above all, they tried to pervert the principles of Parliament by raising divisions among the people, by influencing the elections, by separating representatives from their constituents, and by undermining the control of the legislature over the executive. They maintained that all political connections were in their nature factious; but free commonwealths were ever made by parties, *i.e.*, bodies of men united for promoting by their joint endeavors the national interest upon great leading principles in which they were agreed; government by parties was the very soul of representative institutions; it had raised England to her present power and protected the liberty of the people; while the cant, "measures not men," had always been the pretext for getting loose from every honorable engagement.

Burke finds the remedy in restoring the Constitution to its original principles; all patriots must form a firm combination against the cabal; a just connection between representatives and constituents must be re-established; Parliament ought not to meddle with the privileges of the executive, but exercise real control upon the acting powers of the state, and if necessary, not be afraid to resort to impeachment, " that great guardian of the purity of the Constitution ;" finally, if all means fail, there must be an interposition of the body of the people itself—"an unpleasant remedy but legal, when it is evident that nothing else can hold the Constitution to its true principles."

He at the same time displayed a prominent activity in Parliament, where soon all internal questions gave way to the great contest with America. In 1771 he had accepted the place of an agent for New York, had become intimately acquainted with Franklin, and won a deep insight into American affairs. Of the six duties imposed by Townshend's Revenue Act (1767) five had been repealed; the tea duty alone remained. December 18, 1773, the cargo of an East Indian tea-ship was thrown into the sea at Boston, and the first armed conflict ensued. Court and government were resolved to put down this rebellion ; Burke, on the contrary, supported in his great speech " On American Taxation " Rose-Fuller's motion (April, 1774) for suppressing the last duty. England had no right to tax the colonies, nor had she ever pretended to do so before Grenville's Stamp Act ; that, as well as the most important duties of the Revenue Act, had been repealed ; the tea-duty was slight and it produced short of nothing, the cost of collection devouring it to the bone ; for the Americans refused to buy imported tea, and they were right to do so ; having inherited English principles they resisted for the same reason for which Hampden had resisted the payment of the trifling ship-money, because the principle on which it was demanded would have made him a slave. It would be a signal folly to maintain the shadow of a duty and to risk the loss of an empire merely because the preamble of the Revenue Act said it was expedient that a revenue should be raised in his majesty's dominions in America.

The blindness of the majority turned away from those wise counsels. Parliament was dissolved. Burke, elected for Bristol, forthwith introduced thirteen resolutions, which he defended in his celebrated speech for "Conciliation with the Colonies" (March 22, 1775). As he had told his constituents his aim was to reconcile British superiority with American liberty, he proposed to remove the ground of the difference in order to restore the former confidence of the colonies in the mother-country. "Fighting is not the best way of gaining a people of more than two millions, in which the fierce spirit of liberty is probably stronger than in any other country, and that liberty is founded upon English principles." Now, a fundamental point of our Constitution is that the people have power of "granting their own money ;" the colonial assemblies have uncontested competence to raise taxes, and have frequently granted them for imperial purposes ; sometimes so liberally that, in 1743, the Commons resolved to reimburse the expense ; no method for procuring a representation in Parliament of the colonies has hitherto been advised, consequently no revenue by imposition has been raised before the Stamp Act ; we therefore ought to acknowledge that only the general assemblies can grant " aids to his Majesty." To enforce the reverse principle is not only unjust, but impossible, " when three thousand miles of ocean lie between us and them. Seas roll and months pass between the order and the execution.

DOYLE PINXIT.

BURKE, JOHNSON AND THEIR FRIENDS.

We may impoverish the colonies and cripple our own most important trade, but it is preposterous to make them unserviceable, in order to keep them obedient." The motions were rejected ; three years afterward, when it was too late, Burke's opponent, Lord North, proposed a similar plan.

In 1780 Burke introduced his bill for " Economical reform in support of several petitions to correct the gross abuses in the management of public expenditure before laying fresh burdens upon the people." His speech derives a particular interest from its defining the difference of timely and gradual reformation from hasty and harsh, making clear work. The former was an amicable and temperate arrangement with a friend in power, leaving room for growth ; the latter was imposing terms upon a conquered enemy under a state of inflammation. In 1782 Lord North was obliged to resign, and Rockingham became again premier, Burke paymaster-general of the army. He now carried his economical reform, abolishing sinecures, suppressing useless expenses, and cutting down salaries, among which was his own.

After Rockingham's death and the overthrow of the short Shelburne administration, Burke turned his activity to the misgovernment of India ; his speeches in support of Fox's East-India Bill (December 1, 1783), and on the Nabob of Arcot's debts (February 15, 1783), show that he had thoroughly mastered that intricate subject. He violently denounced the oppression exercised by the company, a prelude to his campaign against Warren Hastings, which he continued for eight years. His speech justifying the impeachment of the governor-general, said Erskine, "irresistibly carried away its brilliant audience by a superhuman eloquence."

Burke in this contest was, as always, animated by the purest motives, but his passion went too far in comparing Hastings to Verres, and did not sufficiently allow for the difficult circumstances in which his adversary was placed. Without the latter's unscrupulous energy, India would have been lost. Hastings finally was acquitted, but Burke's attacks nevertheless had the effect of uncovering and redressing the prevailing abuses.

The last period of Burke's life is filled up by his great struggle against the French revolution. Already in 1769 he had prophetically asserted that the derangement of French finances must infallibly lead to a violent convulsion, the influence of which upon France and even Europe could be scarcely divined ; now he directed the attention of the House (February 4, 1790) to the dangers of the revolution, by which the French had shown themselves "the ablest architects of ruin," pulling down all their domestic institutions, making "a digest of anarchy" called "the rights of men," and establishing a ferocious, tyrannical, and atheistical democracy. It might be said that they had done service to England, a rival, by reducing their country to impotence and expunging it out of the system of Europe ; but, by the vicinity of the two countries, their present distemper might prove more contagious than the gilded tyranny of Louis XIV. had been, and "much as it would afflict him, he would abandon his best friends and join with his worst enemies to oppose all violent exertions of the spirit of innovation, which by tearing to pieces the contexture of the state prevented all real reformation ;" the last passage alluding to the apology of Fox, hitherto his closest friend, for French proceedings.

These ideas Burke more fully developed in his famous " Reflections on the Revolution in France " (1790) ; liberals maintained that by this work he had deserted the cause of liberty ; conservatives asserted that he had become the stoutest champion of order combined with rational freedom. It must be acknowledged that Burke erred by judging the state of France before the revolution too favorably ; if he justly appreciated the pernicious influence of Rousseau, " that great professor and hero of vanity," he ought to have discerned that a nation, the higher classes of which were undermined by materialism and unbelief, while the masses lived in deep misery, was incapable of a temperate reform ; the follies and terrors of the revolution were the children of the sins of the "ancien régime." But how amply has history confirmed his judgment on the revolution itself ! While Fox admired the constitution of 1791 as " the most astonishing and glorious edifice of liberty that ever was erected," Burke foresaid that this constitutional king would be torn from his throne by the mob, that the wildest anarchy would put France in confusion, and that after its exhaustion an unlimited military despotism would be established.

This work, which produced a European sensation, receives its true light by Burke's " Appeal from the New to the Old Whigs " (1791). His former friends having sided with Fox, he refuted the reproach of having abandoned his principles by an elaborate comparison of the English revolution of 1688 with that of France. His later writings, among which the " Thoughts on French Affairs " (1791) and " Thoughts on a Regicide Peace " (1796) are the principal, were directed against the foreign influence of the revolutionary system, " France being no more a state but a faction, which must be destroyed or will destroy Europe." Here again Burke was wrong ; if France was a revolutionary crater, the safest way was to let it burn out in itself, while the insane aggression of continental powers only confirmed the reign of terror. Burke would go to war for the idea of prescriptive right ; Pitt declined to fight for the French monarchy, and would make war only for the defence of English interests.

Although Burke had the satisfaction of gaining the majority for his views, he retired from Parliament in 1794 ; a pension which he obtained he defended in the " Letter to a Noble Lord," a dignified plea, " pro domo." One of his last works was " Thoughts and Details on Scarcity " (1795). In a time when political economy was still in a state of infancy, he held the most enlightened opinions on all questions relating to it ; his doctrines on prices, wages, rent, etc., are still worth reading. Above all, he opposes indiscreet government tampering with the trade of provisions. " Once habituated to get cheap bread, the people will never be satisfied to get it otherwise, and on the first scarcity they will turn and bite the hand that fed them."

Burke died July 8, 1797. His was a character of unblemished purity, manly uprightness, and perfect disinterestedness. He was a conservative of the truest and best kind, but in his later years went too far in supporting existing institutions merely because they existed. Lacking practical accommodation to circumstances, he would probably not have been a great minister ; neither was he a consummate parliamentary tactician and debater, nevertheless he stands in the first ranks of statesmen and orators. Lord Brougham goes too far in calling his speeches spoken dissertations ; they were carefully prepared set speeches. In them, as in his writings, we admire the most varied information, philosophical acuteness, penetrating sagacity, curious felicity of expression, and an eloquence embracing the full range and depth of the subject. Fox avowed that he had learned more from Burke than from all other men and authors, and for the same reason his works will remain a mine of political wisdom. The only drawback is that in his eagerness he sometimes overstated his case, and, embittered by the struggles of his later years, occasionally condescended to expressions bordering upon scurrility.

Heinrich Jeffcken 93

BENJAMIN FRANKLIN

(1706–1790)

THOUGH eminent qualities are generally necessary to the acquisition of permanent fame, the life of Franklin affords signal proof that moderate talents, judiciously directed, when aided by industry and perseverance, will enable a man to render signal services to his country and his kind, and give him a claim to the homage of posterity. He was the fifteenth child of a tallow-chandler in Boston, where he was born January 17, 1706. His father at first intended to educate him for the church, but finding that the expense was likely to exceed his means, he took the boy home after he had acquired little more than the elements of learning, to assist him in his own trade. The boy greatly disliked the nature of the employment, and was very anxious to become a sailor. Fortunately for him his friends controlled his inclinations ; instead of going to sea he was apprenticed to his eldest brother, James, who was a printer. Franklin records in his Memoirs that though he had only at this time entered his twelfth year he paid so much attention to his business that he soon became proficient in all its details, and, by the quickness with which he executed his work, obtained a little leisure, which he devoted to study. His studious habits were noticed by a gentleman named Adams, who had a large collection of books, which he placed at the disposal of Franklin; among these were some volumes of poetry, which fired his emulation, and he began to compose little pieces in verse. Two of these were printed by his brother and sold as street-ballads, but they were, as he informs us, wretched doggerel, and the ridicule thrown on them by his father deterred him from similar attempts. But though he laid aside poetry, he did not abandon his ambition to become a good English writer; he studied the art of composition with great labor, being rewarded by the consciousness of improvement.

Franklin's self-denial and power of control over his appetites were not less remarkable than his industry. Having, at the age of sixteen, read a work which recommended vegetable diet, he determined to adopt the system, and undertook to provide for himself upon his brother's allowing him one-half of the ordinary expenses of board. On this pittance he not only supported himself, but contrived, by great abstemiousness, to save a portion of it, which he devoted to the purchase of books. He soon had an opportunity of testing his literary progress; in 1720 his brother commenced the publication of a newspaper, the second which had appeared in America, called the *New England Courant*. This paper, at a time when periodicals were rare, attracted most of the literary men of Boston to the house of the proprietor; their conversation, and particularly their remarks on the authorship of the various articles contributed to the paper, revived Franklin's literary ambition; he sent some communications to the journal in a feigned hand; they were inserted, and he tells us that "he had the exquisite pleasure to find that they met with approbation, and that, in the various conjectures respecting the author, no one was mentioned who did not enjoy a high reputation in the country for talents and genius." He was thus encouraged to reveal his secret to his brother, but he did not obtain the respect and fraternal indulgence which he had anticipated. James Franklin was a man of violent temper; he treated Benjamin with great harshness, and often proceeded to the extremity of blows.

An article which appeared in the *Courant* having given offence to the authorities, James was thrown into prison for a month, and the management of the paper devolved on Benjamin. He conducted it with great spirit, but with questionable prudence, for he made it the vehicle of sharp attacks on the principal persons in the colony. This gave such offence that when James was liberated from prison, an arbitrary order was issued that he should no longer print the paper called the *New England Courant.* To evade this order it was arranged that Benjamin's indentures should be cancelled in order that the paper might be published in his name, but at the same time a secret contract was made between the parties, by which James was entitled to his brother's services during the unexpired period of apprenticeship. A fresh quarrel, however, soon arose, and Benjamin separated from his brother, taking what he has confessed to be an unfair advantage of the circumstance that the contract could not be safely brought forward.

The circumstance produced an unfavorable impression on the minds of the printers in Boston, and Franklin, finding it impossible to obtain employment in his native town, resolved to seek it in New York. Aware that his father would be opposed to this measure, he was compelled to sell his books to raise money for defraying the expenses of his journey. America was at this time very thinly inhabited; there were no public conveyances on the roads, the inns were few, and their accommodations miserable; but Franklin had accustomed himself to hard fare, and he did not allow the inconvenience he endured to interfere with his enjoyment of new scenery. On reaching New York he found that the printers there had no occasion for his services, and he continued his journey to Philadelphia. Having obtained employment in that city from a printer named Keimer, Franklin continued to devote his leisure hours to literature. The respectability of his appearance and the superior tone of his conversation began soon to be remarked; they led to his being introduced to several eminent men, and particularly to Sir William Keith, the Governor of Pennsylvania, who frequently invited him to his table. Keith urged Franklin to commence business on his own account, and when the young man had ineffectually applied for assistance to his father in Boston, he advised him to go to London and form a connection with some of the great publishing houses, promising him letters of credit and recommendation. Franklin sailed for London, but the promised letters were never sent; and he found himself, on his arrival in England, thrown entirely on his own resources.

Having soon obtained employment, he exhibited to his fellow-workmen an edifying example of industry and temperance, by which many of them profited. He also published a little work of a sceptical tendency, which procured him introductions to some eminent men, but which he afterward lamented as one of the greatest errors of his life. After remaining about eighteen months in England, he returned to Philadelphia as a clerk to Mr. Denham, and on the death of that gentleman went back once more to his old employer, Keimer. About this time he established a debating society, or club of persons of his own age, for the discussion of subjects connected with morals, politics, and natural philosophy. These discussions gradually assumed political importance, and had a great effect in stimulating the public mind during the War of Independence.

Having quarrelled with Keimer, Franklin entered into partnership with a young man named Meredith, and commenced publishing a paper in opposition to one which had been started by his former employer. Meredith proving negligent of business, Franklin was enabled by his friends to dissolve the partnership, and to take the entire business into his own hands. His steady adherence to habits of industry and economy had brought him comparative wealth; and he now married Miss Read, whom he had met on his first arrival in Philadelphia.

In 1732 Franklin began the publication of " Poor Richard's Almanac," which soon became celebrated for its important lessons of practical morality. These were subsequently collected in a little volume, and are still highly esteemed both in England and America. His high character for probity and intelligence induced the citizens of Philadelphia to intrust him with the management of public affairs; he was appointed clerk of the general assembly, postmaster, and alderman, and was put by the governor into the commission of the peace. All the hours he could spare from business he now devoted to objects of local utility, and the city of Philadelphia is indebted to him for some of its finest buildings and best institutions. As his wealth increased he obtained leisure to devote himself to the study of philosophy, and to take a leading part in political life.

We shall first look at his philosophical labors, by which his name first became known abroad. His attention was drawn to the subject of electricity in 1746, by some experiments exhibited by Dr. Spence, who had come to Boston from Scotland. These isolated experiments were made with no regard to system, and led to no results. A glass tube, and some other apparatus that had been sent to Franklin by a friend in London, enabled him to repeat and verify these experiments. He soon began to devise new forms of investigation for himself, and at length made the great discovery, which may be said to be the foundation of electrical science, that there is a positive and negative state of electricity. By this fact he explained the phenomenon of the Leyden phial, which at that time excited great attention in Europe, and had foiled the sagacity of its principal philosophers. In the course of his investigations he was led to suspect the identity of lightning and the electric fluid; and he resolved to test this happy conjecture by a direct experiment. His apparatus was simply a paper-kite with a key attached to the tail. Having raised the kite during a thunder-storm, he watched the result with great anxiety; after an interval of painful suspense, he saw the filaments of the string exhibit by their motion signs of electrical action; he drew in the kite, and, presenting his knuckles to the key, received a strong spark, which of course decided the success of the experiment. Repeated sparks were drawn from the key, a phial was charged, a shock given, and the identity of lightning with the electric fluid demonstrated beyond all possibility of doubt.

Franklin had from time to time transmitted accounts of his electrical experiments to his friend, Mr. Collinson, in England, in order that they should be laid before the Council of the Royal Society; but, as they were not published in the "Transactions" of that learned body, Collinson gave copies of the communications to Cave, for insertion in the *Gentleman's Magazine.* Cave resolved to publish them in a separate form, and the work, soon after its appearance, became generally recognized as the text-book of electrical science. It was translated into French, German, and Latin; the author's experiments were repeated, and verified by the leading philosophers of France, Germany, and even Russia; the Royal Society atoned for its former tardiness by a hearty recognition of their value, and Franklin was elected a member of their body without solicitation or expense. The universities of St. Andrews, Edinburgh, and Oxford subsequently conferred upon him the honorary title of Doctor of Laws.

We must pass more briefly over Franklin's political career. In 1753 he was appointed Deputy Post-master of the American colonies. The post-office, which had previously supplied no revenue to the Government, became very productive under his management, and yielded three times as much as the post-office in Ireland. Nor was this the only service he rendered to the Government. At the time of Braddock's unfortunate expedition against the French and Indians, he provided conveyances for the troops and stores at his own risk; he took a leading part in obtaining a militia bill, and he proposed a plan for the union of the several colonies in a common system of defence against the Indians. These measures greatly increased his influence and popularity.

Pennsylvania was at this period a proprietary government, and the proprietary body claimed exemption from taxation. In consequence of the disputes to which these claims gave rise, he was sent to England by the General Assembly, as agent for the provinces. He performed his duties with such zeal and ability, that he was appointed agent for the provinces of Massachusetts, Georgia, and Maryland; and, on his return to America in 1762, received not only the thanks of the House of Assembly, but a grant of £5,000. Previous to his return he made a short visit to the continent, and was everywhere received with great honor, especially at the court of Louis XV.

In the year 1764, the American colonies, alarmed at the system of taxation with which they were menaced by the British, resolved that Franklin should be sent to England, no longer as an agent, but as the general representative of the States. In this character he arrived in London about forty years after his first appearance in that city as a distressed mechanic. His own mind was strongly impressed by the contrast; he went to the printing-office where he had worked, introduced himself to the men employed there, and joined in a little festival in honor of printing. He officially presented to Mr. Grenville a petition against the Stamp Act, but finding that the minister was not deterred from his purpose, he zealously exerted himself to organize an opposition to the measure. When it was proposed to repeal the bill in the following year, Franklin was examined before the House of Commons; the effect of his evidence was decisive, and the Stamp Act was repealed.

The quarrel with the colonies, however, grew more and more bitter; and while Franklin's words were always of peace, he championed the American cause with power and dignity. Attempts were made to win him over to the side of the Government, by offers of high honors and liberal emoluments; but threats and promises were alike unavailing to divert him from his course. He lingered in England, hoping that some turn in public affairs would avert the fatal necessity of war; but when the petition of the American Congress was rejected, and Lord Chatham's plan of reconciliation outvoted, he resolved to return home and share the fortunes of his countrymen. His departure was hastened by the intelligence that the ministers intended to arrest him on a charge of fomenting rebellion in the colonies; he narrowly escaped this danger, and on landing in America, he was elected a member of Congress.

Soon after the declaration of independence was issued, Dr. Franklin was sent as ambassador to France, to solicit aid for the infant republic. On his first arrival, in 1776, he was not officially received ; but when the intelligence of the English losses had given courage to the French court, negotiations were formally commenced, and on February 7, 1778, he had the honor of signing the first treaty between the United States and a foreign power. He remained at the French court as ambassador until the end of the war, when, as an American plenipotentiary, he signed the treaty of Paris, by which Great Britain recognized the independence of the United States. At the close of the negotiations (November, 1782), he was anxious to be recalled ; but his diplomatic services were too highly valued to be spared, and he remained at Paris three years longer, during which period he negotiated treaties with Sweden and with Prussia. His residence in France was cheered by the enthusiasm with which he was regarded by all classes, particularly persons of literature and science ; his departure from that city was lamented as a general loss to society.

Honors of every kind awaited him on his return to his native land ; he was appointed President of the State of Pennsylvania, and a member of the Federal Convention, by which the American Constitution was framed. But old age, and a painful disease, to which he had been long subject, compelled him to retire into the bosom of his family. Notwithstanding his sufferings, he preserved his affections and faculties unimpaired to the last, and died tranquilly, April 17, 1790. The American Congress, and the National Assembly of France, both went into mourning on receiving the intelligence of his death.

Franklin's powers were useful rather than brilliant ; his philosophical discoveries were the result of patience and perseverance ; with a warmer imagination he would probably have been misled by speculative theory, like so many of his contemporaries. His industry and his temperance were the sources of his early success, and they nurtured in him that spirit of independence which was the leading characteristic of his private and public career.

PATRICK HENRY *

By General Bradley T. Johnson

(1736–1799)

PATRICK HENRY was born in Hanover County, Virginia, May 29, 1736; died in Charlotte County, Virginia, June 6, 1799. He was the son of Colonel John Henry, of Mount Brilliant, a Scotchman by birth, who was the nephew of Dr. William Robertson, the historian. Henry received only the limited education accessible in the rural locality in which he was born, consisting of the rudiments of an English training and absolutely no acquaintance with the classics. His early youth was

* Copyright, 1894, by Selmar Hess.

spent on the plantation, occupied with the amusements of his age and his epoch ; fishing and hunting gave him acquaintance with the fields, the streams, and the forests, and the observation of nature, her changes, her forces, and her moods.

The habits thus formed evolved in part the great power of introspection and analysis of the feelings of men which afterward gave him such control of them.

At the age of fifteen he was placed in a country store as assistant salesman, or clerk. After a year's experience, his father purchased a small stock of goods for him, and set him up on his own account in partnership with his brother William.

This adventure came to grief in a year, and then Henry, at the age of eighteen, married Miss Shelton, the daughter of a neighboring farmer.

The young couple were settled on a farm by the joint efforts of their parents, where they endeavored to win a subsistence with the assistance of two or three servants. In two years he sold out and invested in another mercantile undertaking. In a few years this ended in bankruptcy, leaving him without a dollar and with a wife and an increasing family to support. He was devoted to music, dancing, and amusement, and was incapable of continuous physical or intellectual labor. He had devoted himself to desultory reading of the best kind, and made himself acquainted with the history of England, of Greece, and of Rome. He therefore undertook to win a support by the profession and the practice of the law, and after a brief pretence of preparation, by the generosity of the bar at that period, was admitted to practice. The vigor of his intellect, his powerful logic, and his acute analysis induced the examining committee to sign his certificate.

That committee consisted of Mr. Lyons, then the leader of the Provincial bar, afterward president-judge of the Supreme Court of Appeals of Virginia ; Mr. John Lewis, an eminent lawyer, and John Randolph, afterward knighted and as Sir John Randolph, the king's Attorney General for Virginia. Henry was twenty-four when admitted to the bar, and for three years did nothing.

Under the law of Virginia the people, without regard to religious belief, were bound to pay a tax of so many pounds of tobacco per poll for the support of the clergy. The parson of each parish was entitled to sixteen thousand pounds of tobacco per annum. When the price of tobacco was low this imposition was borne not without grumbling. When short crops or increased demand raised the price, the General Assembly of the colony by law allowed the people the option to pay their poll-tax in tobacco, or to commute it at the fixed price of 16s. and 8d. per hundred. When the market price was above that the tax was paid in currency ; when it was below, in tobacco. When tobacco rose to 50s. per hundred the parsons demanded tobacco for their salaries instead of 16s. 8d. per hundred. The King in council declared the Commutation Act void, and the parsons brought suit for their salaries. The defendants pleaded the Commutation Act in defence; to this plea the plaintiffs demurred; and the court, as it was bound to do, gave judgment for the plaintiff on the demurrer. The only question then left was the *quantum* of damages, to be assessed by a jury. The case selected for a test was the case of the Rev. James Maury against the sheriff of Hanover County and his sureties. It was set for trial at the December term of the County Court of Hanover, 1763. Henry was retained for the defendant, and made an argument so forcible, so conclusive, and so eloquent that it has made his fame as "the greatest orator who ever lived," as Mr. Jefferson wrote of him. He took the ground that allegiance and protection in government are reciprocal, that the King of Great Britain had failed to protect the people of Virginia in their rights as Englishmen, and that therefore they owed no allegiance to him and he had no right to declare laws made by them void, therefore his nullification of the Commutation Act was void and of no effect. The jury found for the plaintiff with one penny damages, and thus ended the attempt to rely upon the power of the king to set aside laws made by Virginia for her own government.

It was the first announcement in America of the radical revolutionary doctrine that government is a matter of compact with the people, and when the former breaks the agreement, the latter are absolved from obedience to it.

The next year Henry removed to Louisa County and was employed by Dandridge in the contested election case of Dandridge v. Littlepage before the House of Burgesses for a seat in that body. When the Stamp Act passed in 1765, Mr. William Johnson, member of the House of Burgesses for Louisa County, resigned his place to make way for Henry, who was elected to fill the vacancy.

This body consisted of some of the ablest and most illustrious Americans who ever lived. George Washington, Peyton Randolph, Richard Bland, Edmund Pendleton, George Wythe, Richard Henry Lee were all members, and Henry at the first session won a place in the front rank among them. In May, 1765, he introduced a series of resolutions, reiterating and enlarging the propositions of the parson's case, and declaring that the people of Virginia are entitled to all the rights of British subjects, and that they alone, through their General Assembly, "have the sole right and power to lay taxes and impositions on this colony," and that any attempt by any other authority "has a manifest tendency to destroy British as well as American freedom." They were opposed by the old members, but the eloquent logic of Henry, backed by Johnston, a member from Fairfax, carried them by a close vote, the last one by a majority of one.

In this debate, Henry in a passion of eloquence exclaimed, "Cæsar had his Brutus, Charles the First his Cromwell, and George III.——" "Treason," cried the Speaker and the House——"may profit by their example. If this be treason, make the most of it."

The next day, the House in a panic, reconsidered, rejected, and expunged from the *Journal* the last resolution, which asserted the sole right of taxation in Virginia, and denied it to Parliament.

Henry continued a member of the House of Burgesses from Louisa County until the close of the Revolution. He led Virginia in resistance to the tax on tea, and in organizing armed resistance to the Mother Country by all the colonies. He was among the first of the Americans who understood that liberty could only be preserved by defending it by force.

He was sent as a deputy from Virginia to the first Continental Congress, which met at Philadelphia in September, 1774. He at once took a commanding influence in that body, and on its adjournment in October, returned home.

In March, 1776, he attended the Convention of Virginia held in Richmond. Here he moved that "this colony be immediately put in a state of defence, and that a committee be appointed to prepare a plan for embodying, assigning, and disciplining such a number of men as may be sufficient for that purpose." Bland, Harrison, Pendleton, and Nicholas, all vigorously opposed these resolutions as leading inevitably and logically to revolution and separation ; but Henry, in a storm of patriotic, eloquent enthusiasm, carried everything, uttering those deathless sentences, "Our brethren are already in the field! Why stand we here idle. What is it that gentlemen wish? What would they have?

"Is life so dear or peace so sweet, as to be purchased at the price of chains and slavery?

"Forbid it, Almighty God! I know not what course others may take, but as for me, give me liberty or give me death!"

The resolutions were carried and Henry made chairman of the committee to organize the colony. He proceeded with great vigor to form companies of cavalry or infantry in every county. On April 20, 1775, Lord Dunmore, the royal governor, seized the powder of the colony and placed it on the armed schooner Magdalene. The country rose at once. Henry, as captain, marched the independent company of Hanover on Williamsburgh, to compel the governor to pay for or restore the powder. Five thousand armed men were marching from the counties to reinforce him, when Lord Dunmore, through the intercession of Peyton Randolph, paid Henry for the powder and induced the volunteers from Hanover, Frederick, Berkeley, and other counties to return to their homes. As soon as they had returned, Dunmore issued a proclamation denouncing Henry and his comrades as traitors and rebels.

Henry was elected by the Virginia Convention one of the deputies to the second Continental Congress. He was also elected colonel of the first Virginia Regiment, and "commander-in-chief of all the forces raised and to be raised for the defence of the colony." Lord Dunmore having erected a fortification south of Norfolk, at Great Bridge, Colonel Woodford, with the second Virginia Regiment, was sent by the Committee of Safety to drive him away, which he did promptly and well. Henry claimed the right to command this expedition himself, but his claim was not admitted by the committee, and his authority was disclaimed by Colonel Woodford. Henry insisted upon having the question of rank between them decided, and the committee decided in favor of Colonel Henry. Yet when brigadiers were selected by Congress to command the troops of Virginia in the Continental Army, Andrew Lewis was made brigadier, Henry colonel of the first regiment. He promptly refused the Continental commission, and resigned the one held in the service of Virginia. Henry's conduct was justified in the opinion of his contemporaries and of posterity. He had led the colony at the risk of life and fortune, he had organized and led the first movement of troops against the royal authority, he had been appointed commander-in-chief and colonel of the First Regiment, and then had been superseded in command by another, without excuse or justification. He was thus driven out of the military service by petty intrigues and small jealousies of smaller men, and the country deprived of his great abilities in the military field.

On May 15, 1776, the Virginia Convention instructed their deputies in Congress "to declare the United Colonies free and independent States," and on June 29th adopted a form of State government and elected Mr. Henry governor. During the winter of 1776–77 was the darkest period of the revolution, and it has been charged that it was proposed to create him dictator; but his friends have always denied this, and it seems with truth, for he was re-elected governor, May 30th, 1777. He was a firm supporter of General Washington through all the trials of that period, and firmly stood by him against the intrigue in the army to supersede him with Gates. He was again elected governor in the spring of 1778, and the next year declined a re-election because in his opinion he was ineligible. His wife, Miss Shelton, died in 1775, leaving him the father of six children, and in 1777 he married Dorothea, daughter of Nathaniel W. Dandridge.

After the expiration of his gubernatorial service he retired to his estate in Henry County. He was elected to the General Assembly for that County in 1780, and he continued to represent it until after the revolution. He took the ground of amnesty to the Tories and the resumption of commercial intercourse with Great Britain. In 1784, he introduced and urged the passage of a bill to promote inter-marriages with the Indians, which failed to pass from his being again elected governor on November 17, 1784, for the term of three years.

He declined a re-election, and was appointed one of the deputies from Virginia to the Constitutional Convention to meet in Philadelphia. The order of appointment being George Washington, Patrick Henry, Edmund Randolph, John Blair, James Madison, George Mason and George Wythe. He, however, was too poor to perform the duties of the office and was obliged to return to the practice of the law. He was sent as a member from Prince Edward to the convention to consider the Federal Constitution which had been framed at Philadelphia. The convention met at Richmond, June 2, 1788.

It was composed of the most illustrious men that Virginia ever produced, and was probably the ablest body that ever convened in any country in any age. James Madison, John Marshall, James Monroe, Edmund Pendleton, George Nicholas, George Mason, Jarvis, Grayson, and Henry, Lee, and Randolph were among the members. Henry vigorously opposed the ratification of the new constitution on the ground that it would establish a government of the people in place of a government of the States, and would create a consolidated government with omnipotent power, without check or balance, and lead to a great and mighty empire and an absolute despotism. The Federal party carried the ratification under the lead of Madison and Marshall by a majority of ten.

In the ensuing General Assembly Henry opposed the election of Madison as one of the first senators under the new constitution, and secured that of Richard Henry Lee and Grayson to represent Virginia in the first Congress. He also drafted and had passed resolutions calling upon Congress to call a Constitutional Convention of the States to cure by amendments the many defects in the Federal Constitution which were indicated by the amendments proposed to it by Virginia. The Convention was never called, but ten of the amendments were adopted by Congress and ratified by the States.

He declined a re-election to the General Assembly in 1791, and retired to private life. In November, 1791, he appeared before the Federal Court in Richmond, for the defendant in the case of the British debts. The question involved was the right of Virginia to confiscate, during the war, debts due by her citizens to subjects of Great Britain. With Henry was John Marshall, and in the argument Henry made the greatest legal effort of his life.

In November, 1795, he was again elected Governor of Virginia, but declined on account of his age. He was offered the mission to Spain by Washington during his first term, and to France during his second—both of which positions he declined. Alarmed at the position taken by the Virginia resolutions of 1798, he became a candidate for, and was elected to the General Assembly from Charlotte County in 1799. But the Virginia Legislature was opposed to his views, and reiterated those set forth in the resolution of 1798.

His health had been infirm for several years, and he died June 6, 1799. The General Assembly passed resolutions recording their love and veneration for his name and fame, and ordered a bust of him to be procured and set up in one of the niches of the hall of the House of Delegates. It is now in the capitol at Richmond.

16

GEORGE WASHINGTON

(1732–1799)

GEORGE WASHINGTON was born at Bridge's Creek, in Westmoreland County, Va., on February 22, 1732. The first of the family who settled in Virginia came from Northampton, but their ancestors are believed to have been from Lancashire, while the ancient stock of the family is traced to the De Wessyngtons of Durham. George Washington's father, Augustine, who died, after a sudden illness, in 1743, was twice married. At his death he left two surviving sons by the first marriage, and by the second, four sons (of whom George was the eldest) and a daughter. The mother of George Washington survived to see her son President. Augustine Washington left all his children in a state of comparative independence ; to his eldest son by the first marriage he left an estate (afterward called Mount Vernon) of twenty-five hundred acres and shares in iron works situated in Virginia and Maryland ; to the second, an estate in Westmoreland. Confiding in the prudence of his widow, he directed that the proceeds of all the property of her children should be at her disposal till they should respectively come of age ; to George were left the lands and mansion occupied by his father at his decease ; to each of the other sons, an estate of six or seven hundred acres ; a suitable provision was made for the daughter.

George Washington was indebted for all the education he received to one of the common schools of the province, in which little was taught beyond reading, writing, and accounts. He left it before he had completed his sixteenth year ; the last two years of his attendance had been devoted to the study of geometry, trigonometry, and surveying. He had learned to use logarithms. It is doubtful whether he ever received any instruction in the grammar of his own language ; and although, when the French officers under Rochambeau were in America, he attempted to acquire their language, it appears to have been without success. From his thirteenth year he evinced a turn for mastering the forms of deeds, constructing diagrams, and preparing tabular statements. His juvenile manuscripts have been preserved ; the handwriting is neat, but stiff. During the last summer he was at school, he surveyed the fields adjoining the school-house and the surrounding plantations, entering his measurements and calculations in a respectable field-book. He compiled about the same time, from various sources, " Rules of Behavior in Company and Conversation." Some selections in rhyme appear in his manuscripts, but the passages were evidently selected for the moral and religious sentiments they express, not from any taste for poetry. When a boy he was fond of forming his school-mates into companies, who paraded and fought mimic battles, in which he always commanded one of the parties. He cultivated with ardor all athletic exercises. His demeanor and conduct at school are said to have won the deference of the other boys, who were accustomed to make him the arbiter of their disputes.

From the time of his leaving school till the latter part of 1753, Washington was unconsciously preparing himself for the great duties he had afterward to discharge. An attempt made to have him entered in the Royal Navy, in 1746, was frustrated by the interposition of his mother. The winter of 1748–49 he passed at Mount Vernon, then the seat of his brother Lawrence, in the study of mathematics and the exercise of practical surveying. George was introduced about this time to the family of Lord Fairfax, his brother having married the daughter of William Fairfax, a member of the Colonial Council, and a distant relative of that nobleman. The immense tracts of wild lands belonging to Lord Fairfax, in the valley of the Alleghany Mountains, had never been surveyed ; he had formed a favorable estimate of the talents of young Washington, and intrusted the task to him. His first essay was on some lands situated on the south branch of the Potomac, seventy miles above its junction with the main branch. Although performed in an almost impenetrable country, while winter yet lingered in the valleys, by a youth who had only a month before completed his sixteenth year, it gave so much satisfaction that he soon after received a commission as public surveyor, an appointment which gave authority to his surveys, and enabled him to enter them in the county offices.

The next three years were devoted without intermission, except in the winter months, to his profession. There were few surveyors in Virginia, and the demand for their services was consequently great, and their remuneration ample. Washington spent a considerable portion of these three years among the Alleghanies. The exposures and hardships of the wilderness could be endured only for a few weeks together, and he recruited his strength by surveying, at intervals, tracts and farms in the settled districts. Even at that early age his regular habits enabled him to acquire some property ; and his probity and business talent obtained for him the confidence of the leading men of the colony.

At the time he attained his nineteenth year the frontiers were threatened with Indian depredations and French encroachments. To meet this danger the province was divided into military districts, to each of which an adjutant-general with the rank of major was appointed. George Washington was commissioned to one of these districts, with a salary of £150 per annum. There were many provincial officers (his brother among the number) in Virginia, who had served in the expedition against Carthagena and in the West Indies. Under them he studied military exercises and tactics, entering with alacrity and zeal into the duties of his office. These pursuits were varied by a voyage to Barbadoes, and a residence of some months in that colony, in company with his brother Lawrence, who was sent there by his physicians to seek relief from a pulmonary complaint. Fragments of the journal kept by George Washington on this excursion have been preserved; they evince an interest in a wide range of subjects, and habits of minute observation. At sea the log-book was daily copied, and the application of his favorite mathematics to navigation studied; in the island, the soil, agricultural products, modes of culture, fruits, commerce, military force, fortifications, manners of the inhabitants, municipal regulations and government, all were noted in this journal. Lawrence Washington died in July, 1752, leaving a wife and infant daughter, and upon George, although the youngest executor, devolved the whole management of the property, in which he had a residuary interest. The affairs of the estate were extensive and complicated, and engrossed much of his time and thoughts for several months. His public duties were not, however, neglected. Soon after the arrival of Governor Dinwiddie the number of military divisions was reduced to four and the northern division allotted to Washington. It included several counties, which he had visited at stated intervals, to train and instruct the military officers, inspect the men, arms, and accoutrements, and establish a uniform system of manœuvres and discipline.

In 1753 the French in Canada pushed troops across the lakes, and at the same time bodies of armed men ascended from New Orleans to form a junction with them, and establish themselves on the upper waters of the Ohio. Governor Dinwiddie resolved to send a commissioner to confer with the French officer in command, and inquire by what authority he occupied a territory claimed by the British. This charge required a man of discretion, accustomed to travel in the woods, and familiar with Indian manners. Washington was selected, notwithstanding his youth, as possessed of these requisites. He set out from Williamsburg on October 31, 1753, and returned on January 16, 1754. He discovered that a permanent settlement was contemplated by the French within the British territory, and notwithstanding the vigilance of the garrison, he contrived to bring back with him a plan of their fort on a branch of French Creek, fifteen miles south of Lake Erie, and an accurate description of its form, size, construction, cannon, and barracks.

In March, 1754, the military establishment of the colony was increased to six companies. Colonel Fry, an Englishman of scientific acquirements and gentlemanly manners, was placed at the head of them, and Washington was appointed second in command. His first campaign was a trying but useful school to him. He was pushed forward, with three small companies, to occupy the outposts of the Ohio, in front of a superior French force, and unsupported by his commanding officer. Relying upon his own resources and the friendship of the Indians, Washington pushed boldly on. On May 27th he encountered and defeated a detachment of the French army under M. De Jumonville, who fell in the action.

Soon after Colonel Fry died suddenly, and the chief command devolved upon Washington. Innis, the commander of the North Carolina troops, was, it is true, placed over his head, but the new commander never took the field. An ill-timed parsimony had occasioned disgust among the soldiers, but Washington remained unshaken. Anticipating that a strong detachment would be sent against him from Fort Duquesne as soon as Jumonville's defeat was known there, he intrenched himself on the Great Meadows. The advance of the French in force obliged him to retreat, but this operation he performed in a manner that elicited a vote of thanks from the House of Burgesses. In 1755 Colonel Washington acceded to the request of General Braddock to take part in the campaign as one of his military family, retaining his former rank. When privately consulted by Braddock, " I urged him," wrote Washington, " in the warmest terms I was able, to push forward, if he even did it with a small but chosen band, with such artillery and light stores as were necessary, leaving the heavy artillery and baggage to follow with the rear division by slow and easy marches." This advice prevailed. Washington was, however, attacked by a violent fever, in consequence of which he was only able to rejoin the army on the evening before the battle of the Monongahela. In that fatal affair he exposed himself with the most reckless bravery, and when the soldiers were finally put to rout, hastened to the rear division to order up horses and wagons for the wounded. The panic-stricken army dispersed on all sides, and Washington retired to Mount Vernon, which had now, by the death of his brother's daughter without issue, become his own property. His bravery was universally admitted, and it was known that latterly his prudent counsels had been disregarded.

In the autumn of the same year he was appointed to reorganize the provincial troops. He retained the command of them till the close of the campaign of 1758. The tardiness and irresolution of provincial assemblies and governors compelled him to act during much of this time upon the defensive; but to the necessity hence imposed upon him of projecting a chain of defensive forts for the Ohio frontier, he was indebted for that mastery of this kind of war, which afterward availed him so much. Till 1758 the Virginia troops remained on the footing of militia; and Washington having had ample opportunities to convince himself of the utter worthlessness of a militia in time of war, in the beginning of that year prevailed upon the Government to organize them on the same footing as the royal forces. At the same time that Washington's experience was extending, his sentiments of allegiance were weakened by the reluctance with which the claims of the provincial officers were admitted, and the unreserved preference uniformly given to the officers of the regular army. At the close of 1758 he resigned his commission and retired into private life.

On January 6, 1759, he married Mrs. Martha Custis, a young widow with two children. " Mr. Custis," says Mr. Sparke, " had left large landed estates, and £45,000 sterling in money. One-third of this property she held in her own right; the other two-thirds being equally divided between her two children." Washington had a considerable fortune of his own at the time of his marriage, consisting of the estate at Mount Vernon, and large tracts of land which he had selected during his surveying expeditions and obtained grants of at different times. He now devoted himself to the management of this extensive property, and to the guardianship of Mrs. Washington's children, and till the commencement of 1763 was, in appearance at least, principally occupied with these private matters. He found time, however, for public civil duties. He had been elected a member of the House of Burgesses before he resigned his commission, and although there were commonly two, and sometimes three sessions in every year, he was punctual in his attendance from beginning to end of each. During the period of his service in the Legislature he frequently attended on such theatrical exhibitions as were then presented in America, and lived on terms of intimacy with the most eminent men of Virginia. At Mount Vernon he practised on a large scale the hospitality for which the Southern planters have ever been distinguished. His chief diversion in the country was the chase. He exported the produce of his estates to London, Liverpool, and Bristol, and imported everything required for his property, and domestic establishment. His industry was equal to his enterprise ; his day-books, ledgers and letter-books were all kept by himself and he drew up his own contracts and deeds. In the House of Burgesses he seldom spoke, but nothing escaped his notice, and his opinion was eagerly sought and followed. He assumed trusts at the solicitation of friends, and was much in request as an arbitrator. He was, probably without being himself aware of it, establishing a wide and strong influence, which no person suspected till the time arrived for exercising it.

On March 4, 1773, Lord Dunmore prorogued the intractable House of Burgesses. Washington had been a close observer of every previous movement in his country, though it was not in his nature to play the agitator. He had expressed his disapprobation of the Stamp Act in unqualified terms. The non-importation agreement, drawn up by George Mason in 1769, was presented to the members of the dissolved House of Burgesses by Washington. In 1773 he supported the resolutions instituting a committee of correspondence and recommending the legislatures of the other colonies to do the same. He represented Fairfax County in the Convention which met at Williamsburg, in August, 1774, and was appointed by it one of the six Virginian delegates to the first General Congress. On his return from Congress he was virtually placed in command of the Virginian Independent Companies. In the spring of 1775 he devised a plan for the more complete military organization of Virginia ; and on June 15th of that year, he was elected commander-in-chief of the continental army by Congress.

The portion of Washington's life which we have hitherto been passing in review, may be considered as his probationary period—the time during which he was training himself for the great business of his life. His subsequent career naturally subdivides itself into two periods—that of his military command and that of his presidency. In the former we have Washington the soldier ; in the latter, Washington the statesman. His avocations from 1748 to 1775 were as

DUMARESQ PINXIT.

THE SURRENDER OF CORNWALLIS TO WASHINGTON.

good a school as can well be conceived for acquiring the accomplishments of either character. His early intimacy and connection with the Fairfax family had taught him to look on society with the eyes of the class which takes a part in government. His familiarity with applied mathematics and his experience as a surveyor on the wild frontier lands, had made him master of that most important branch of knowledge for a commander—the topography of the country. His experience as a parade officer, as a partisan on the frontier, and as the commander of considerable bodies of disciplined troops, had taught him the principles both of the war of detail and the war of large masses. On the other hand, his punctual habits of business, his familiarity with the details both of agriculture and commerce, and the experience he had acquired as trustee, arbitrator, and member of the House of Burgesses, were so many preparatory studies for the duties of a statesman. He commenced his great task of first liberating and then governing a nation, with all the advantages of this varied experience, in his forty-third year, an age at which the physical vigor is undiminished, and the intellect fully ripe. He persevered in it, with a brief interval of repose, for upward of twenty years, with almost uniform success, and with an exemption from the faults of great leaders unparalleled in history.

Washington was elected commander-in-chief on June 15, 1775; he resigned his commission into the hands of the President of Congress on December 23, 1783. His intermediate record as a general, and as the steadfast and undismayed leader of an apparently hopeless struggle, we pass over here. It is the entire history of the American Revolution.

We must also pass briefly over the interval which separates the epoch of Washington the soldier from that of Washington the statesman—the few years which elapsed between the resignation of his command in 1783, and his election as first President of the United States, in February, 1789. It was for him no period of idleness. In addition to a liberal increase of hospitality at Mount Vernon, and indefatigable attention to the management of his large estates, he actively promoted in his own State, plans of internal navigation, acts for encouraging education, and plans for the civilization of the Indians. He also acted as delegate from Virginia to the Convention which framed the first constitution of the United States. We now turn to contemplate him as president.

Washington left Mount Vernon for New York, which was then the seat of Congress, on April 16, 1789. His journey was a triumphal procession. He took the oath of office on April 30th, with religious services, processions, and other solemnities.

The new president's first step was to request elaborate reports from the Secretary of Foreign Affairs, the Secretary of War, and the Commissioners of the Treasury. The reports he read, and condensed with his own hand, particularly those of the Treasury board. The voluminous official correspondence in the public archives, from the time of the treaty of peace till the time he entered on the presidency, he read, abridged, and studied, with the view of fixing in his mind every important point that had been discussed, and the history of what had been done.

His arrangements for the transaction of business and the reception of visitors were characterized by the same spirit of order which had marked him when a boy, and when at the head of the army. Every Tuesday, between the hours of three and four, he was prepared to receive such persons as chose to call. Every Friday afternoon the rooms were open in like manner for visits to Mrs. Washington. He accepted no invitations to dinner, but invited to his own table foreign ministers, officers of the government, and others, in such numbers as his domestic establishment could accommodate. The rest of the week-days were devoted to business appointments. No visits were received on Sunday, or promiscuous company admitted ; he attended church regularly, and the rest of that day was his own.

The organization of the executive departments was decreed by act of Congress during the first session. They were the Departments of Foreign Affairs (afterward called the Department of State, and including both foreign and domestic affairs), of the Treasury, and of War. It devolved upon the president to select proper persons to fill the several offices. Jefferson was appointed Secretary of State ; Hamilton, Secretary of the Treasury ; and Knox, Secretary of War. Randolph had the post of Attorney-General. Jay was made Chief-Justice. After making these appointments he undertook a tour through the Eastern States, and returned to be present at the opening of Congress, in January, 1790.

In his opening speech he recommended to the attention of the Legislature a provision for the common defence ; laws for naturalizing foreigners ; a uniform system of currency, weights, and measures ; the encouragement of agriculture, commerce, and manufactures ; the promotion of science and literature ; and an effective system for the support of the public credit. The last topic gave rise to protracted and vehement debates. At last Hamilton's plan for funding all the domestic debts was carried by a small majority in both Houses of Congress. The president suppressed his sentiments on the subject while it was under debate in Congress, but he approved the act for funding the public debt, and was from conviction a decided friend to the measure. It now became apparent to the most unreflecting that two great parties were in the process of formation, the one jealous of anything that might encroach upon democratic principles ; the other distrustful of the power of institutions so simple as those of the United States to preserve tranquillity and the cohesion of the state. Jefferson was the head of the Democratic, Hamilton of what was afterward called the Federalist party. Washington endeavored to reconcile these ardent and incompatible spirits. His own views were more in accordance with those of Hamilton ; but he knew Jefferson's value as a statesman, and he felt the importance of the president remaining independent of either party. The two secretaries, however, continued to diverge in their political course, and ultimately their differences settled into personal enmity.

The president's term of office was drawing to a close, and an anxious wish began to prevail that he should allow himself to be elected for a second term. Jefferson, Hamilton, and Randolph—who did not exactly coincide with either—all shared in this anxiety, and each wrote a long letter to Washington, assigning reasons for his allowing himself to be re-elected. He yielded; and on March 4, 1793, he took the oath of office in the senate chamber.

The first question that came before the cabinet after the re-election, rendered more decided the differences which already existed. The European parties, of which the court of England and the French republic were the representatives, were eager to draw the United States into the vortex of their struggle. The president and his cabinet were unanimous in their determination to preserve neutrality, but the aristocratic and democratic sections of the cabinet could not refrain from displaying their respective biases and their jealousy of each other. Foreign affairs were mingled with domestic politics, and the Democratic and Federalist parties became avowedly organized. Washington was for a time allowed to keep aloof from the contest—not for a long time. A circumstance insignificant in itself increased the bitterness of the contest out of doors. Democratic societies had been formed on the model of the Jacobin clubs of France. Washington regarded them with alarm, and the unmeasured expression of his sentiments on this head subjected him to a share in the attacks made upon the party accused of undue fondness for England and English institutions.

Advices from the American minister in London representing that the British cabinet was disposed to settle the differences between the two countries amicably, Washington nominated Mr. Jay to the Senate as Envoy-extraordinary to the court of Great Britain. The nomination, though strenuously opposed by the Democratic party, was confirmed in the Senate by a majority of two to one. The treaty negotiated by Jay was received at the seat of government in March, 1795, soon after the session of Congress closed. The president summoned the Senate to meet in June to ratify it. The treaty was ratified. Before the treaty was signed by the president it was surreptitiously published. It was vehemently condemned, and public meetings against it were held to intimidate the executive. The president, nevertheless, signed the treaty on August 18th. When Congress met in March, 1796, a resolution was carried by a large majority in the House of Representatives, requesting the president to lay before the house the instructions to Mr. Jay, the correspondence, and other documents relating to the negotiations. Washington declined to furnish the papers; a vehement debate ensued, but in the end the hostile majority yielded to the exigency of the case and united in passing laws for the fulfilment of the treaty.

The two houses of Congress met again in December. Washington had published on September 15th his farewell address to the United States. He now delivered his last speech to Congress, and took occasion to urge upon that body the gradual increase of the navy, a provision for the encouragement of agriculture and manufactures, the establishment of a national university, and of a military academy. Little was done during the session; public attention was engrossed by the presidential election. Adams, the Federalist candidate, had the highest number of votes; Jefferson, the Democratic candidate (who was consequently declared vice-president), the next. Washington's commanding character and isolation from party, had preserved this degree of strength to the holders of his own political views. He was present as a spectator at the installation of his successor, and immediately afterward returned to Mount Vernon.

He survived till December 14, 1799, but except when summoned in May, 1798, to take the command of the provincial army, on the prospect of a war with France, did not again engage in public business.

The character of Washington is one of simple and substantial greatness. His passions were vehement but concentrated, and thoroughly under control. An irresistible strength of will was combined with a singularly well-balanced mind, with much sagacity, much benevolence, much love of justice. Without possessing what may be called genius, Washington was endowed with a rare quickness of perception and soundness of judgment, and an eager desire of knowledge. His extremely methodical habits enabled him to find time for everything, and were linked with a talent for organization. During the War of Independence he was the defensive force of America ; wanting him, it would almost appear as if the democratic mass must have resolved itself into its elements. To place Washington as a warrior on a footing with the Cæsars, Napoleons, and Wellingtons, would be absurd. He lost more battles than he gained. But he kept an army together and kept up resistance to the enemy, under more adverse circumstances than any other general ever did. His services as a statesman were similar in kind. He upheld the organization of the American state during the first eight years of its existence, amid the storms of Jacobinical controversy, and gave it time to consolidate. No other American but himself could have done this, for of all the American leaders he was the only one whom men felt differed from themselves. The rest were soldiers or civilians, Federalists or Democrats ; but he was Washington. The awe and reverence felt for him were blended with affection for his kindly qualities, and except for a brief period toward the close of his second presidential term, there has been but one sentiment entertained toward him throughout the Union—that of reverential love. His was one of those rare natures which greatness follows without their striving for it.

The following extract is from a letter written by him to his adopted daughter, Nellie Custis, on the subject of love :*

" Love is said to be an involuntary passion, and it is therefore contended that it cannot be resisted. This is true in part only, for like all things else, when nourished and supplied plentifully with aliment it is rapid in progress ; but let these be withdrawn and it may be stifled in its birth or much stunted in its growth. For example : a woman (the same may be said of the other sex) all beautiful and accomplished, will, while her hand and heart are undisposed of, turn the heads and set the circle in which she moves on fire. Let her marry, and what is the consequence ? The madness ceases and all is quiet again. Why ? Not because there is any diminution in the charm of the lady, but because there

* Copied by kind permission of the publishers, Messrs. Harper & Bros., from Benson Lossing's " Mary and Martha Washington."

is an end of hope. Hence it follows that love may, and therefore ought to be, under the guidance of reason, for although we cannot avoid first impressions, we may assuredly place them under guard ; and my motives for treating on this subject are to show you, while you remain Eleanor Parke Custis, spinster, and retain the resolution to love with moderation, the propriety of adhering to the latter resolution, at least until you have secured your game, or the way by which it may be accomplished.

"When the fire is beginning to kindle, and your heart growing warm, propound these questions to it : Who is this invader ? Have I a competent knowledge of him ? Is he a man of good character ; a man of sense ? For, be assured, a sensible woman can never be happy with a fool. What has been his walk in life ? Is he a gambler, a spendthrift, or drunkard ? Is his fortune sufficient to maintain me in the manner I have been accustomed to live, and my sisters do live ? and is he one to whom my friends can have no reasonable objection ? If these interrogatories can be satisfactorily answered there will remain but one more to be asked ; that, however, is an important one : Have I sufficient ground to conclude that his affections are engaged by me ? Without this the heart of sensibility will struggle against a passion that is not reciprocated—delicacy, custom, or call it by what epithet you will, having precluded all advances on your part. The declaration, without the *most indirect* invitation of yours, must proceed from the man, to render it permanent and valuable, and nothing short of good sense, and an easy, unaffected conduct can draw the line between prudery and coquetry. It would be no great departure from truth to say that it rarely happens otherwise than that a thorough-paced coquette dies in celibacy, as a punishment for her attempts to mislead others by encouraging looks, words, or actions, given for no other purpose than to draw men on to make overtures that they may be rejected. . . . Every blessing, among which a good husband when you want one, is bestowed on you by yours affectionately."

JOHN ADAMS

By Edwin Williams

(1735–1826)

 OHN ADAMS, the second president of the United States, was born on the 19th of October (old style), 1735, in that part of the town of Braintree (near Boston), Massachusetts, which has since been incorporated by the name of Quincy. He was the fourth in descent from Henry Adams, who fled from persecution in Devonshire, England, and settled in Massachusetts about the year 1630. Another of the ancestors of Mr. Adams was John Alden, one of the Pilgrim founders of the Ply-

mouth colony in 1620. Receiving his early education in his native town, John Adams, in 1751, was admitted a member of Harvard College, at Cambridge, where he graduated in regular course four years afterward. On leaving college

he went to Worcester, for the purpose of studying law, and at the same time to support himself, according to the usage at that time in New England, by teaching in the grammar-school of that town. He studied law with James Putnam, a barrister of eminence, by whom he was afterward introduced to the acquaintance of Jeremy Gridley, then attorney-general of the province, who proposed him to the court for admission to the bar of Suffolk County, in 1758, and gave him access to his library, which was then one of the best in America.

Mr. Adams commenced the practice of his profession in his native town, and by travelling the circuits with the court, became well known in that part of the country. In 1766, by the advice of Mr. Gridley, he removed to Boston, where he soon distinguished himself at the bar by his superior talents as counsel and advocate. At an earlier period of his life his thoughts had begun to turn on general politics, and the prospects of his country engaged his attention. Soon after leaving college he wrote a letter to a friend, dated at Worcester, October 12, 1755, which evinces so remarkable a foresight that it is fortunate it has been preserved. We make the following extracts : " Soon after the Reformation a few people came over into this new world for conscience' sake. Perhaps this apparently trivial incident may transfer the great seat of empire into America. It looks likely to me, if we can remove the turbulent Gallics, our people, according to the exactest computation, will, in another century, become more numerous than England herself. The only way to keep us from setting up for ourselves is to disunite us. *Divide et impera.* Keep us in distinct colonies, and then some great men in each colony, desiring the monarchy of the whole, will destroy each other's influence, and keep the country in equilibrio. Be not surprised that I am turned politician ; the whole town is immersed in politics. I sit and hear, and, after being led through a maze of sage observations, I sometimes retire and, by laying things together, form some reflections pleasing to myself. The produce of one of these reveries you have read above." Mr. Webster observes : " It is remarkable that the author of this prognostication should live to see fulfilled to the letter what could have seemed to others, at the time, but the extravagance of youthful fancy. His earliest political feelings were thus strongly American, and from this ardent attachment to his native soil he never departed."

In 1764 he married Abigail Smith, daughter of Rev. William Smith, of Weymouth, and granddaughter of Colonel Quincy, a lady of uncommon endowments and excellent education. He had previously imbibed a prejudice against the prevailing religious opinions of New England, and became attached to speculations hostile to those opinions. Nor were his views afterward changed. In his religious sentiments he accorded with Dr. Bancroft, a Unitarian minister of Worcester, of whose printed sermons he expressed his high approbation. In 1765 Mr. Adams published an essay on canon and feudal law, the object of which was to show the conspiracy between Church and State for the purpose of oppressing the people.

In 1770 he was chosen a representative from the town of Boston, in the Legislature of Massachusetts. The same year he was one of the counsel who defended Captain Preston and the British soldiers who fired at his order upon the inhabitants of Boston. Captain Preston was acquitted, and Mr. Adams lost no favor with his fellow-citizens by engaging in this trial. As a member of the Legislature he opposed the royal governor, Hutchinson, in his measures, and also wrote against the British Government in the newspapers. In 1774 he was elected a member of the Massachusetts Council, and negatived by Governor Gage. In this and the next year he wrote on the Whig side, the pamphlets called "Nov Anglus," in reply to essays, signed "Massachusitensis," in favor of the British Government, by Sewall, the attorney-general. The same year he was appointed a member of the Continental Congress, from Massachusetts, and in that body, which met at Philadelphia, he became one of the most efficient and able advocates of liberty. In the Congress which met in May, 1775, he again took his seat, having been reappointed as a delegate. In 1775 he seconded the nomination of Washington as commander-in-chief of the army, and in July, 1776, he was the adviser and great supporter of the Declaration of Independence. It was reported by a committee composed of Thomas Jefferson, John Adams, Benjamin Franklin, Roger Sherman, and Robert R. Livingston. During the same year he, with Dr. Franklin and Edward Rutledge, was deputed to treat with Lord Howe for the pacification of the colonies. He declined at this time the offer of the office of Chief-Justice of the Supreme Court of Massachusetts.

In December, 1777, Mr. Adams was appointed a commissioner to the court of France; and with the exception of one short interval, during which he aided in the framing of the Massachusetts State Constitution, he spent the following eleven years in diplomatic services abroad. He arranged the treaties of the United States with most foreign nations during that time, was associated with Franklin and Jay in signing the treaty of peace with England, and was our first English minister.

The services of Mr. Adams in the cause of his country, at home and abroad, during the period to which we have referred, it is believed, were not excelled by those of any other of the patriots of the Revolution. In the language of one of his eulogists (Mr. J. E. Sprague, of Massachusetts), "Not a hundred men in the country could have been acquainted with any part of the labors of Mr. Adams—they appeared anonymously, or under assumed titles; they were concealed in the secret conclaves of Congress, or the more secret cabinets of princes. Such services are never known to the public; or, if known, only in history, when the actors of the day have passed from the stage, and the motives for longer concealment cease to exist. As we ascend the mount of history, and rise above the vapors of party prejudice, we shall all acknowledge that we owe our independence more to John Adams than to any other created being, and that he was the Great Leader of the American Revolution."

When permission was given him to return from Europe, the Continental Congress adopted the following resolution: "Resolved, That Congress entertain a high sense of the services which Mr. Adams has rendered to the United States, in the execution of the various important trusts which they have from time to time committed to him; and that the thanks of Congress be presented to him for the patriotism, perseverance, integrity, and diligence with which he has ably and faithfully served his country." Such was the testimonial of his country, expressed through the national councils, at the termination of his revolutionary and diplomatic career.

During the absence of Mr. Adams in Europe, the Constitution of the United States had been formed and adopted. He highly approved of its provisions, and on his return, when it was about to go into operation, he was selected by the friends of the Constitution to be placed on the ticket with Washington as a candidate for one of the two highest offices in the gift of the people. He was consequently elected vice-president, and on the assembling of the Senate he took his seat, as president of that body, at New York, in April, 1789. Having been reelected to that office in 1792, he held it, and presided in the Senate with great dignity, during the entire period of the administration of Washington, whose confidence he enjoyed, and by whom he was consulted on important questions. In his valedictory address to the Senate he remarks: "It is a recollection of which nothing can ever deprive me, and it will be a source of comfort to me through the remainder of my life that, on the one hand, I have for eight years held the second situation under our Constitution, in perfect and uninterrupted harmony with the first, without envy in the one, or jealousy in the other, so, on the other hand, I have never had the smallest misunderstanding with any member of the Senate."

In 1790 Mr. Adams wrote his celebrated "Discourses on Davila;" they were anonymously published at first, in the *Gazette of the United States*, of Philadelphia, in a series of numbers; they may be considered as a sequel to his "Defence of the American Constitutions." He was a decided friend and patron of literature and the arts, and while in Europe, having obtained much information on the subject of public institutions, he contributed largely to the advancement of establishments in his native State for the encouragement of arts, sciences, and letters.

On the retirement of General Washington from the presidency of the United

States, Mr. Adams was elected his successor, after a close and spirited contest with two rivals for that high office ; Mr. Jefferson being supported by the Democratic or Republican party, while a portion of the Federal party preferred Mr. Thomas Pinckney, of South Carolina, who was placed on the ticket with Mr. Adams. The result was the election of Mr. Adams as president, and in March, 1797, he entered upon his duties in that office. He came to the presidency in a stormy time. In the language of Colonel Knapp, "the French revolution had just reached its highest point of settled delirium, after some of the paroxysms of its fury had passed away. The people of the United States took sides, some approving, others deprecating, the course pursued by France. Mr. Adams wished to preserve a neutrality, but found this quite impossible. A navy was raised with surprising promptitude, to prevent insolence and to chastise aggression. It had the desired effect, and France was taught that the Americans were friends in peace, but were not fearful of war when it could not be averted. When the historian shall come to this page of our history, he will do justice to the sagacity, to the spirit, and to the integrity of Mr Adams, and will find that he had more reasons, and good ones, for his conduct, than his friends or enemies ever gave him."

In his course of public policy, when war with France was expected, he was encouraged by addresses from all quarters, and by the approving voice of Washington. He, however, gave dissatisfaction to many of his own political party, in his final attempts to conciliate France, and in his removal of two members of his cabinet toward the close of his administration. Under these circumstances, notwithstanding Mr. Adams was the candidate of the Federal party for re-election as president, and received their faithful support, it is not strange that his opponents, with the advantage in their favor of the superior popularity of Mr. Jefferson, succeeded in defeating him. For this event, the correspondence of Mr. Adams shows that he was prepared, and he left the arduous duties of chief magistrate probably with less of disappointment than his enemies expected.

Immediately after Mr. Jefferson had succeeded to the presidency, in 1801, Mr. Adams retired to his estate at Quincy, in Massachusetts, and passed the remainder of his days in literary and scientific leisure, though occasionally addressing various communications to the public. He gave his support generally to the administration of Mr. Jefferson, and the friendship between these distinguished men was revived by a correspondence, and continued for several years previous to their death. When the disputes with Great Britain eventuated in war, Mr. Adams avowed his approbation of that measure, and in 1815 he saw the second treaty of peace concluded with that nation, by a commission of which his son was at the head, as he had been himself in that commission which formed the treaty of 1783.

In 1816 the Republican party in Massachusetts, which had once vehemently opposed him as president of the United States, paid him the compliment of placing his name at the head of their list of presidential electors. In 1820 he was chosen a member of the State Convention to revise the constitution of Massachusetts, which body unanimously solicited him to act as their president. This he declined on account of his age, but he was complimented by a vote of the convention acknowledging his great services, for a period of more than half a century, in the cause of his country and of mankind.

The last years of the long life of Mr. Adams were peaceful and tranquil. His mansion was always the abode of elegant hospitality, and he was occasionally enlivened by visits from his distinguished son, whom, in 1825, he had the singular felicity of seeing elevated to the office of President of the United States. At length, having lived to a good old age, he expired, surrounded by his affectionate relatives, on July 4, 1826, the fiftieth anniversary of that independence which he had done so much to achieve. A short time before his death, being asked to suggest a toast for the customary celebration, he replied, " I will give you—Independence forever." Mr. Jefferson died on the same day. A similar coincidence occurred five years afterward, in the death of President Monroe, July 4, 1831.

Mr. Adams was of middle stature and full person, and when elected president, was bald on the top of his head. His countenance beamed with intelligence, and moral as well as physical courage. His walk was firm and dignified to a late period of his life. His manner was slow and deliberate, unless he was excited, and when this happened he expressed himself with great energy. He was ever a man of purest morals, and is said to have been a firm believer in Christianity, not from habit and example, but from diligent investigation of its proofs.

THOMAS JEFFERSON *

By Hon. John B. Henderson

(1743–1826)

THOMAS JEFFERSON was born April 2, 1743, at Shadwell, Albemarle County, Va. His father, Peter Jefferson, was a descendant of a Welsh family which came to Virginia before the Pilgrims landed in Massachusetts. The father's income was derived from a large farm adjoining that of William Randolph, whose daughter, Jane, he married in 1738. Monticello, the future residence of his son Thomas, was a part of this farm. Peter Jefferson was a leader among the men of his day and received expressions of public confidence from the voters of his county. He died in 1759, having directed that Thomas should complete his education in William and Mary College at Williamsburg, then the capital of the colony.

Thomas entered the college and by assiduous application he soon built upon the learning acquired in the public and private schools of his county, an education quite liberal and advanced for that period.

He was tall, and in youth somewhat awkward in manner. What he lacked, however, in personal grace was at once forgotten in the vivacity of his conversation, made doubly charming by the extent and variety of his learning. During his collegiate days he formed a close friendship with Patrick Henry, John Marshall, and others who afterward became distinguished in American history. He was always welcome in the house of Governor Fauquier, from whom he learned much of the social, political, and parliamentary life of the old world. It was here that he first met George Wythe, a gifted and talented young lawyer, who afterward became Chancellor of the State.

After leaving college he entered upon the study of the law in the office of his friend Mr. Wythe, and with this and the management of his father's estate he found himself abundantly occupied.

In 1767 he was admitted to the bar, and for several years devoted himself to the practice of his profession. It is quite probable that, in consequence of his inability to speak and his utter incapacity for forensic controversy, his career at the bar would not have reached the highest distinction. What he lacked, however, in the power of speech, found ample compensation in the strength, beauty, and elegance of expression which he commanded with the pen. This extraordinary talent was destined soon to find abundant employment in defending the rights of the people against the oppressive acts of the mother-country. Patrick Henry had already argued the "Parsons' Cause" in December, 1763, and Jefferson himself, as a college student at Williamsburg, had listened to the impassioned speech of Henry in the Virginia House of Burgesses against the Stamp Act of Parliament. But the fiery eloquence of his friend Henry only fanned a flame that already burned in the breast of Jefferson. Impulsive by nature, by education and training a democrat, he naturally espoused the cause of his countrymen. The peculiar condition of the colonies furnished the opportunity to Jefferson's wonderful faculty for writing. The orator could not be heard by all the people of the colonies; but the products of the pen could be carried to the most secluded hamlet. And truly in Jefferson's hands the pen was "mightier than the sword."

The first year after opening his law office, at the age of twenty-five, he was elected a member of the House of Burgesses from Albemarle, his native county, and on taking his seat the following May, the controversy between the royal governor and the assembly at once began. Jefferson prepared the resolutions in reply to the executive speech; and on the third day of the session the passage of other resolutions, in the form of a bill of rights, caused the governor to dissolve the assembly. Jefferson was again elected to the House of Burgesses, and in 1774, was elected a delegate to the State convention.

17

On account of illness he failed to reach the convention, but he prepared and forwarded to its president a draft of instructions which he hoped would be adopted for the guidance of those to be sent by the body as delegates to the General Congress of the colonies. For this paper, afterward published as " A Summary View of the Rights of British America," the name of Jefferson was inserted in a bill of attainder brought into the English Parliament.

After a short detention in the House of Burgesses, in which he drafted the reply of Virginia to the " conciliatory proposition " of Lord North, he proceeded to Philadelphia as a delegate to the General Congress, in which he took his seat on June 21, 1775.

When Jefferson entered the Congress, conditions existing between the mother country and the colonies had already reached the point of open rebellion. It is true that the taxes had all been repealed except the import tax on tea, but the repeals had been invariably accompanied with the assertion of an unlimited right to tax without the consent of the colonies. English troops had been quartered in Boston, and English war-ships occupied its harbor. The right of deportation to, and trial in, England for offences committed in America, was still claimed by both king and Parliament. The battles of Lexington and Bunker Hill had now been fought, and Washington had already been commissioned as commander-in-chief of the colonial armies.

In this condition of affairs Massachusetts and Virginia, in which had been most keenly felt the oppressive acts of the mother country, were quite ready for open and avowed rebellion. But in many of the other colonies the sense of loyalty and the ties of friendship were yet sufficiently strong to induce the hope of continued union.

It was therefore not until June 7, 1776, that Virginia, through Richard Henry Lee, introduced into Congress at Philadelphia the resolutions for a final separation ; and a few days thereafter a committee was appointed to prepare the Declaration of Independence. Jefferson was placed at the head of this committee, his colleagues consisting of Adams, Franklin, Roger Sherman, and Robert R. Livingston. The declaration was prepared by Jefferson, and when submitted to Dr. Franklin and John Adams for criticism, some verbal amendments suggested by them were made. It was then reported to Congress on June 28th, and after debate and other slight amendments by the body itself, it was adopted and signed on July 4, 1776.

Whatever the merits or demerits of the paper, it is essentially the work of Jefferson. It has been much criticised, both in its substance and its form. It is quite certain, however, that since its promulgation there has been, not only in the United States but abroad, a continually increasing tendency to accept and apply its principles in the practical affairs of government. As an eloquent arraignment of tyranny, a denunciation of oppression and an inspiration to resistance, it stands perhaps unequalled among the products of human intellect. As appropriately said by another, the paper is " consecrated in the affections of Americans and praise may seem as superfluous as censure would be unavailing."

So soon as the colonies had become united in the cause of forcible resistance, Jefferson returned to his own State to commence perhaps the most useful and beneficent work of his life. He had again been elected to Congress, but with the prescience of the seer, he chose the seemingly less important place of representative to the Legislature of his State. He took his seat on October 7, 1776. On the 11th of the same month he asked leave to present a bill to establish courts of justice in the State of Virginia; on the next day, to authorize tenants *en tail* to convey their estates in fee simple. This was immediately followed by other bills for the utter overthrow of primogeniture and the whole law of entails.

His reformatory spirit did not stop with these radical measures. He found another danger in the conservatism and aristocratic tendencies of the established church of the State. In his judgment the whole body of law and custom inherited from England must be thoroughly exterminated, to the end that English influence might be driven from the land. In his judgment English institutions had been cunningly devised in the interest of monarchy. Their purpose, he believed, was to create and maintain distinctions in society, and to perpetuate and strengthen an aristocratic caste as the ally and support of the crown. So long as they existed there was constant danger of relapse from the high purposes of the rebellion. In Jefferson's regard, they were inconsistent with the principles of the revolution now proclaimed, and sooner or later would be found its open or secret enemies.

For these reforms the old aristocracy of his State denounced him as a Jacobin, and the established church denounced him as an infidel.

Jefferson continued to serve in the House of Delegates during the years 1777 and 1778, and in addition to the measures already named, he secured laws to establish elementary and collegiate education in the State, and to prohibit the further importation of slaves into Virginia. He also sought to inaugurate a system of gradual emancipation; but slavery was already so thoroughly engrafted on the social system of the people, that even Jefferson, Wythe, and Mason could not dislodge it. Jefferson, in 1821, referring to his failure in this regard, said: "it was found that the public mind would not yet bear the proposition, nor will it bear it, even to this day; yet the day is not distant, when it must bear and adopt it, or worse will follow. Nothing is more certainly written in the book of fate than that these people are to be free."

On retiring from the Legislature he was elected governor of the State. The period of his service in this position was unfortunate for his fame. He was essentially a civilian, neither having, nor pretending to have, military skill or knowledge. The war had now been transferred to the Southern States. Cornwallis had overrun Georgia and South Carolina, defeated Gates at Camden, and was pushing north for the desolation of Virginia. The State had already become impoverished by its liberal contributions of money, men, and arms to the general cause, and was now powerless for its own defence. The hated Benedict Arnold was able to ascend the James River to Richmond, dispersing the Legislature and burning the town. Tarleton afterward penetrated as far as Charlottesville—Jefferson and the Legislature narrowly escaping capture. Jefferson felt keenly the situation, and at the expiration of his term retired to Monticello, humiliated and overwhelmed by unjust criticism and undeserved censure. His gloom and melancholy were made still more sad at this period, by the death of his wife, whom he had married in 1772. But the privilege of neither obscurity nor rest was reserved for him. The winter session of 1783 found him again in the General Congress abolishing the English system of coinage and providing for the government of the Northwestern territory, which had been ceded to the confederation by Virginia.

In 1784 he was named as a minister plenipotentiary to Europe at large, to assist Adams and Franklin in the negotiation of commercial treaties. In 1785 he became minister to France in the place of Dr. Franklin, who had resigned; and in March, 1790, in pursuance of a previous acceptance, he entered the Cabinet of President Washington as Secretary of State.

Already the germs of two great conflicting parties had been sown. The debates in the convention that framed the Constitution, and still more manifestly the controversies in the State Conventions called to consider the adoption of the instrument, had developed the differences, which, in theory at least, have distinguished political parties ever since. The colonies had been chiefly settled by Englishmen. No people are more tenacious than they of preconceived opinions, or more averse to the abandonment of ancient forms and customs. A strong attachment to the institutions of England still remained with the people of the colonies. With many of them the whole object of the revolution was political separation from the mother country. They heartily desired independence and freedom, and they had willingly risked their lives to secure them. But the freedom they sought was the right, if they chose, to establish and perpetuate those cherished institutions of the mother-country for themselves. They would enjoy them still, and make them a lasting inheritance for their posterity, but free from the power and dominion of Europe.

Such persons had revolted not against England, but against England's wrongful acts; not against the authority of law, but against the perversion of law. To them the Declaration of Independence was a splendid piece of rhetoric intended only to inflame the mind with a sense of injury, and to nerve the heart to determined resistance. Like the Marseillaise hymn, it was merely to be repeated on entering the battle. Like the bugle blast, it served only to stimulate the soul and shut out all other sounds while the contest lasted. Not so with Jefferson and his followers. The Declaration of Independence truly reflected their political sentiments. To them the revolution meant something more than mere separation. It looked to the total repudiation of the English system of government, and the substitution of the rule of the people. They admitted the inefficiency of the articles of confederation, and were willing to accept nationality in a modified form. But to them the Constitution as framed in 1787 was armed with the most dangerous powers. They accepted it merely as a choice of evils, trusting by strict construction and future amendment to give it eventually the form and mould of their own views.

The President, in selecting his ministers, sought to compromise these antagonisms by giving the parties equal representation in his Cabinet. Between two such men, however, as Jefferson, his Secretary of State, and Alexander Hamilton, his Secretary of the Treasury, there could be no permanent co-operation. So eager, indeed, was Jefferson to inaugurate the controversy, that he really began the battle of strict construction before his peculiar principles had been seriously invaded. Time has long since demonstrated that, in his opposition to Hamilton's financial measures, he was clearly wrong. The truth seems to be, that in this branch of politics, Jefferson was without knowledge or practical skill.

In his discussions with the English minister touching violations of the late treaty of peace, and in the controversy with Spain in respect to the right of navigating the Mississippi River through her territory to the Gulf, Jefferson displayed his usual ability.

The declaration of war by France, now a republic, against England, precipitated upon the Government of the United States a number of difficult and troublesome questions of international law. They were especially irritating because of the personal feelings involved in their discussion and settlement. A profound sense of gratitude to France for assistance in the late revolutionary struggle, was felt by all classes in America, while the Republicans were especially open and undisguised in their expressions of sympathy for the French people. And but for the imprudent conduct of the French minister, Genet, the supremacy of the Federal party might have been seriously jeopardized in the beginning of Washington's second term. The conduct of this functionary was so insolent and exacting as to excite disgust for himself, and to cool in a marked degree the zeal of the Republicans in their support of the new republic.

While Jefferson's sympathy with France was perhaps too manifest, and while his personal conduct in the Cabinet touching this question was not altogether kind to the president, and in other respects liable to criticism, his correspondence with the French Government, when finally published, was found to have been based upon the highest principles of international right and dictated by a proper sense of the dignity and character of his own country.

Jefferson's proud nature had for several years, chafed under the continued success of Federal measures. Washington had manifestly ignored his counsel in the Cabinet, and favored Hamilton in the administration of the Government. Jefferson was piqued and chagrined beyond further endurance. He hated Hamilton with an intensity due only to an open enemy of the country.

In this state of mind, on December 31, 1793, he resigned from the Cabinet, and again sought the seclusion and quiet of his farm at Monticello. But his pen was never idle. He was untiring in the dissemination of his peculiar views of government. With emotions intensified by strong convictions of right, his contributions to the political literature of the day were vigorous and peculiarly attractive. He continued to be the acknowledged leader of the Republican party, and was promptly named as its candidate for president in 1796, to succeed General Washington, who had declined a third term. Between him and John Adams, the candidate of the Federal party, the vote was very close, Adams receiving 71 electoral votes and Jefferson 68. Under the provisions of the Constitution as they existed at the time, Adams became President and Jefferson Vice-President.

During Adams' term were passed the Alien and Sedition laws, as well as others, unnecessary and of doubtful constitutionality, which proved to be fatal and ruinous mistakes of the Federal party. Jefferson and Madison's threats of State repudiation against Federal legislation, as enunciated in the Kentucky and Virginia resolutions, furnished good arguments, of course, for the continued existence of a truly national party. But the seeds of decay had been sown. Adams was vain, impulsive, rash, and violent. Jefferson was far more deliberate, with larger views of statesmanship and a better knowledge of the people. He had abundant cunning and the ready adaptation of partisan skill.

In a contest of four years between such leaders, it is not strange that when the election of 1800 came on, Jefferson should receive 73 electoral votes while Adams received but 65.

Although Jefferson was elected over Adams, he was not yet elected over Aaron Burr, who had received an equal number of votes for president with himself. In reality no vote had been intended for Burr as President—the purpose being to elect Jefferson President and Burr Vice-President.

Under the constitutional provision already referred to, the election was remitted to the House of Representatives. Finally, by the aid of Hamilton, who only hated Jefferson less than he hated Burr, the controversy was decided in favor of the former.

The moment Jefferson became president his whole character seemed to be changed. Instead of the relentless partisan of the past, he became the apostle of benevolence and charity. His inaugural address, in that florid rhetoric of which he was master, enunciated principles of government to which no friend of human liberty could object. The spirit of conciliation breathed in every sentence. "Every difference of opinion," he said, "is not a difference of principle. We have called by different names brethren of the same principles. We are all Republicans—we are all Federalists. . . . Let us then, with courage and confidence, pursue our own Federal and Republican principles, our attachment to our Union and representative government."

The short-lived peace of Europe had re-established American commerce on the ocean, and general prosperity pervaded all departments of business. Indeed, the wise moderation of the president had brought the most agreeable disappointment to his enemies. Federalists were not removed from office for political reasons, and the country settled down into the conviction that Republican success after all, might prove to be a beneficent change.

As already stated, the Northwest territory, extending from the Ohio to the Mississippi River, had formerly belonged to Virginia, and perhaps no public man of his day so well understood as did Jefferson, the importance and needs of that vast domain.   Spain, as the owner of Louisiana, held supreme control of New Orleans and the lower Mississippi.

While Secretary of State under Washington, Jefferson would have been content with the acquisition of the Island of New Orleans, and the free navigation of the Mississippi River.   Circumstances had now changed.   He was himself president.   Spain had suddenly conveyed Louisiana to France, and Napoleon was meditating the abrogation of the peace of Amiens and the declaration of war against England.   In such a war France could not well retain her distant possessions against the superior naval power of her old and grasping enemy.   Napoleon had a property which in case of war, he was likely to lose.   He had resolved on war, and for that purpose needed money, which, fortunately, the American Treasury could furnish at once.

Instead of the Island of New Orleans the President's dream now embraced the whole of the Louisiana purchase, extending from the Mississippi River to the Pacific Ocean.

Livingston, of New York, the associate of Jefferson, in 1776, on the Committee to frame the Declaration of Independence, was now Minister to France, but he was unfortunately embarrassed by his committal to the acquisition of New Orleans alone.   Monroe's term, as Governor of Virginia, had just expired. He had formerly served the country most acceptably at the French court.   He was the devoted friend, personally and politically, of Jefferson.   They were both committed to the " strict construction " theory of the Constitution.   This narrow view of the instrument, on which their party had come into power, absolutely forbade the acquisition of territory by purchase.   But Louisiana was necessary not only to the growth, but to the maintenance of the Union.   It mattered not that the professions of the Republican party had to be violated.   The prize outweighed the virtue of party consistency.   Jefferson himself was forced to admit the want of power, but having resolved on the act, he said : " The less that is said about any constitutional difficulty the better."   Again he said : " It will be desirable for Congress to do what is necessary in silence."

With these views he despatched Monroe to Paris.   For obvious reasons written instructions were avoided ; but it is quite certain that unlimited discretion to the Minister had resulted from a careful comparison of views.

It was under these circumstances that in 1803 the vast domain known as "The Louisiana Purchase" was obtained by the United States for the paltry consideration of fifteen million dollars.

This of itself added immensely to Jefferson's popularity.   Internal taxation had been abolished.   Rigid economy of administration had been introduced. The public debt was in the course of rapid extinction.   The rigorous ceremonials of former administrations had given place to the simplest forms, and the temples of power had been made accessible to the humblest citizen.   The country enjoyed great prosperity, and a spirit of contentment pervaded the land.

Jefferson's second election, in 1804, was almost without opposition—his vote being 162 to 14 for C. C. Pinkney, the Federal candidate.

The second term of the President was far less successful than the first. A political exigency in France had forced the sale of Louisiana, and its opportune purchase had given Jefferson unbounded popularity, and linked his name with the future greatness of his country. But the impending hostilities producing that exigency had now been declared. France and England were again in open war, and each, to wound the other, had recklessly trampled upon the rights of the United States. English orders in council blockaded the ports of France, and Napoleon's Berlin decrees equally closed those of England against neutral commerce. The right of search was claimed by both powers, and offensively exercised by England. Time had now brought its inevitable revenges. Jefferson was again confronted by conditions in which he manifested more or less of weakness and incapacity. In peace his statesmanship was always creditable, and at times, truly magnificent. In the presence of war he was too often vacillating and incompetent. The embargo on the commerce of his own country, which he suggested, was hardly less injurious than the wrongs of which he complained. The remedy was worse, if possible, than the disease.

Aaron Burr, in contesting for the presidency in 1801, had forfeited the confidence of his own party, and for killing Hamilton in a duel in 1804, he had incurred the hatred of the Federalists, and lost the respect of all parties. In his desperation he had organized an expedition to proceed down the Ohio and Mississippi rivers with a view, as was supposed, of invading Mexico, or segregating from the United States a portion of its territory. He was arrested for treason and brought to Richmond, where he was finally tried for a high misdemeanor in organizing forces against Spain within the United States. In this prosecution, as in the impeachment of Judge Chase of the Supreme Court, executive encouragement and aid were offensively open and notorious.

When the embargo had almost ruined the commercial States of the Union, it was modified by a non-intercourse act with France and England, to take effect on March 4, 1809, the last day of Jefferson's term.

At the close of his second term Jefferson permanently retired from office, and spent his remaining years at Monticello.

By a singular coincidence both he and John Adams died on July 4, 1826, just fifty years after they had signed the Declaration of Independence.

The brief facts already recited clearly indicate the character of the man. He was a bold and original thinker. With him mere precedent was without weight. By nature he was a democrat, plain, simple, and unostentatious. He not only believed in the capacity of the people for self-government, but in their honest wish to govern aright. In the struggle of the Revolution his devotion to the rights of the people against English tyranny took the form of religious enthusiasm. In France he witnessed the sufferings and misery of the down-trodden poor, whose wild vengeance he believed to be justified by the long ages of oppression and wrong under which they had groaned.

He distrusted power and naturally sought to restrict its exercise. Hating monarchy, he feared to delegate large powers of government even in republican forms.   Hating an aristocracy, he encouraged the masses to demand equality in civil, political, and social rights.

His political inconsistencies resulted from the usual impossibility of reconciling theory and practice.   When his opponents were in power, their purposes, he thought, were accomplished through violations of the constitution.   An equally dangerous exercise of power by his friends failed to excite his alarm.   Feeling conscious within himself of an honest purpose to subserve the good of the people and to perpetuate their liberties, he found ready justification for every act having, in his judgment, those ends in view.

America has produced no man so dear to the masses of its people as Thomas Jefferson.   He was an iconoclast, but the images broken by him were the idols of a past age, and no longer deserved the worship of a free people.

ALEXANDER HAMILTON

(1757–1804)

THE parentage of Alexander Hamilton is given by his son and biographer as of mingled Scottish and French ancestry— Scottish on the father's side, Huguenot on the mother's.   Students of the doctrine of temperaments may find something to ponder over in such a fusion under the genial ray of the southern sun.   Given the key, they may unlock with it many cabinets in the idiosyncrasy of the future Hamilton ; Scottish perseverance and integrity, French honor and susceptibility, tropical fervor.   Be that as it may, Alexander Hamilton first saw the light in the West India island, St. Christopher, January 11, 1757.   His father was a trader or captain, sailing between the islands of the archipelago, whose business brought him into relation with Nicholas Cruger, a wealthy merchant of Santa Cruz, in intimate relation with New York, in whose counting-house the son was placed at the age of twelve.   He was a boy of quick intellect, in advance of his years, and had already made much of limited opportunities of instruction, as we may learn from an exceedingly well-penned epistle, addressed thus early to a school-fellow who had found his way to New York.   In this remarkable letter, the boy seems to have written with prophetic instinct. "To confess my weakness, Ned," he says, "my ambition is prevalent, so that I contemn the grovelling condition of a clerk or the like, to which my fortune condemns me, and would willingly risk my life, though not my character, to exalt my station. . . . I mean to prepare the way for futurity. . . . I shall conclude by saying, I wish there was a war." This may be regarded as a boyish rhapsody; but all boys are not given to such rhapsodies.

The clerk had his hours for study as well as for the counting-room, and doubtless practised his pen in composition, for we hear of his writing an account of a fearful hurricane which visited the island, a narrative which appears to have been published, since it attracted the attention of the governor. These evidences of talent determined his friends to send him to New York to complete his education. He came, landing at Boston in the autumn of 1772, and was received at New York by the correspondents of Dr. Knox, a clergyman who had become interested in his welfare in Santa Cruz. He was immediately introduced to the school of Francis Barber, at Elizabethtown, where he enjoyed the society of the Boudinots, Livingstons, and other influential people of the colony. He studied early, and at the close of the year presented himself to Doctor Witherspoon, at Princeton, with a request to be permitted to overleap some of the usual collegiate terms according to his qualifications. As this was contrary to the usage of the place, he entered King's College, now Columbia, in New York, with the special privileges he desired. In addition to the usual studies, he attended the anatomical course of Clossey. Colonel Troup, at this time his room-fellow, testifies to his earnest religious feeling, a very noticeable thing in a youth of his powers. He wrote verses freely—among them doggerel burlesques of the productions of the ministerial writers of the day.

The Revolution was now fairly getting under way, and in the opening tumultuous scenes in New York, strong hands were wanted at the wheel. Hamilton, at the age of seventeen, in 1774, did not hesitate in making his decision. He entered the field against the dashing young president of the college, Myles Cooper, of convivial memory, in a reply in Holt's *Gazette* to some Tory manifesto of that divine. About this time, after the adjournment of Congress, at the close of the year, he also published a pamphlet in vindication of the measures of Congress, against the attacks of Seabury and Wilkins. The contest, however, was one which was not to be decided by the pen alone. The old prerogative lawyers and divines were not to be shaken out of their seats by the constitutional arguments of such young counsellors as Hamilton and Jay. The hard hands of the committee of mechanics were much more demonstrative. Myles Cooper, Seabury, and their brethren very naturally suspected the logic, and laughed at the novel measures of the day by which the popular party in their restrictive, non-importation measures proposed to dispense with the wisdom of Lords and Commons, and starve themselves into independence. It is well sometimes to look at that side of the question, too.

But all the pooh-poohing in the world over the best wine in the colony, was not to stop the affair which had commenced. Volunteers were drilling, men of sound heads and stout hearts were getting ready for action. There were certain cannon to be removed from the Battery; Hamilton was engaged in the duty with his comrades, "Hearts of oak" they called themselves; a boat approached from the man-of-war Asia, in the harbor; the citizens fired; the fire was returned from the ship, and one of Hamilton's company was killed. The Liberty Boys spread the alarm and gathered in a mob, threatening to attack the college and seize its president, Myles Cooper. Hamilton, who was no friend to riot, little as he was afraid of discussion or of force, interposed with a speech from the college steps, while the president, roused from his bed, half naked, took refuge on the shore, wandering over the island in the night to the old Stuyvesant mansion, whence he was the next day finally removed from America in his Majesty's vessel, the Kingfisher. The royal governor, Tryon, took refuge in the Asia shortly after.

Hamilton now turned his attention in earnest to military affairs, making choice of the artillery service, in which he gained some instruction from a British soldier, and by aid of the popular leader, McDougal, received from the convention the appointment of captain of the Provincial Company of Artillery. He had only recently completed his nineteenth year. It was early, but not so very early for a man of genius; for the child in such cases is the father of the man, and youth is an additional spur to exertion. But this was not all. The young captain was engaged, not only in the gymnastics of drilling recruits, but he was reading, thinking, and working out problems in political economy for himself— and the future. Dr. Johnson said that he learned little after eighteen; Hamilton would seem to have laid the foundation at least, of all his knowledge before twenty. "His military books of this period," says his son, "give an interesting exhibition of his train of thought. In the pay-book of his company, amid various general speculations and extracts from the ancients, chiefly relating to politics and war, are intermingled tables of political arithmetic, considerations on commerce, the value of the relative productions which are its objects, the balance of trade, the progress of population, and the principles on which depends the value of a circulating medium; and among his papers there remains a carefully digested outline of a plan for the political and commercial history of British America, compiled at this time." There is the germ in all this of the Secretary of the Treasury.

The battle of Long Island now ensued on the vain attempt to resist the landing of Howe and his British troops, followed by the masterly retreat of Washington, in which Hamilton brought up the rear. The subsequent American proceedings in the evacuation of the city, the passage from the island to Westchester, and the subsequent retreat before Cornwallis through the Jerseys under Washington, if they had little of glory, at least required their full share of military determination and endurance. Hamilton was active throughout the campaign. At White Plains and on the Raritan, at Trenton and Princeton, his artillery did good service. When he entered Morristown, his original company of a hundred was reduced by the accidents of war to twenty-five. Here, on March 1, 1777, leaving the line of the army, he became attached to the staff of Washington as his aid. This was the commencement of that half military, half civil relation which identified Hamilton in joint labors and councils with the Father of his Country.

Hamilton became, in fact, the right-hand man of Washington, not only during the war, but throughout his subsequent political career, and no better proof than this can be had at once of the sagacity of Washington in selecting his instruments, and of the honor and worth of Hamilton in so long and so successfully maintaining this distinguished position. In the staff of the commander-in-chief, Hamilton, we are told, acquired the title, " The Little Lion." His spirit and courage were shown in numerous instances, particularly in the battle of Monmouth, where Lee exposed bravery to such violent hazards, an affair out of which grew a duel between that officer and Colonel John Laurens, one of Washington's aids, in which Hamilton was the second of his friend and associate. Nor was Hamilton's counsel less serviceable in interviews with the French officers, and those frequent negotiations with the different portions of the army, and with Congress, which were among the hardest necessities of Washington's campaigns.

The relation of Hamilton to Washington, as a member of his military family, was suddenly brought to a termination at head-quarters on the Hudson, in February, 1781. The difference arose in a momentary forgetfulness of temper on the part of Washington. For some purpose of consultation he required the presence of Hamilton, who was detained from keeping the appointment on the instant, for it appears to have been a delay of but a few moments. Washington, however, was impatient, and meeting Hamilton at the head of the stairs, angrily exclaimed, " Colonel Hamilton, you have kept me waiting at the head of the stairs these ten minutes; I must tell you, sir, you treat me with disrespect." Hamilton firmly replied, " I am not conscious of it, sir ; but since you have thought it necessary to tell me so, we part." " Very well, sir," said Washington, " if it be your choice," or something to that effect, and the friends separated. Washington immediately opened the way for the Secretary's continuance at his post, but, without any feeling of asperity, the overture was declined. Hamilton, however, proffered his services and counsel. With no other man than Washington, indeed, could the subordinate relation have continued so long, and Hamilton had often thought of renouncing it ; but he saw in Washington the man for the times, the great representative of a great cause, for which minor considerations must be sacrificed. Writing at this moment to Schuyler, he says, " The General is a very honest man ; his competitors have slender abilities and less integrity. His popularity has often been essential to the safety of America, and is still of great importance to it. These considerations have influenced my past conduct respecting him, and will influence my future. I think it is necessary he should be supported."

Hamilton was now desirous to resume active service in the line, and after some discussion as to rank, received the command of a New York battalion of light infantry, which he led right manfully at the siege of Yorktown. He was anxious to signalize himself at this crowning act of the war by some distinguished exercise of bravery, and when, at an advanced period of the approaches, a redoubt was to be stormed, he eagerly solicited the forlorn hope from Washington. Advancing to the charge with characteristic spirit, at the point of the bayonet, exposed to a heavy fire, he struggled through the ditch, and surmounting the defences, took the work in the most brilliant manner. He gallantly arrested the slaughter at the first moment, and thus placed his humanity upon a level with his bravery.

The war being now brought to an end, Hamilton turned his attention to the law, and in a few months' ardent devotion—the devotion of Hamilton was always ardent—at Albany to the study with the aid of his friend, Colonel Troup, and the stimulus of his recent marriage, qualified himself thoroughly for the practice of the profession. He was admitted to the Supreme Court at its July term, 1782. About the same time, at the solicitation of Robert Morris, the financier of Congress, he accepted the appointment of receiver of the continental taxes in the State of New York, with the understanding that his exertions were to be employed in impressing upon the Legislature the wants and objects of the Government. In pursuance of this, he urged resolutions which were unanimously adopted in July, 1782, recommending the call of a convention for the purpose of revising and amending the Articles of Confederation. He was also elected by the Legislature of this year a member of Congress. He bore an active part in its debates, and was greatly employed in its important financial measures.

On the final departure of the British from New York, in 1783, Hamilton became a resident of the city with his family, and devoted himself assiduously to the practice of his profession. He was constantly, however, looked to as a public man. We find him, in 1784, appealing to the public under the signature of Phocion, in favor of more liberal and enlightened views in regard to the loyalists of the late Revolution, and their rights of property. In 1786 he is a member of the State Assembly, and in September of the same year among the delegates of the five States which, at the instance of Virginia, met at Annapolis to confer on the commercial interests of the country; a too limited representation, indeed, to achieve the objects in view, but the precursor of the great Federal Convention at Philadelphia of the following year.

We have seen Hamilton's early studies of the theoretical workings of government. His practical experience, in the army of Washington, of the imperfections of Congress and the defects of the old confederation, was not likely to let him forget the subject. Authority in government, rules in legislation, financial measures, taxes, loans, and a bank, were topics constantly before his mind. The Convention of 1787 gave him, at length, the wished-for opportunity to enter upon a full discussion of his plans in a cause and before an audience worthy of his powers. Washington was the presiding officer, Franklin was in attendance; it was a congregation of notables—Rufus King, Oliver Ellsworth, Roger Sherman, William Livingston, Robert Morris, Gouverneur Morris, John Dickinson, Luther Martin, James Madison, George Wythe, John Rutledge, and others as worthy. Much has been said of Hamilton's course in this Convention, and of his advocacy of monarchical views. It is true that a plan of government which he supported in a speech of length and eloquence, provided several features, as the life tenure of the President and senators, and the appointment of State officers by the General Government, which, in the interpretation of some minds, as Patrick Henry used to express it, "was an awful squinting toward monarchy;" but, on the other hand, it should be remembered that the Convention was a meeting for consultation, with closed doors, in a committee of the whole, in which perfect freedom in the interchange of views was desirable; that, in the view of our own day, other members displayed heresies quite as obnoxious, and that in the final resolves of the Constitution, Hamilton, with the others, yielded his prejudices, and became the firm defender of the instrument as it was adopted, and substantially now stands.

Remember the age of Hamilton at this time—twenty-nine; a greater prodigy in the Convention at Philadelphia than the youth in the army of Washington. To no one probably are we more indebted for the Constitution than to Hamilton. The Convention which laid the instrument before the country for its adoption had scarcely adjourned, when, in company with Madison and Jay, he took up the pen in its explanation and defence, in the celebrated series of papers, "The Federalist," originally published in the New York *Daily Advertiser*. Hamilton began and closed the work. Of its eighty-five papers much the greater portion, it is believed, were written by him.

The discussion of the financial and military powers, the executive and the judiciary, fell to his pen. In the New York Convention he was again the efficient advocate of the adoption of the Constitution. In a separate series of papers, signed Philo Publius, published in another journal, Hamilton, assisted by his friends, met various objections, the discussion of which would have marred the unity of "The Federalist," which was thus left a classical commentary upon the Constitution.

Having been thus instrumental in forming the Constitution, Hamilton was destined to be one of the most active agents of its powers. When the new government went into operation, under its provisions he was summoned by Washington, to the discharge of one of the most onerous duties of the department, in his appointment as Secretary of the Treasury. He continued in office six years, marking his administration—for such it was in his province—by his report and measures for the funding of the public debt, the excise revenue system, which he was called upon to assert in arms during the insurrection of Western Pennsylvania, and the creation of a National Bank. His reports on these subjects, and on manufactures, in which he advocated protection, are among the most important contributions of their kind to our national archives. In allusion to the financial measures of Hamilton, and their success at the time in the welfare of the country, Daniel Webster, in a speech at New York, half a century afterward, exclaimed: "He smote the rock of the national resources, and abundant streams of revenue gushed forth. He touched the dead corpse of the public, and it sprung upon its feet."

The measures of Hamilton, however, were not adopted without opposition. Jefferson was their persistent opponent ; local interests and State pretensions arose to thwart the measures of Government, and gave birth to the party feuds of Federalism and its opponents.   A growing element of disaffection was added to the political caldron in the relations with England and the disturbing influences of the principles of the French Revolution.   Hamilton bore the brunt of much of this popular opposition, which came to a crisis in the discussions attending the British Treaty of Jay, in 1794, as he defended its provisions in the papers signed "Camillus," while it was before the country, and advocated its leading neutrality principles in "The Letters of Pacificus," published by him the previous year. When France had wearied out all indulgence by her aggressions on the high seas, and by her treatment of our ministers at Paris, and Washington was again called to the field in anticipation of an expected invasion, Hamilton was appointed second in command, and now employed himself in the organization of the army.   On the death of Washington he became commander-in-chief.   On the conclusion of a treaty with France the army disbanded.

In the intervals of these public duties, Hamilton was actively employed in his profession in the higher courts of the State.   The late Chancellor Kent afterward recalled his " clear, elegant, and fluent style and commanding manner.   He never made any argument in court without displaying his habit of thinking and resorting at once to some well-founded principle of law, and drawing his deductions logically from his premises.   Law was always treated by him as a science, founded on established principles.   His manners were gentle, affable, and kind. He appeared to be frank, liberal, and courteous in all his professional intercourse."

The last important trial in which Hamilton was engaged, the case of the People against Harry Croswell, in the Supreme Court, a few months before his untimely death, is memorable also for his maintenance of the right of juries to determine the law as well as the fact in cases of libel.

The party politics of the time had been broken up in the simplicity of their outline by the administration of John Adams.   Aaron Burr was the most prominent intriguer in the field.   He had attained the vice-presidency, and the choice hung for a while suspended between him and Jefferson for the presidency.   Between the two, Hamilton, who had formed an unfavorable opinion of the character of Burr, preferred his old antagonist, Jefferson, and cast his influence accordingly.   When Burr afterward sought the office of Governor of New York, in a contest with a member of his own Republican party, in which he relied upon the support of the Federalists, he was defeated by Hamilton, who made no secret of his opposition.   Smarting under the failure of his intrigue, Burr determined to challenge the honest man who stood in his way to power.   He had no ground of personal offence bringing Hamilton within any justifiable pretensions even of the lax code of the duellist.   The expressions which he called upon him to avow or disavow, were vague, and were based upon the report of a person who specified neither time, place, nor the words.   It was a loose matter of hearsay which was alleged—evidently a wanton provocation to a murderous duel. Burr demanded so broad a retraction from Hamilton of all he might have said, that compliance was impossible. It was an attempt to procure an indorsement of his character at the cost of the moral character of the indorser. Hamilton despised the manœuvre, but perceiving that a meeting was forced upon him, and unhappily determining, contrary to his better judgment, that his usefulness would be destroyed in the public affairs of the times if he avoided the contest, fell into the fatal snare.

He executed his will, in which he made provision for his family and creditors, thinking tenderly of his wife, enjoining his children to bear in mind she had been to them the most devoted and best of mothers. On the night preceding the appointment he wrote a paper declaring his intention to throw away his fire, and acquitting himself before the world of the malice of the duellist, while he rested his conduct upon his usefulness to his country. The next morning, July 11th, they met at Weehawken ; the weapons were pistols, the distance ten paces. The duel was fought within a few feet of the shore, in a woodland scene beneath the cliff opposite the present inhabited portion of New York, at a spot now traversed or closely approached by the river road, but then readily accessible only by water. Hamilton fell at the first fire, mortally wounded, his pistol-shot striking at random a twig some seven feet above the head of his antagonist. Burr fled, a wanderer over the earth. Hamilton was carried across the river, supported by Pendleton and Dr. Hosack, to the house of his friend, Mr. Bayard, at Greenwich. He was there enabled to take farewell of his family, and receive the last consolations of religion from the hands of Bishop Moore. He died on the afternoon of Thursday, July 12, 1804.

The reception of the fatal news sent a thrill of horror through the community. The brilliant, fiery youth of Hamilton, which had lighted his countrymen to victory and a place among the nations—Hamilton, the counsellor of Washington, the consummate statesman of the Constitution, the reliance of the State, the hope of the future : visions such as these were contrasted in the popular mind with his wretched fall. We perhaps darken the shades of the picture, for time and proof have added to the greatness of Hamilton, and Burr waited not for death to exhibit the penury of his fame. But the men who knew the heart of Hamilton, who saw in him the bulwark of the State, his contemporaries, wept his fate with no common lamentation. New York gave her public honors to his grave. Gouverneur Morris, with strenuous words, delivered the funeral oration by the side of his bier, under the portico of old Trinity ; and Mason, the pulpit orator of his time, thundered his strong sentences at the crime which had robbed the world of Hamilton.

COUNT DE MIRABEAU*

By Charles S. Hathaway

(1749–1791)

Honoré Gabriel Riquetti, Count de Mirabeau, one of the most eminent among the great authors, orators, and statesmen of France, was born on March 9, 1749, on his father's estate at Bignon, near Nemours.

The earliest of Mirabeau's ancestors of whom there is any notable record, was Jean Riquetti, a prominent merchant at Marseilles, who, in 1570, bought the château and estate of Mirabeau, near Pertuis, from the well-known Provençal family of Barras, and who, a few years later, acquired the title of Esquire.

In 1685, one hundred and fifteen years after the purchase above mentioned, Honoré Riquetti, lineal descendant of the Marseilles merchant, obtained the title of Marquis de Mirabeau, and there was born to this marquis a son, Jean Antoine Riquetti, who achieved a worthy record as a soldier, but whose prominent place in history is due to the fact that he was the grandfather of the great Mirabeau.

Victor Riquetti, son of this second Marquis de Mirabeau and father of the great, the Count de Mirabeau, was in his early manhood an indifferent soldier, but he afterward became distinguished as a writer and leader in French politics. His wife (the mother of Count de Mirabeau) was Marie Geneviève, daughter of M. de Vassan, a brigadier in the French army, she being, also, the widow of the Marquis de Saulyebœuf. This union, entered into without a previous meeting between the principals to the contract, and at a time when the Marquis de Mirabeau was well started in his career as a politician, was not a happy one. The new husband was more loyal to politics than to his wife, so that, when their son, who was destined to achieve fame, was but thirteen years old, there was a separation between the parents by mutual consent.

Thus, in outline, is indicated the ancestry of Mirabeau through a period of nearly two centuries, and, meagre as the showing is, it is evident that he was the scion of a long line of wealth and nobility, his paternal ancestors having served with credit as soldiers, while his father was eminent as a politician. There is a second group of facts which bear interestingly upon the career under discussion.

18

Mirabeau the great was born at a time when more than two-thirds of France was in the hands of privileged classes—the king, the nobility, and the clergy—and at a time, too, when the structure founded upon years of feudalism and absolutism was about to be shaken to its base by the magic of popular public opinion.

Under such conditions, at such a time, and from such stock, occurred the birth of Mirabeau the great; a coming into the world of a babe "scarce half made up;" a child with a head so large that it was a dire deformity, with one foot sadly twisted, and with a tongue that was tied; in brief, an infant ogre born with teeth. So great was the chagrin of the father that he made no effort to conceal his dislike for the misshapen child. Hence, when at three years of age the little one was left wretchedly pitted by a severe attack of small-pox, its fate was listed. It must not, could not, bear the name of Mirabeau.

Accordingly, when the youngster was fourteen years old—after several years of instruction under the private tutorship of Lachabeaussière, *père*—he was entered under the fictitious name of "Pierre Buffière," at a private military school in Paris. Here, strong of limb, body, and mind, industrious and aggressive, he remained for four years. Then his father placed him in the Berry regiment of cavalry, which regiment had been commanded, sixty-two years before, by his grandfather.

This event marked the end of a boyhood which had been clouded by an almost entire absence of paternal favor, and wholly free from maternal care—the mother's absence having been secured by the father, by a *lettre de cachet*. In addition, that boyhood had been irritated and embittered by a continuous and exasperating development of his natural personal disfigurement. His enormous head grew less in harmony with his torso, his lips and nose became thick and heavy, great moles revealed themselves upon his cheeks, and in every way, physically, his growth was a perpetual disappointment.

However, he was now (1767) the eighteen-year old "Pierre Buffière," a lieutenant of cavalry, conscious of his exceptional mental strength and somewhat vain thereof, and full of ambition and determination to win as he wished and in spite of all of his many obstacles. Unfortunately, but most naturally, considering his temperament, the first test of his will, his passion, and his determination, resulted in his victory. He won the affection of a young woman to whom his colonel had long been devoted, and the scandal resulting therefrom caused the father to obtain a *lettre de cachet*, by authority of which the indiscreet young man was placed in confinement in the Isle of Rhé. Immediately the prisoner began his first illustration of his ability to gain to his own purposes the ability and influence of others—one of his strongest and most useful characteristics. Within two months he had secured the esteem and confidence of his jailer, so that that official soon made a most favorable report, upon the strength of which Mirabeau was accepted as a volunteer to accompany the French expedition sent (in 1769) to conquer Corsica. So well did the young soldier conduct himself during this campaign, that he was not only promoted to a captaincy in the dragoons, but he effected a partial reconciliation with his father, returned to Provence, was permitted to assume his true name and title, and was presented at court. In June, 1772, he married, by his father's advice, Marie Emile de Covet, only daughter of the Marquis de Marignane. She came to him portionless, and he, impetuous, ambitious, and extravagant, became, during the next two years, deeply involved in debt. The marriage was a failure. Again the father utilized the *lettre de cachet*, and a second time was Mirabeau a prisoner (August 23, 1774), this time in the Château d'If, at Marseilles. Here it was that he wrote his first work of which we have any exact knowledge, its title being: " Essai sur le Despotisme."

In the following year he was transferred from the Château d'If to the Castle of Joux, where he was less strictly confined. He had the freedom of the place and frequent opportunities for visiting the near-by town of Pontarlier. It was in this town that he first met Marie Thérèse, the Marchioness de Monnier, the young and attractive wife of an aged magistrate. A love affair was the result, and it culminated in August, 1776, in an elopement, first to Switzerland and then to Amsterdam. For over nine months the fugitive pair lived together in the Dutch capital, Mirabeau, under the assumed name of St. Mathieu, earning a livelihood as a pamphleteer and by making translations for Holland publishers. Meanwhile the tribunal of Pontarlier had condemned both parties—Mirabeau to be beheaded and his companion (his " Sophie," as she is most widely known) to imprisonment for life. On May 14, 1777, they were arrested at Amsterdam, and Mirabeau was imprisoned by a *lettre de cachet* in the Castle of Vincennes, while Sophie was surrendered to the Pontarlier authorities.

For three and a half years thereafter Mirabeau was in confinement, a term which proved sufficient to temper his passion, and during which he wrote his well-known " Letters to Sophie," the " Erotica Biblion," and " My Conversion." He also wrote, during this time, his first worthy political production, the " Lettres de Cachet." He was released from this imprisonment on December 13, 1780, and at once sought out Sophie, to quarrel with and leave her, and so, fortunately, end the most disgraceful portion of his life.

Mirabeau, now thirty-one years old, and, according to the times, most liberally experienced in the ways of the then turbulent world, undertook, as his first task, the removal of the sentence of death which still confronted him. Not only did he succeed in this, but, by his plausibility and eloquence, he shifted the entire cost of the proceedings to the shoulders of the complainant—the aged magistrate he had so grossly wronged. His next venture was an effort before the tribunal of Aix, to compel his wife to return to him. Here he failed, as also he failed in an effort to compromise a suit pending between his father and mother. Not only that, but by his pleadings his mother became forever alienated from him, and by reason of his bitter attacks upon the rulings of the court he was forced to leave Paris. Locating at Amsterdam, he began his lasting and respectable relations with Madame de Nehra, daughter of Zwier van Haren, a Dutch writer and politician. She was a woman of education and refinement, who exercised a valuable influence over his rapidly growing celebrity, bringing out his good qualities, subduing his undesirable characteristics, and encouraging all of his better ambitions.   It was at her suggestion that he went to England, after a brief stay in Holland, while she repaired to Paris.   His mission—which he accomplished—was to publish his " Considérations sur l'Ordre de Cincinnatus " and his " Doutes sur la Liberté de l'Escaut ; " while her mission, also successful, was to establish peace between Mirabeau and the authorities at the French capital.

During twenty years of the thirty-six years he had lived, Mirabeau had been, either through his father's intervention or by his own acts, a constant topic of consideration by the French authorities.   On the other hand, by virtue of his writings, his declared enmity to all forms of tyranny and oppression, and his distaste for pretence, he had become a popular idol.   He was, as Carlyle puts it, "a swallower of formulas," and it seems he had the ability to digest such food thus taken.   Therefore, upon his return to Paris in April, 1785, he made a series of attacks upon agiotage, or stock jobbing, most effectively assaulting the Compagnie des Eaux and the Banque de St. Charles.   While such efforts proved offensive to the government, it caused such an appreciation of his ability that he was sent, in June, 1786, on a secret mission to Berlin.   He remained there for half a year, and during that time he secured the material for his notable work, " Histoire Secrète de la Cour de Berlin."   Among other writings which he produced about this time were his " Moses Mendelssohn, ou la Réforme politique des Juifs," and his pamphlet "Dénonciation de l'Agiotage," aimed against the policy of Calonne.   Again he was in danger of the *lettre de cachet*, and so he repaired to Brunswick, where he finished his work " De la Monarchie Prussienne," which was published in 1788.

Up to 1789, Mirabeau had been a dramatic character, an individual revelation of theatric passion, a figure-piece single and alone; but the climax was at hand. The achievement of American independence had been an object-lesson most potent.   Louis and his queen, Marie Antoinette, could not check the storm, and for the first time in one hundred and seventy-three years, France was to have an assembly of the nation by its representatives.   The "third estate" was aroused and the States-General was summoned.   Mirabeau, having a deep-rooted desire to provide for France a government in accord with the wishes and intent of a majority of the people, and having been rejected by the noblesse of his own district, presented himself to the " third estate," as a candidate.   He was elected both for Aix and for Marseilles, and he decided to sit for Aix.   Naturally an enthusiast, he was present (May 4, 1789) at the opening of the States-General, but with excellent sagacity he entered that body as an independent.   To the end of his life, twenty-three months later, he maintained that independence.

When, being shut out in the rain from the great hall of the Estates, the " third estate " established themselves in the adjacent tennis-court, and when, being ejected from there, they came together again and forced the king to recognize them as the representatives of the nation ; through all these earlier and wiser stages of the great revolt, Mirabeau was the leader and director.   But when, on June 5, 1789, a resolution was passed by the delegates declaring themselves—the people, the Commons of France—to be the National Assembly, he spoke and worked bravely

THE THIRD ESTATE TAKES REFUGE IN THE TENNIS COURT

BY

ÉTIENNE-LUCIEN MÉLINGUE

THE THIRD ESTATE TAKES REFUGE IN THE TENNIS COURT

BY

ÉTIENNE-LUCIEN MÉLINGUE

and eloquently against abandoning the old order of things before formulating an exact and sufficient policy as its successor. He declared the action a hasty one, and finally avoided the issue in the only way possible, by absenting himself when the vote was taken. And yet, eight days later, at the close of the royal sitting, he bade the grand master of ceremonies: "Go and tell your master we are here by the power of the people, and that we are only to be driven out by that of the bayonet."

He advised the Assembly against the publication of pompous proclamations, and classed the demonstration of the night of August 4th as a theoretical display of liberty wholly without practical value. He was opposed to mob-law, and in no sense was he dazzled by the fall of the Bastille. He pleaded in favor of the royal right to veto, and proclaimed that he was willing, even, to advocate a "restoration of the king's legitimate authority as the only means of saving France."

He was a leader of magnificent power, enthusiastic in the advocacy and support of his convictions; a statesman who would not speak, write or do, in politics, anything not in accord with his estimate as to what was right. True, he was accused of treason for speaking in support of the king's right to proclaim war or peace, but three days thereafter he defended himself against the charge, and with overwhelming success. He was a leader who worked prodigiously. In addition to his duties as a member of the Assembly, he was also publisher and editor of a paper first called the *Journal des États-Généraux*, later the *Lettres à mes Constituants*, and at last the *Courrier de Provence*. As clerk of the Comité Diplomatique of the Assembly and because of his thorough knowledge of foreign affairs, he was the constant adviser of Montmorin, the foreign secretary. Thus, by his wise appreciation of the subject, he established harmony between the Assembly and Montmorin, and so prevented foreign intervention, at the same time maintaining the honor of France abroad. But this bulwark to the nation's safety was about to topple and fall, precipitated by its own decay. As in all things, Mirabeau had been colossal in his excesses, and like them, the punishment was great. He wished to live, but he did not fear death. Early in 1791 the structure began to weaken, and realizing that the time was at hand, Mirabeau carefully collected all of his writings, and after classifying them, forwarded them to his firm friend and companion, Sir Gilbert Elliott, in England. So far as he was able, he continued to contribute to the guidance and protection of his country. He was patient and fearless, his only regret taking the form of a pardonable conceit that, could he but live, the Revolution could be controlled and guided, that the awful Reign of Terror, so soon to follow, could be averted. The progress of his decline was without hindrance, in spite of all that science could devise. It is reported that, as he looked out from his sick-room, on the day of his death, on the brilliant spring-time sun, he said: "If he is not God, he is at least his cousin-german." Those were, it is said, his last spoken words, although some time later when unable to articulate, he feebly held a pen in his hand as he wrote the single word: "dormir." And so, on April 2, 1791, he died. Thus ended the life of a wondrous statesman ; a singular career, of which Carlyle (in his " French Revolution ") says : " Strange lot ! Forty years of that smouldering with foul fire-damp and vapor enough ; then victory over that ;—and like a burning mountain, he blazes heaven high ; and for twenty-three resplendent months pours out, in flame and molten fire-torrents, all that is in him, the Pharos and the Wondersign of an amazed Europe ;—and then lies hollow, cold, forever."

Chas S Hathaway

MAXIMILIEN ROBESPIERRE

(1758–1794)

Maximilien Isidore Robespierre, the leader of the most violent of those theorizers who overthrew the French monarchy, the exponent of all that deep-rooted hatred which the commoners of France, as the result of long centuries of oppression, harbored against their king, nobles, and clergy ; Robespierre, who ruled the infant republic during her first bold defiance of united Europe, yet whose name has become, even among his countrymen, a symbol of horror, was born at Arras, in 1758. His father was an advocate in the supreme council of Artois, and, ruined by his dissipation, had left France long before the revolution. An orphan at the age of nine, and without fortune, Maximilien was indebted to the benevolent protection of the Bishop of Arras, M. de Conzié, for the situation of bursar of the College of Louis XIV. We are assured that from his infancy he manifested a cruel, reserved, and timid disposition, and an ardent love of liberty and independence. After having passed through his studies, and obtained the honor of being chosen by his fellow-students to address Louis XVI., upon the entrance of that prince into Paris, he returned to Arras, where, having become an advocate of the council of Artois, he composed strictures against the magistrates of that province. A daring enthusiast, in 1789 he was elected, on account of his revolutionary principles, by the third estate of Artois, to a seat in the Constituent Assembly. We shall not follow him in detail in that assembly : we shall simply remark, that he spoke much without obtaining any particular influence, and evinced himself constantly the enthusiastic champion of the people. Robespierre, in all his harangues, appears to foresee events. The avowed enemy of royalty, we behold him on the side of republicanism, of which he ventured to alter the name on the day when the Assembly decreed the French government monarchical. We behold him again, after the arrest of the king at Varennes, resuming his projects for the destruction of that monarch, preparing the movements which took place at the Champ-de-Mars, on July 14, 16, 17, 1791, and attacking, on the 14th, in the Assembly, the principle of the inviolability of the sovereign, in the hope of having him arraigned; but at the end of the sitting, finding his opinion rejected, he began to tremble for his temerity, and required that they should not provoke the ruin of persons who had engaged in that affair.

If Robespierre was unable to distinguish himself among the orators of the Constituent Assembly; if his principles appeared obnoxious to the innovators acting from sentiment in 1789; if they often drew upon him the indignation of his colleagues; they were the means of his acquiring among the Jacobins that reputation and favor which, daily increasing, rendered him at last the idol of the people and the ruler of the government. He was called "The Incorruptible." The day of the closing of the Assembly, the populace surrounded him on his coming out of the hall, put a crown of oak upon his head, placed him in a carriage, and, taking out the horses, dragged him to his house, exclaiming as they moved, "Behold the friend of the people, the great defender of Liberty!" Robespierre was fully sensible of the advantages which might result from his alliance with the Jacobins. He devoted himself entirely to the direction of a club bearing that name, and refused, in order to give up his whole time to the objects they had in view, the office of accuser in the criminal tribunal at Paris, to which he had been appointed. Until his election to a seat in the Convention, he was never seen personally to engage in those insurrections which produced the atrocious attack upon the king, nor in the horrible massacres which, in 1792, covered Paris with murder and blood, and the French name with eternal opprobrium. He refused even to preside at the tribunal of August 10th, because, as he said, " He had long since denounced and accused the conspirators, whom this tribunal was ordained to judge." But he had scarcely entered the Convention when he resolved to raise his faction upon the ruins of all the others, and his power upon the destruction of those factions which he might employ. To attain this end, he was seen at first to strengthen the ties by which he had already been united to Marat and Danton, and to avail himself particularly of the latter, in order to overthrow the Girondins, who, from the fifth session, had suspected his ambition, and accused him of aspiring to the dictatorship. It was during this struggle that Louvet pronounced against him that very eloquent harangue, which Madame Roland called the "Robespierreiad." Assisted by his brother and by Danton, Robespierre, in the sitting of November 5th, overpowered the Girondins, and went to the Jacobins to enjoy the fruits of his victory, where Merlin de Thionville declared him an eagle, and a barbarous reptile. From that moment he never ceased to promote the death of Louis XVI., with an asperity and a perseverance almost incredible.

In short, until the fatal day of the martyrdom of that amiable and unfortunate prince, he continually importuned the tribune to pronounce upon him (according to the expression of one of his colleagues) *des vociférations de cannibale*, and the most atrocious prejudgments. It is almost superfluous to add, that he voted for his death on the day of the nominal appeal to the nation.

Within any moderate limits, it would be impossible to give the details of this monstrous proceeding. Of all the disorders which had occurred during the stormy period which had seen him on the throne of France, Louis was accused. He was assigned counsel ; and MM. Tronchet, Lamoignon, Malesherbes, and De Séze, with his approbation, undertook his defence. Their exertions, though creditable to themselves, were of no avail ; and on January 16, 1793, after hearing them in his defence, and his solemn denial of the crimes laid to his charge, and after a sitting of nearly thirty-four hours, the punishment of death was awarded.

Constant in his hatred of the Girondins, Robespierre attacked them with great vehemence until May 31st, when he obtained a complete triumph. His most dangerous enemies among the men of that faction were outlawed, and others arrested. The success of this day rendered him absolute ruler of the Convention, and founded that tyrannical empire which only terminated with his life.

Among the factions which had lent him their assistance, the Hebertistes were the first that separated from his cause. This faction aspired to sole dominion, but the good fortune or the address of Robespierre was able at once to oppose to it the Jacobins and the Cordeliers, and it sunk in March, 1794, under their united efforts. Danton, who had been particularly serviceable on this occasion, whose energy had been of such utility, who had aided him in sweeping away the other factions ; Danton, in short, whom he ought to have considered as the instrument of his power, became a formidable enemy, after being for a length of time a most devoted friend and faithful ally. The two parties were at issue ; one or the other must necessarily be overcome. The cunning of Robespierre triumphed over the inconsiderate ardor of his rival, whom he took pains to render unpopular by sending him to enrich himself in Belgium. A few days afterward he was accused, arrested, and conveyed to the scaffold with Desmoulins, La Croix, Fabre, and others. In the course of the same month (April, 1794) he delivered over to the Revolutionary Tribunal the remainder of the party of the Hebertistes, and that of the Cordeliers, whom he degraded by the name of Atheists, and from that moment to the period of his downfall he met no opposition. It was then that his language assumed a different tone. " I must be," "it is necessary," " I will," were his general expressions ; and the Convention, as he himself called it, was only his *machine à décrets*. What is worthy of remark is, that France, groaning under the struggles of different parties, should applaud the conduct of Robespierre, from an idea that she would be less miserable under a single tyrant. His new plan of religion, ridiculous as it was, gained him some adherents ; but it must be evident to every reflecting mind that Robespierre must have conceived himself at the head of the government, since he, whose sole object had hitherto been to destroy, attempted to rebuild. It is impossible to conjecture how long his power might

FRANCOIS FLEMING PINXIT.

ROBESPIERRE'S ARREST.

have continued, had he spared his colleagues, and if he had not incited to resistance men who, until then, had blindly executed his orders, and who desired nothing more than to continue to serve and obey him; but in sacrificing the leaders of the Revolutionary Government, Robespierre sought a support in the moderate party. This policy ruined him; those whose destruction he had meditated occasioned his downfall. Danger, however, inspired him with courage. From June 10th, Ruamps and Bourdon de l'Oise, in particular, had expressed some distrust of the Committee of Public Safety, which produced a discussion in which Robespierre, speaking with an air of despotism, had the good fortune to silence them. This was the moment he should have chosen to overwhelm the party, which redoubled its intrigues for his destruction; and at whose head Tallien rendered himself remarkable. His friend, St. Just, advised him to strike the first blow. Robespierre had passed several days in retirement, occupied in projecting, at a moment when he ought to have acted. When he reappeared on the 26th, at the Convention, his partisans abandoned him; he in vain endeavored to regain the ground he had lost. Sensible of the danger which threatened him, he called together his most intimate friends on the night of the 26th. St. Just pressed him immediately to act. He hesitated for twenty-four hours, and this delay was the sentence of his death. The next day Billaud-Varennes removed the veil, and Robespierre having rushed to the tribune to reply to him, the cries of "Down with the tyrant!" drove him instantly from the assembly. A few minutes after a decree was passed for his arrest, and that of St. Just, Couthon, and Lebas. "The robbers triumph," he exclaimed, on turning to the side of the conquerors. He was afterward conducted to the Luxembourg, and in a little time removed from that palace and conveyed to the tribune which had delivered him up. He for some instants cherished the hopes of a triumph; the national guard, under the command of Henriot, assembled in his defence. But the Convention having put him out of the protection of the law, the Parisians abandoned him, and at three o'clock in the morning he found himself with his accomplices in the power of the officers of the Convention. At the moment he was about to be seized he discharged a pistol at his head, which only fractured his lower jaw; others say it was fired by Medal, one of the gendarmes, who had stepped forward to arrest him, and against whom he defended himself. He was immediately conducted to the Commune, from thence conveyed to the Conciergerie, and executed on the same day, July 28, 1794.

His last moments presented a terrific scene; his mouth full of blood, his eyes half closed, his head bound up with a bloody handkerchief, he was thrown into the same cell which had been successively inhabited by Hébert, Danton, and Chaumette. When he quitted the prison to meet his punishment, the proscribed persons obstructing the passage, the jailer cried out, "Make way for monsieur the incorruptible!" He was conveyed in a cart between Henriot and Couthon; the people halted before the house, two women danced before the wagon, and one of them exclaimed; "Your sufferings intoxicate us with joy! You will descend to hell, accompanied by the curses of all wives and mothers." The executioner, in order to dispatch him, rudely tore away the bandage from his wound. He uttered a cry of horror ; his lower jaw separated itself from the upper. The blood again flowed, and his head exhibited a spectacle of the most frightful kind. He died at the age of thirty-six.

Robespierre was not a monster ; his life attests it ; nor was he solely guilty of the atrocities which signalized his reign. By his downfall he was loaded with all those iniquities which, had he triumphed, he would have attributed to his opponents.

JEAN HENRI PESTALOZZI

By Harriet Martineau

(1746–1827)

THOSE of us who can look back forty years must well remember the fancy that society took, on a sudden, to interrogate children. It is an odd thing to recall now one of the strangest fashions of a period full of wild fashions. After a long term of insular seclusion, through the war, we welcomed all sorts of foreigners to our soil, and all manner of foreign notions to our minds. The grand discovery of the benefit of questioning children made great way in the country, and among some of the best-hearted people in it. Wherever one went, among the educated classes, one found the same thing going on. Children of all ages, but especially the younger, were undergoing cross-examination from morning till night. It was a terrible time for them. I have seen some fall into a habit of tears when asked a question which they could not answer. I have seen more fall into a habit of glib lying, under the teazing constraint. I have seen tempers ruined for life by the constant irritation, and most old people can probably say that they have seen promising intellects frittered away ; minds above the average at the outset of life rendered incurably desultory, shallow, and conceited. If there are readers of Wordsworth who are puzzled at this day about the drift of his poem, called "Anecdote for Fathers, Showing how the Practice of Lying May be Taught,"

let them remember that it was written at a time when "the Pestalozzian system" was in vogue in England, and throughout Europe ; and then they will see what a good lesson it yields. If, at this day, the image flits across our memories of some pale child, with a fretful brow, red eyes, and a constant disposition to get out of the room, or to hide behind the window curtains, when spoken to, we may refer that image back to the days of the "Pestalozzian system," as it was fashionably understood in this country.

It was a cruel injustice to Pestalozzi to render him responsible for all this mischief. His mission was, not to craze children's brains and break their hearts, but the very contrary. We, in fact, gave his name to a mere reaction from a mistake of our own—to one kind of ignorance into which we fell in our escape from another.

In our desire for popular education, early in the century, we had supposed the thing to be done was to put certain facts into the learner's mind—to lay them upon his memory, as it were. To quicken and spread the process, we set children who had learned a thing one minute to teach it to other children the next. This did not answer. We called it "the Lancasterian system," and supposed the nation would be educated in a trice. When we found, at the end of ten or twenty years, that boys and girls left school after sitting nine years on the benches, unable to do any good with book or pen, while they had lost their home-training in the workshop, the field, or the dairy, we were ready for a reaction ; and to that reaction we most unjustly gave the name of "Pestalozzian system."

The notion was that we had been all wrong in putting knowledge into children's heads ; and that the right way was to get ideas out of them. Henceforth we were to develop faculties, and not impose knowledge. It was a great day for us when the conception was formed, and began to spread. Without it, education would never have advanced even as far as it has. But we blundered over it sadly at first ; and among our mistakes, it was not the least that we christened our follies after Pestalozzi. Every great step in social progress is taken in the name of some representative man. It is the business of those who come after to absolve those representatives from the disrepute of mistakes which were none of theirs ; and we may hope that Pestalozzi's memory has long been clear from the charge of torturing on the rack of cross-examination the generation of children whom he loved so well. What it was that he did propose is best seen by looking at his life ; for, if he was not a very practical man in the sense of wisely conducted affairs, he was still less of a theorist. He knew very well what he meant and what he wanted ; but he had no compact system to propose, grounded on any new theory of the human faculties. The foremost man in the educational revolution of modern times, he obeyed his instincts, and left it for incompetent followers to make a scheme of doctrine out of what he said and did.

What were those instincts? And how did he use them?

We first see him as a very peculiar little boy, whose best friend was his mother's maid, Barbara. His name is Italian, but he was a Swiss. His ancestors had been citizens of Milan ; but one of them, becoming Protestant at the time of the

Reformation, had to seek a Protestant country to live in, and went to Zurich. The father of this little John Henry was a physician. He died so early that he left a very bare provision for his widow and their only son ; and, aware of the prudence that their circumstances would require, he recommended them, on his death-bed, to the care of the trusty maid Barbara, who fully justified the confidence. She carried them through with an appearance of respectability on the smallest means, and nourished the pride of narrow circumstances in the boy, in striving to avoid the opposite fault of meanness. She told him that no Pestalozzi had ever eaten the bread of dependence, and that his mother's self-denial raised him above the degradation suffered by many another orphan in Zurich. These lessons and Barbara's own character, account for much of the passionate advocacy of the claims and the independence of the poor, and of the respect for their virtue, which were the chief features of the whole life of the man. From six years old, when his father died, he looked upon all orphans with an interest compounded of fellow-feeling and of lofty pity for their inferiority in independence. His great, but as yet unconscious, desire was to help the whole class to independence.

It does not appear why he devoted himself, as he grew up, to the study of languages. Probably he had no choice as to the course of his training ; but we find him, so early as the age of eighteen, leaving that study and preparing himself with great zeal for the pulpit. His deeply religious nature might well indicate this career ; but he early failed in it and gave it up. His first attempt to preach ended in mortification, and it is not difficult to perceive why. His education must have been defective, for, to the end of his long life, he spoke a jargon of German or French, sometimes mixing the two ; a kind of language which none but his intimates could comprehend. His articulation was defective ; his countenance was so ugly as to be forbidding ; and, during the latter part of his life at least, his personal habits were worse than slovenly. The failure in the pulpit is not wonderful ; nor yet that in the law, which he tried next. He turned again to his first pursuit, and published some philological writings. While eager about a new method of teaching Latin, he one day took up Rousseau's " Emile," and the book determined the whole course of his life.

Insisting that the pursuit of learning was the most unnatural of human occupations, he not only gave it up, but burned all his papers ; not only his notes, but manuscripts on Swiss law and Swiss history. He would live henceforth as a son of the soil. He sold his small patrimony to buy a bit of land to farm ; married the daughter of a merchant of Zurich, and began domestic life at two and twenty. His wife's connection gave him an interest in a cotton manufactory ; and he became well acquainted with two classes of laborers at once. The discovery of their intellectual degradation shocked him. Both the farm-laborers and the spinners were so inferior to the poor of his imagination, that he was at once stimulated and dismayed. He was thirty when he set about the sort of work which made him the world's benefactor. He collected about fifty poor and desolate children on his little estate, lived with them in a state of hardship, taught them

to work, and to think, and to read, and made friends of them.   In the absence
of other assistants, he adopted the plan of setting them to teach one another; a
feature of his method which recommended it where the Lancasterian system
existed.   Having no skill, and no prudence in the management of affairs, he was
soon ruined, and the establishment was broken up.

This was the occasion of his giving us the book which made his name famous
all over Europe.   To explain his views, and to get immediate means of support,
he wrote " Leonard and Gertrude," which might soon after be seen on the tables
of all benevolent and literary persons in all countries.   Its disclosure of continental peasant life was perhaps the first charm to us; but it also changed the
character of educational effort in England as elsewhere.   Perhaps this popularity
gave the good man honor in his own country.

After the Revolutionary War in Switzerland, the Canton of Unterwalden was
overrun with wretched children who seemed to belong to nobody.   They prowled
about the burned hamlets, and infested town and country like little wolves.   The
government asked Pestalozzi to take charge of some of them, and offered him
some little aid.   It was a singular spectacle when this uncouth man, then in the
vigor of his years (it was in 1798), entered the ruins of a ravaged convent, with
his mob of one hundred and fifty outcast children.   He was all alone with them ;
and some of them were sickly and stunted ; many were fretful ; and not a few
ferocious, or malicious, or impudent, or full of suspicion and falsehood.   He
lived and labored among them, nursed them, taught them, and soon began to
open their minds and gain their hearts.   In a little while their avidity for knowledge astonished him.   The facts of the case indicate that he had an aptitude for
communicating with children's minds that amounted to genius.   Our mistake,
twenty years later, was in supposing that the virtue lay in that part of the method
which could be imitated.   Pestalozzi, conversing with young creatures who had
never supposed that anybody cared for them, surprised them by his interest in
what they felt and thought.   His questions roused their faculties, and sent a
glow through their feelings ; and their improvement transcended all precedent.
Reports of his conversation and his achievements set others to work ; and there
was such an interrogation of children as was never dreamed of before.

One question which Pestalozzi asked of this set of pupils is memorable.
They had seen Altdorf in flames.   About those blackened ruins there were again
desolate children, living as they could.   Pestalozzi sounded the minds of his
pupils as to doing something in the case.   When they eagerly desired to take in
twenty among them, Pestalozzi asked them whether they could bear the consequences.   They must work harder even than now; they must live yet more
barely ; they might have to share their dinners and their clothes with strangers
whom they might not like.   He would not allow a rash decision.   He made
them fully understand what they were undertaking, and put off the settlement of
the question.   Still, the pupils said, " Let them come !"

The ravage of the war swept away this institution ; but Pestalozzi could never
again be overlooked.   His special function was recognized at home and abroad.

His books were translated into many languages ; and the emperors and kings of Europe were eager to apply his wisdom to the education of their people.   He was summoned to Paris to join a consultation on the interests of Switzerland, ordered by Napoleon.   But he made his escape from Paris at the first possible moment ; he did not want imperial patronage which interfered with his work at home ; but he would have nothing to do with politics.   He desired to live with children and the poor, to open their minds, and make them good and happy.

It seemed as if he had attained his utmost wishes when the town of Yverdun offered him its castle and grounds for a school, with perfect freedom as to the management.   For a few years the promise of educational advancement was truly splendid.   Some of Pestalozzi's own pupils became able and devoted assistants ; and other young men of the highest qualifications devoted themselves as apostles of his mission.   Here and there over Europe establishments arose where boys, and sometimes girls, were trained at once in industry and intellectual progress. Those who were in the gardens, or the harvest field, or the dairy at one time of the day, were studying languages, mathematics, or music at other hours.   And where this direct imitation of the Swiss establishments was not attempted, there was a visible improvement in methods of instruction.   We learned to see that books and education, books and teaching, are not the same thing.   Oral instruction came into use elsewhere than at mothers' knees ; and amid some gross abuses, " the Pestalozzian system " began to work great good.

There is almost always some dreary chapter in the history of these representative men.   In Pestalozzi's there were several ; but the dreariest of all was the last.

There never was a movement which depended more entirely for success on the personal qualifications of its agents.   We need not look further than the next street, or the next house, to see how one person differs from another in the faculty of genuine intercourse with children's minds.   The smallness of the number of the well-endowed with this power, is the best reason for the large use of books in schools ; and Pestalozzi's genius for companionship with inferior minds caused a too exclusive recourse to oral instruction.   Thus, when assistants came upon the scene, there was diversity, disagreement, disappointment, and no little disorder.   We need not go into the painful story of warring tempers and incompatible interests.   The institution declined for some years, and then was broken up—the government of the Canton warning the manager of the concern, who acted in Pestalozzi's name, to leave the country.

It needs no explanation that Pestalozzi was in some respects weak.   The failure of all his establishments and his inability to keep out of debt show this. His faculties of imagination and sympathy overpowered the rest of his mind. He early seized a great truth—that of the claim of every human being to the full development of his faculties, whatever they may be ; and the concentration of his strongest powers on this great truth made him a social reformer of a high order.   He was not a philosopher ; he was not a man of good sense, or temper, or practical ability, generally speaking ; though sense, temper, and ability appeared to be all transcendent in the particular direction taken by his genius. Among his inferiors—and particularly friendless children—he was a prophet and apostle ; among men he was a child, and sometimes a perverse one.

He died at the age of eighty-one, preserving, in the midst of great pain, his enthusiasm for justice, his special love for children and the poor, and his strong religious sentiment.   Two days before his death he spoke long and nobly, while taking leave of his family and his enterprises.   His country, and we hope the world, has remembered his good offices to society, and forgiven his foibles.

GEORGES CUVIER

By John Stoughton, D.D.

(1769–1832)

Georges Chrétien Léopold Dagobert Cuvier was born at Montbéliard, a place of manufacturing industry about forty miles from Besançon, now within the French dominions, then a little principality pertaining to the Duke of Wurtemberg. Young Cuvier was remarkable for his intelligence and precocity ; and an incident in his boyish days indicated the bent of his genius, and the sphere of knowledge and discovery in which as a man he was destined to excel. He found one day, among his father's books, Buffon's work on natural history, and it suggested the idea of copying and coloring the plates, after he had carefully studied the text. The contents formed his chief reading for many years.   The relatives of Cuvier were poor. His father was a pensioned officer in a Swiss regiment in the service of France. His mother was an affectionate, godly, wise woman.   To her early lessons in Latin, geography, and drawing, and to her communications of religion, he always acknowledged himself much indebted.   He went to the public gymnasium at the age of ten, and remained there for four years, bearing off prizes for learning and athletics.   Through the patronage of a Wurtemberg princess he was sent to the university of Stuttgart, where he pursued a course of scientific study, particularly in the division relating to natural history.   There he acquitted himself with distinction, not only in that special department, but also in the most sacred branch of learning.   "The young Cuvier," said his examiners, "has shown just notions of Christianity well adapted to his years," and "considerable skill" in reading the Greek Testament.

Circumstances compelled him in early life to do something toward earning a livelihood, and in 1794 he became tutor in a French Protestant family living in the castle of Fiquainville, near Fécamp.   In that little Norman fishing-town he found much to gratify his curiosity; and he might often be seen scouring the country after birds, butterflies, and other insects; or prying into nooks and corners on the shore, after shell-fish and other marine productions; while the treasures of the boundless sea inspired wonder, with a longing to explore its depths and to become acquainted with the forms of life hidden under its waters.

He appears to have continued in the family of Count d'Hericy for nearly seven years.   He was introduced to the *savants* of Paris by his researches, and accepted an invitation to remove thither in 1795.   He reached the French metropolis just after the horrors of the Revolution.   Papers written by him already on his favorite subject had brought him into notice; and he found congenial employment in the Jardin des Plantes—the home of his after-studies and the sphere of his scientific exploits.   There he worked and lectured, and obtained the office of assistant to the aged professor of comparative anatomy.   In the year of his appointment, he made a mark in the study which he rendered so famous, by a memoir on the Megalonyx, a fossil animal known by a few of its bones, and which, contrary to received opinion, he boldly proved to have been a gigantic sloth.   This was the first of those able comparisons of the fossil with the present world which revolutionized geology, extended comparative anatomy, and absolutely created the science of palæontology.   He was also appointed to a professorship of natural philosophy in the College of France; then he rose, step by step, under the favor and patronage of Napoleon, who made him an inspector-general of schools; secretary to the French Institute; councillor of the new Imperial University, and organizer of reformed colleges in Italy, Holland, and Germany, after the vast extension of the empire.   Even at Rome he was thus employed in 1813; and though a Protestant, he there won the good opinion of the authorities.   The conquest and banishment of the great ruler of France did not spoil the fortunes of Cuvier; for, after the restoration of Louis XVIII., he was confirmed by that monarch in the office of state councillor, to which he had been appointed by the emperor, and in 1819 he was made a baron of France.

Just before this he visited England, and was received with the highest honors. Another visit followed in 1830.   An amusing circumstance occurred on one of these occasions, indicative of his wide-spread fame amid the lower as well as the upper classes of society.   When in London, owing to the absence of his valet, he sent for a barber to shave him.   When the operation was finished he offered

PESTALOZZI, THE CHILDREN'S FRIEND

BY

KONRAD GROB

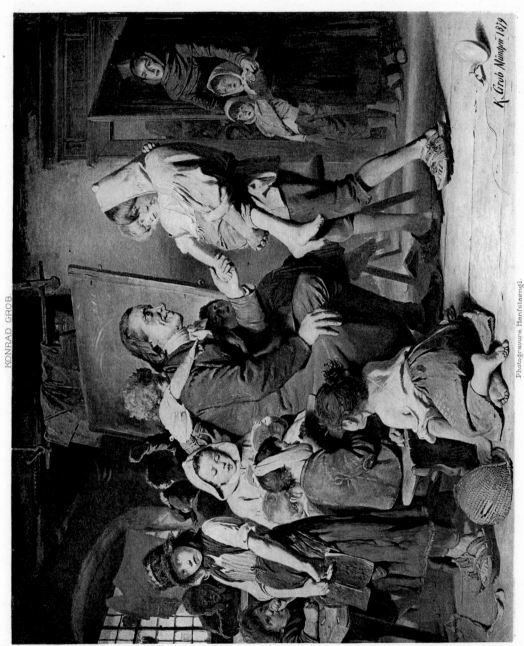

KONRAD GROB.

K. Grob München 1879

Photogravure. Hanfstaengl.

payment. "I am too much honored," replied the Gascon—for such the operator happened to be, "by having shaved the greatest man of the age, to accept any recompense." M. Cuvier allowed him the honor to the full extent, and engaged him to perform the function repeatedly, for which, at length, he was willing to pocket payment.

Cuvier's life must have been most laborious. The same year in which he was made baron, he became president of the Committee of the Interior ; and the numerous and various affairs which there passed under his review, and required his examination, were perfectly wonderful ; together with his scientific employments, they seem more than any mortal man could accomplish. But by economy of time and distribution of labor, concentration of thought, retentiveness of memory, and a profound knowledge of principles in every department, he acquitted himself in a manner which secured universal admiration.

Charles X., of France, and the King of Wurtemberg, vied with each other in the honors they conferred on Cuvier ; and on the accession of Louis Philippe to the French throne the new sovereign continued the favors shown by his predecessors, and in 1832 made the baron a French peer. But his end was now drawing nigh. " Gentlemen," he said one day to his hearers, in opening a new course of lectures, "these will be the objects of our future investigations, if time, health, and strength shall be given to me to continue and finish them with you." But an overwrought brain the very next day produced paralysis, and the distinguished statesman and philosopher died at the age of sixty-three, on May 13, 1832.

Down to the time of Cuvier, the classification of animal life had been most imperfect and unsatisfactory. The basis adopted by Ray was open to criticism. Comparative anatomy, rising into importance during the eighteenth century, continued through that period in a state of infancy. Linnæus and Buffon rendered valuable service ; but all former students in this branch of science were surpassed by Cuvier. A curious anecdote is recorded of the ignorance of natural objects which continued even after the opening of the present century. When the committee of the French Academy were employed in preparing the well-known Academy dictionary, Cuvier came one day into the room where they were holding a session. "Glad to see you, M. Cuvier," said one of the forty ; "we have just finished a definition which we think quite satisfactory, but on which we should like to have your opinion. We have been defining the word 'crab,' and explained it thus : 'Crab, a small red fish, which walks backward.'" "Perfect, gentlemen," said Cuvier ; "only, if you will give me leave, I will make one small observation in natural history. The crab is not a fish, it is not red, and it does not walk backward. With these exceptions your definition is excellent."

Cuvier was the first to give a really philosophical view of the animal world in reference to the plan on which each animal is constructed. There are, he says, four such plans—four forms on which animals appear to have been modelled, and of which the ulterior divisions, with whatever titles naturalists have decorated them, are only very slight modifications, founded on the development or addition of some parts which do not produce any essential change in the plan. These

19

four great branches of the animal world are the *vertebrata, mollusca, articulata,* and *radiata.*

Comparative anatomy found in Cuvier a student who appreciated its importance and revived its efficiency and honors. He saw more distinctly than anyone before, that large classes of animals, when carefully examined, are but modifications of a common type; that, for example, there is after all a strong resemblance, when their skeletons are looked at, between a man and a bird, and also a complete analogy between the human skull and the head of a fish. It was in the pursuit after such analogies that Cuvier was led into the track where he found the basis of his new anatomical classifications.

For his wonderful volumes on fossil animals, Cuvier had made some preparation by an essay, presented in 1810 to the Academy, on the geology of the basin of Paris, a district singularly rich in fossil remains. Montmartre and its vicinity, covered with buildings and crowded with people, would not strike many observers as a promising field for scientific exploration; but it is the peculiarity of genius to read instruction where others can find only a blank, or a record of commonplace character. Cuvier discovered in the geological construction and the fossil remains of the Paris basin, elements for the solution of the most critical scientific questions, relative not only to that locality, but to the globe at large. Long before, he had begun to treasure up facts, the collocation of which ultimately constituted his marvellous additions to human knowledge. In 1800 he finds a few teeth, in following years a few bones; and after many years' patience and skill he ascertains and demonstrates the existence and place of a number of tapir-like animals which he classed as *Lophiodon Paleotherium* and *Anoplotherium,* formerly abounding on the banks of the ponds which have left their mud and marl in the tertiary strata of the Paris basin. His anticipations seemed like prophecies, based, as they were, on a tooth or a bone; but subsequent discoveries enabled him to verify them all, so that they became parts of scientific and general knowledge. The effect of these discoveries on the scientific world was prodigious.

"The great work of Cuvier," says Lord Brougham, "stands among those rare monuments of human genius and labor, of which each department of exertion can scarcely ever furnish more than one, eminent therefore above all the other efforts made in the same kind. In the stricter sciences, the 'Principia' of Newton, and in later times its continuation and extension in La Place's 'Mécanique Céleste;' in intellectual philosophy, Locke's celebrated work; in oratory, Demosthenes; in poetry, Homer, leave all competitors behind by the common consent of mankind; and Cuvier's researches in fossil osteology will probably be reckoned to prefer an equal claim to distinction among the works on comparative anatomy."

"If," says Cuvier, "you have but the extremity of a bone well preserved, you may, by attention, consideration, and the aid of resources which analogy furnishes to skill, determine all the rest as well as if you had the entire skeleton submitted to you."

The great scientific value of the work lies in its comparative anatomy, creating as it were (as we have said) the science of palæontology at a leap; but there are in it also sundry other philosophical deductions in geology, such as the following : that in the strata called primitive there are no remains of life or organized existence ;—that all organized existences were not created at the same time, but at different times, probably very remote from each other, vegetables before animals, the mollusca and fishes before reptiles, and the latter before the mammalia ;—that the transition limestone exhibits remains of the lowest forms of existence ; and the chalk and clay conceal the remains of fishes, reptiles, and quadrupeds, beings of a former order of things, which have now disappeared ;— that among fossil remains no vestige appears of man or his works ; that the fossil remains in the more recent strata are those which approach nearest to the present type of the corresponding living species ; and that these strata show the former prevalence of fresh water as well as sea-water.

The extraordinary sagacity of Cuvier, coupled with his extensive knowledge, qualified him for the execution of this herculean task. His power of geological classification sprang out of his zoölogical skill, and he was a great pioneer in previously unexplored fields of research, where relations between the organic and inorganic changes of the earth were revealed to the eye of the philosopher. "His guiding ideas had been formed, his facts had been studied, by the assistance of all the sciences which could be made to bear upon them. In his geological labors he seems to see some beautiful temple, not only firm and fair in itself, but decorated with sculptures and painting, and rich in all that art and labor, memory and imagination, can contribute to its beauty."

These remarks occur in connection with Whewell's sketch of the contributions to science made by Cuvier : "I may observe, that he is allowed by all to have established on an indestructible basis many of the most important generalizations which zoölogy now contains ; and the principal defect which his critics have pointed out has been that he did not generalize still more widely and boldly. It appears, therefore, that he cannot but be placed among the great discoverers in the studies which he pursued ; and this being the case, those who look with pleasure on the tendency of the thoughts of the greatest men to an intelligence far higher than their own, must be gratified to find that he was an example of this tendency, and that the acknowledgment of a creative purpose, as well as a creative power, not only entered into his belief, but made an indispensable and prominent part of his philosophy."

"Beauty, richness, abundance," says Cuvier, "have been the ways of the Creator, no less than simplicity. We conceive nature to be simply a production of the Almighty, regulated by a wisdom the laws of which can only be discovered by observation."

ALEXANDER VON HUMBOLDT *

By Louis Agassiz

(1769–1859)

Humboldt—Alexander Von Humboldt, as he always called himself, though he was christened with the names of Frederick Heinrich Alexander—was born in 1769, on September 14th, in that memorable year which gave to the world those philosophers, warriors, and statesmen who have changed the face of science and the condition of affairs in our century. It was in that year that Cuvier also and Schiller were born ; and among the warriors and statesmen, Napoleon, the Duke of Wellington, and Canning are children of 1769, and it is certainly a year of which we can say that its children have revolutionized the world.

Of the early life of Humboldt I know nothing, and I find no records except that in his tenth year he lost his father, who had been a major in the army during the seven years' war, and afterward a chamberlain to the King of Prussia. But his mother took excellent care of him, and watched over his early education. The influence she had upon his life is evident from the fact that, notwithstanding his yearning for the sight of foreign lands, he did not begin to make active preparations for his travels during her lifetime. In the winter of 1787–1788 he was sent to the University of Frankfort on the Oder, to study finances. He was to be a statesman ; he was to enter high offices, for which there was a fair chance, owing to his noble birth and the patronage he could expect at court. He remained, however, but a short time there.

Not finding these studies to his taste, after a semestre's residence in the university we find him again at Berlin, and there in intimate friendship with Wildenow, then professor of botany, and who at that time possessed the greatest herbarium in existence. Botany was the first branch of natural science to which Humboldt paid especial attention. The next year he went to Göttingen—being then a youth of twenty years ; and here he studied natural history with Blumenbach, and thus had an opportunity of seeing the progress zoölogy was making in anticipation of the great movement by which Cuvier placed zoölogy on a new foundation.

For it is an unquestionable fact that in first presenting a classification of the animal kingdom based upon a knowledge of its structure, Blumenbach in a

* Written at the time of the death of Baron Von Humboldt, and reprinted, by permission, from " Littell's Living Age."

measure anticipated Cuvier ; though it is only by an exaggeration of what Blumenbach did that an unfair writer of later times has attempted to deprive Cuvier of the glory of having accomplished this object upon the broadest possible basis. From Göttingen he visited the Rhine, for the purpose of studying geology, and in particular the basaltic formations of the Seven Mountains. At Mayence he became acquainted with George Forster, who proposed to accompany him on a journey to England. You may imagine what impression the conversation of that active, impetuous and powerful man had upon the youthful Humboldt. They went to Belgium and Holland, and thence to England, where Forster introduced him to Sir Joseph Banks. Thus the companions of Captain Cook in his first and second voyages round the world, who were already venerable in years and eminent promoters of physical science not yet established in the popular favor, were the early guides of Humboldt in his aspirations for scientific distinction. Yet Humboldt had a worldly career to accomplish. He was to be a statesman, and this required that he should go to the Academy of Commerce at Hamburg. He remained there five months, but could endure it no longer, and he begged so hard that his mother allowed him to go to Freyberg and study geology with Werner, with a view of obtaining a situation in the Administration of Mines. See what combinations of circumstances prepare him for his great career, as no other young man ever was prepared. At Freyberg he received the private instruction of Werner, the founder of modern geology, and he had as his fellow-student no less a man than Leopold Von Buch, then a youth, to whom, at a later period, Humboldt himself dedicated one of his works, inscribing it "to the greatest geologist," as he was till the day of his recent death. From Freyberg he made frequent excursions into the Hartz and Fichtelgeberg and surrounding regions, and these excursions ended in the publication of a small work upon the subterranean flora of Freyberg (" Flora Subterranea Fribergensis "), in which he described especially those cryptogamous plants, or singular low and imperfect formations which occur in the deep mines. But here ends his period of pupilage. In 1792 he was appointed an officer of the mines (Oberbergmeister). He went to Beyreuth as director of the operations in those mines belonging to the Frankish provinces of Prussia. Yet he was always wandering in every direction, seeking for information and new subjects of study. He visited Vienna, and there heard of the discoveries of Galvani, with which he made himself familiar ; went to Italy and Switzerland, where he became acquainted with the then celebrated Professors Jurine and Pictet, and with the illustrious Scarpa. He also went to Jena, formed an intimate acquaintance with Schiller and Goethe, and also with Loder, with whom he studied anatomy. From that time he began to make investigations of his own, and these investigations were in a line which he has never approached since, being experiments in physiology. He turned his attention to the newly-discovered power by which he tested the activity of organic substances ; and it is plain, from his manner of treating the subject, that he leaned to the idea that the chemical process going on in the living body of animals furnished a clew to the phenomena of life, if it was not life itself. This may be inferred from the title of the book published in 1797—" Ueber die gereizte Muskel und Nervenfaser, mit Vermuthungen über den chemischen Process des Lebens, in Thieren und Pflanzen."

In these explanations of the phenomena we have the sources of the first impulses in a direction which has been so beneficial in advancing the true explanation of the secondary phenomena of life; but which, at the same time, in its exaggeration as it prevails now has degenerated into the materialism of modern investigators.

In that period of all-embracing activity, he began to study astronomy. His attention was called to it by Baron Von Zach, who was a prominent astronomer of the time, and who at that time was actively engaged upon astronomical investigations in Germany. He showed Humboldt to what extent astronomy would be useful to him, in his travels, in determining the position of places, the altitude of mountains, etc.

So prepared, Humboldt now broods over his plans of foreign travel. He has published his work on the muscular and nervous fibre at the age of twenty-eight. He has lost his mother; and his mind is now inflamed with an ungovernable passion for the sight of foreign and especially tropical lands. He goes to Paris to make preparation by securing the best astronomical, meteorological and surveying instruments. Evidently he does not care where he shall go, for on a proposition of Lord Bristol to visit Egypt he agrees to it. The war prevents the execution of this plan, and he enters into negotiations to accompany the projected expedition of Captain Baudin to Australia; but when Bonaparte, bent on the conquest of Egypt, started with a scientific expedition, Humboldt wishes to join it. He expects to be one of the scientific party, and to reach Egypt by way of Barbary.

But all these plans failing, he goes to Spain with the view of exploring that country, and finding perhaps some means of joining the French expedition in Egypt from Spain. While in Madrid he is so well received at the court—a young nobleman so well instructed has access everywhere—and he receives such encouragement from persons in high positions, that he turns his thoughts to an exploration of the Spanish provinces of America. He receives permission not only to visit them, but instructions are given to the officers of the colonies to receive him everywhere and give him all facilities, to permit him to transport his instruments, to make astronomical and other observations, and to collect whatever he chooses; and all that only in consequence of the good impression he has made when he appeared there, with no other recommendation than that of a friend who happened to be at that time Danish minister to the court of Madrid. But with these facilities offered to him, he sails in June, 1799, from Corunna, whence he reaches Teneriffe, makes short explorations of that island, ascending the peak, and sailing straightway to America, where he lands in Cumana in the month of July, and employs the first year and a half in the exploration of the basin of the Orinoco and its connection with the Amazon. This was a journey of itself, and completed a work of scientific importance, establishing the fact that the two rivers were connected by an uninterrupted course of water. He established for the first time the fact that there was an extensive low plain, connected by water, which circled the high table-land of Guiana. It was an important discovery in physical geography, because it changed the ideas about water-courses and about the distributions of mountains and plains in a manner which has had the most extensive influence upon the progress of physical geography. It may well be said that after this exploration of the Orinoco, physical geography begins to appear as a part of science. From Cumana he makes a short excursion to Havana, and hearing there of the probable arrival of Baudin on the west coast of America, starts with the intention of crossing at Panama. He arrives at Carthagena, but was prevented by the advance of the season from crossing the Isthmus, and changed his determination from want of precise information respecting Baudin's locality. He determines to ascend the Magdalena River and visit Santa Fé de Bogota, where, for several months, he explores the construction of the mountains, and collects plants and animals ; and, in connection with his friend, Bonpland, who accompanied him from Paris, he makes those immense botanical collections, which were afterward published by Bonpland himself, and by Kunth after Bonpland had determined on an expedition to South America. In the beginning of 1802 he reaches Quito, where, during four months, he turns his attention to everything worth investigating, ascends the Chimborazo, to a height to which no human foot had reached, anywhere ; and, having completed this survey and repeatedly crossed the Andes, he descends the southern slope of the continent to the shore of the Pacific at Truxillo, and following the arid coast of Peru, he visits finally Lima.

I will pass lightly over all the details of his journey, for they are only incidents in that laborious exploration of the country which is best appreciated by a consideration of the works which were published in consequence of that immense accumulation of materials gathered during those explorations. From Lima, or rather from Callao, he sails in 1802 for Guayaquil and Acapulco, and reaches Mexico in 1803, where he makes as extensive explorations as he had made in Venezuela and the Andes, and after a stay of about a year, and having put all his collections and manuscripts in order, revisits Cuba for a short time, comes to the United States, makes a hurried excursion to Philadelphia and Washington, where he is welcomed by Jefferson, and finally returns with his faithful companion Bonpland to France, accompanied by a young Spanish nobleman, Don Carlo de Montufar, who had shared his travels since his visits to Quito.

At thirty-six years of age Humboldt is again in Europe with collections made in foreign lands, such as had never been brought together before. But here we meet with a singular circumstance. The German nobleman, the friend of the Prussian and Spanish courts, chooses Paris for his residence, and remains there twenty-two years to work out the result of his scientific labor ; for since his return, with the exception of short journeys to Italy, England and Germany, sometimes accompanying the King of Prussia, sometimes alone, or accompanied by scientific friends, he is entirely occupied in scientific labors and studies. So passes the time to the year 1827, and no doubt he was induced to make this choice of a residence by the extraordinary concourse of distinguished men in all branches of science with whom he thought he could best discuss the results of his own observations. I shall presently have something to say about the works he completed during that most laborious period of his life. I will only add now, that in 1827 he returned to Berlin permanently, having been urged of late by the King of Prussia again and again to return to his native land. And there he delivered a series of lectures preparatory to the publication of "Cosmos;" for in substance, even in form and arrangement, these lectures, of which the papers of the day gave short accounts, are a sort of prologue to the "Cosmos," and a preparation for its publication. In 1829, when he was sixty years of age, he undertakes another great journey. He accepts the invitation of the Emperor Nicholas to visit the Ural Mountains, with a view of examining the gold mines, and localities where platina and diamonds had been found, to determine their geological relation. He accomplished the journey with Ehrenberg and Gustavus Rose, who published the result of their mineralogical and geological survey, in a work of which he is the sole author; while Humboldt published under the title of "Asiatic Fragments of Geology and Climatology," his observations of the physical and geographical features made during that journey. But he had hardly returned to Berlin when in consequence of the revolution of 1830, he was sent by the King of Prussia as extraordinary ambassador to France, to honor the elevation of Louis Philippe to the throne. Humboldt had long been a personal friend of the Orleans family, and he was selected ambassador on that occasion on account of these personal relations. From 1830 to 1848 he lived alternately in Berlin and in Paris, spending nearly half the time in Paris and half the time in Berlin, with occasional visits to England and Denmark; publishing the results of his investigations in Asia, making original investigations upon various things and especially pressing the establishment of observatories, and connected magnetic observations all over the globe, for which he obtained the co-operation of the Russian government and that of the government of England; and at that time those observations in Australia and in the Russian empire to the borders of China, were established which have led to such important results in our knowledge of terrestrial magnetism. Since 1848 he has lived uninterruptedly in Berlin, where he published on the anniversary of his eightieth year a new edition of those charming first flowers of his pen; his "Views of Nature," the first edition of which was published in Germany in 1808. This third edition appeared with a series of new and remodelled annotations and explanations; and that book in which he first presented his views of nature, in which he drew those vivid pictures of the physiognomy of plants and of their geographical distribution is now revived and brought to the present state of science.

The "Views of Nature" is a work which Humboldt has always cherished, and to which in his "Cosmos" he refers more frequently than to any other work. It is no doubt because there he has expressed his deepest thoughts, his most impressive views, and even foreshadowed those intimate convictions which he never expressed, but which he desired to record in such a manner that those that can read between the lines might find them there ; and certainly there we find them. . His aspiration has been to present to the world a picture of the physical world from which he would exclude everything that relates to the turmoil of human society, and to the ambitions of individual men. A life so full, so rich, is worth explaining in every respect, and it is really instructive to see with what devotion he pursues his work. As long as he is a student he is really a student and learns faithfully, and learns everything he can reach. And he continues so for twenty-three years. He is not one of those who is impatient to show that he has something in him, and with premature impatience utters his ideas, so that they become insuperable barriers to his independent progress in later life. Slowly and confident of his sure progress, he advances, and while he learns he studies also independently of those who teach him. He makes his experiments, and to make them with more independence he seeks for an official position. During five years he is a business man, in a station which gives him leisure. He is superintendent of the mines, but the superintendent of the mines who can do much as he pleases; and while he is thus officially engaged journeying and superintending, he prepares himself for his independent researches. And yet it will be seen he is thirty years of age before he enters upon his American travels—those travels which will be said to have been the greatest undertaking ever carried to a successful issue, if judged by the results; they have as completely changed the basis of physical science as the revolution which took place in France about the same time has changed the social condition of that land. Having returned from these travels to Paris, there begins in his life a period of concentrated critical studies. He works his materials, and he works them with an ardor and devotion which are untiring ; and he is not anxious to appear to have done it all himself. Oltmann is called to his aid to revise his astronomical observations, and his barometrical measurements by which he has determined the geographical position of seven hundred different points and the altitude of more than four hundred and fifty of them.

The large collection of plants which Bonpland had begun to illustrate, but of which his desire of seeing the tropics again has prevented the completion he intrusts to Kunth. He has also brought home animals of different classes, and distributes them among the most eminent zoölogists of the day.

To Cuvier he intrusts the investigation of that remarkable batrachian, the Aæolotel, the mode of development of which is still unknown, but which remains in its adult state in a condition similar to that of the tadpole of the frog during the earlier period of its life. Latreille describes the insects, and Valenciennes the shells and the fishes ; but yet to show that he might have done the work himself, he publishes a memoir on the anatomical structure of the organs of breathing in the animals he has preserved, and another upon the tropical monkeys of America, and another upon the electric properties of the electric eel. But he was chiefly occupied with investigations in physical geography and climatology. The first work upon that subject is a dissertation on the geographical distribution of plants, published in 1817. Many botanist travellers had observed that in different parts of the world there are plants not found in others, and that there is a certain arrangement in that distribution; but Humboldt was the first to see that this distribution is connected with the temperature of the air as well as with the altitudes of the surface on which they grow, and he systematized his researches into a general exposition of the laws by which the distribution of plants is regulated. Connected with this subject he made those extensive investigations into the mean temperature of a large number of places on the surface of the globe, which led to the drawing of those isothermal lines so important in their influence in shaping physical geography, and giving accuracy to the mode of representing natural phenomena. Before Humboldt we had no graphic representation of complex natural phenomena which made them easily comprehensible, even to minds of moderate cultivation. He has done that in a way which has circulated information more extensively, and brought it to the apprehension more clearly than it could have been done by any other means.

It is not too much to say that this mode of representing natural phenomena has made it possible to introduce in our most elementary works the broad generalizations derived from the investigations of Humboldt in South America; and that every child in our schools has his mind fed from the labors of Humboldt's brain, wherever geography is no longer taught in the old routine.

.   .   .   .

Humboldt was born near the court. He was brought up in connection with courtiers and men in high positions of life. He was no doubt imbued with the prejudices of his caste. He was a nobleman of high descent. And yet the friend of kings was the bosom friend of Arago, and he was the man who could, after his return from America, refuse the highest position at the court of Berlin, that of the secretaryship of public instruction, preferring to live in a modest way in Paris, in the society of all those illustrious men, who then made Paris the centre of intellectual culture. It was there where he became one of that Société d'Arceuil, composed of all the great men of the day, to which the paper on "Isothermal Lines" was presented, and by which it was printed, as all papers presented to it were, for private distribution. But from his intimate relations, especially to the court of Prussia, some insinuations have been made as to the character of Humboldt. They are as unjust as they are severe in expression. He was never a flatterer of those in power. He has shown it by taking a prominent position, in 1848, at the head of those who accompanied the victims of the revolution of that year to their last place of rest. But while he expressed his independence in such a manner, he had the kindliest feeling for all parties. He could not offend, even by an expression, those with whom he had been associated in early life; and I have no doubt that it is to that kindliness of feeling we must ascribe his somewhat indiscriminate patronage of aspirants in science, as well as men who were truly devoted to its highest aims. He may be said to have been, especially in his latter years, the friend of every cultivated man, wishing to lose no opportunity to do all the good of which he was capable; for he had a degree of benevolence and generosity which was unbounded. I can well say that there is not a man engaged in scientific investigations in Europe, who has not received at his hands marked tokens of his favor, and who is not under deep obligations to him. May I be permitted to tell a circumstance which is personal to me in that respect, and which shows what he was capable of doing while he was forbidden an opportunity of telling it. I was only twenty-four years of age when in Paris, whither I had gone with means given me by a friend; but was at last about to resign my studies from want of ability to meet my expenses. Professor Mitscherlich was then on a visit to Paris, and I had seen him in the morning, when he asked me what was the cause of my depressed feelings; and I told him that I had to go for I had nothing left. The next morning as I was seated at breakfast in front of the yard of the hotel where I lived, I saw the servant of Humboldt approach. He handed me a note, saying there was no answer and disappeared. I opened the note, and I see it now before me as distinctly as if I held the paper in my hand. It said:—

"My friend, I hear that you intend leaving Paris in consequence of some embarrassments. That shall not be. I wish you to remain here as long as the object for which you came is not accomplished. I enclose you a check of £50. It is a loan which you may repay when you can."

Some years afterward, when I could have repaid him, I wrote, asking for the privilege of remaining forever in his debt, knowing that this request would be more consonant to his feelings than the recovery of the money, and I am now in his debt. What he has done for me, I know he has done for many others; in silence and unknown to the world. I wish I could go on to state something of his character, his conversational powers, etc., but I feel that I am not in a condition to speak of them. I would only say that his habits were very peculiar. He was an early riser, and yet he was seen at late hours in the salons in different parts of Paris. From the year 1830 to 1848, while in Paris, he had been charged by the King of Prussia to send reports upon the condition of things there. He had before prepared for the King of Prussia a report on the political condition of the Spanish colonies in America, which no doubt had its influence afterward upon the recognition of the independence of those colonies. The importance of such reports to the government of Prussia may be inferred from a perusal of his political and statistical essays upon Mexico and Cuba. It is a circumstance worth noticing, that above all great powers, Prussia has more distinguished, scientific, and literary men among her diplomatists than any other state. And so was Humboldt actually a diplomatist in Paris, though he was placed in that position, not from choice, but in consequence of the benevolence of the king, who wanted to give him an opportunity of being in Paris as often and as long as he chose.

But from that time there were two men in him—the diplomatist, living in the Hôtel des Princes, and the naturalist who roomed in the Rue de la Harpe, in a modest apartment in the second story; where his scientific friends had access to him every day before seven. After that he was frequently seen working in the library of the Institute, until the time when the grand seigneur made his appearance at the court or in the salons of Paris.

The influence he has exerted upon the progress òf science is incalculable. I need only allude to the fact that the "Cosmos," bringing every branch of natural science down to the comprehension of every class of students, has been translated into the language of every civilized nation of the world, and gone through several editions. With him ends a great period in the history of science, a period to which Cuvier, Laplace, Arago, Gay-Lussac and De Candolle, and Robert Brown belonged.

DANIEL O'CONNELL *

By Justin McCarthy

(1775–1847)

Daniel O'Connell, undoubtedly one of the greatest Irishmen that ever lived, and according to Mr. Lecky perhaps the greatest political agitator that the modern world has known, was born August 6, 1775, in the county of Kerry, in Ireland. His parents were of good family, but comparatively poor, his father being a second son. Later on, Daniel was adopted by an uncle, through whom he came in for the property of Darrynane, made famous by his name. He was sent when a boy—the fact is worth noticing— to the first school kept openly by a Catholic priest since the establishment of the penal laws. Afterward he became a student in France—in St. Omer and in Douay, until the outbreak of the French Revolution made it unsafe for him to remain longer in France—or at all events until his family believed that it would not be safe for him to remain there any longer. The excesses of the Revolution greatly shocked and horrified the young O'Connell, and indeed the effect of that early shock was felt by him all through his career. He became impressed with an almost morbid detestation of all forms of blood-shedding; and for a while after his return to Ireland he firmly believed himself to be a Conservative in politics. But the system of administration which prevailed in Great Britain and Ireland under Conservative governments soon convinced him that he could have nothing to do with Conservatism, and he very soon became—

what he ever after continued to be—a Liberal as regarded Imperial policy, and indeed something more than a Liberal—what we should now call a Radical. He studied for the bar, and was, to all appearance, little inclined for anything but law and field sports. He was a keen sportsman, and, like another distinguished Irishman, "all his life long he loved rivers, and poets who sang of rivers." He made rapid way in his profession, and soon became one of the foremost advocates in Ireland. He was a safe, shrewd, keen lawyer as well as a great advocate —the two parts do not always go together. He was a master of the art of cross-examination and he was a magnificent speaker—his speeches were aflame with humor, and pathos, and passion. His voice was one of immense power and sweetness and variety of tone. Mr. Disraeli in one of his books, when praising to the highest the superb voice of the great Sir Robert Peel, says that he had never heard its superior "except indeed in the thrilling tones of O'Connell." The Irish advocate had the advantage, too, of a commanding presence. He was tall and moulded in almost herculean form, and he had eyes which were often compared with those of Robert Burns—the light of genius was in them. There is a full-length picture of him in the Reform Club, London, which enables one to understand how stately and imposing his presence must have been.

The career of O'Connell would appear to have been easily marked out for him. He was the foremost advocate in Ireland; he was making a large income; he had inherited a considerable property—what was there for him but to go on and prosper; make money, hunt, shoot, fish, and be happy. He could not indeed obtain any of the honors or dignities of his profession. He could not even be a king's counsel, and wear a silk gown. His religion cut him off from all such marks of distinction—for he was a member of the Catholic Church. But no penal laws prevented him from addressing juries and winning verdicts and attracting popular admiration and making money. He was very happily married —a genuine love-match, it would seem to have been, and the love lasted. Moreover he was strongly and almost unreasonably opposed to all manner of agitation that bordered on rebellion or even on sedition. He was positively unjust, he was utterly unreasonable, in his estimate of the rebellion of 1798 and Robert Emmet's abortive effort in 1803. He never did full justice even to the brave men who were concerned in these movements. He had an absolute detestation for all manner of secret societies. He knew too well that they only ended in betrayal by some traitor who had contrived to be admitted to their ranks. Under such conditions and with such views what was there to induce the successful and prosperous advocate who loved peace and who hated social disturbance, to mix himself up with political affairs at a time when national politics meant for a patriotic Irishman only social exclusion, danger, poverty, and even ruin?

O'Connell could not help himself. He had to walk, as Carlyle says of a very different man, "his own wild road whither that led him." O'Connell's wild road—the road that he had to walk, led him to the leadership of two great national movements.

To understand what O'Connell fought against we must, of course, understand O'Connell's time. It is not easy for an American reader to understand it without some thought and without the endeavor to grasp the reality of a state of things quite outside his own living experience. When O'Connell began his career in politics the Act of Union had but lately been passed. That Act of Union deprived Ireland of the more or less independent Parliament which she had had for generations and even for centuries. It was indeed a Parliament "more or less" independent—less, perhaps, much rather than more. Still there had been always a recognition of Irish nationality in the existence of any form of Irish Parliament. The troubles between England and her American colonies—between England and France—had led to the concession of what we now know as Grattan's Parliament—the nearest form of Home Rule Ireland had ever enjoyed since her conquest by the descendants of the great Norman kings. But it was a Parliament of Protestants—no Catholic, in a nation of which five-sixths were Catholics, could sit in the National Parliament or even give a vote for a member of that National Parliament. Grattan's Parliament was exclusively Protestant; but yet, with all its imperfections, so nationalist was it in spirit that it was willing, under Grattan's inspiration, to enable Roman Catholics to vote for the election of members of the Irish House of Commons. But Grattan and his friends were anxious to go much farther. They demanded a complete political equality for the Roman Catholics. A society was formed for the purpose of conducting the agitation. Its leaders were almost all Protestants—many of them were Protestants from Ulster. The stupid bigotry of George the Third bluntly refused Catholic Emancipation; and the Society of United Irishmen became a rebellious organization. The rebellion of 1798 broke out and was crushed after terrible bloodshed. Then, when Ireland was wholly at the mercy of England, Pitt brought in his proposal for an Act of Union. After much resistance from all that was patriotic in Ireland and all that was sympathetic in England, the Act of Union was carried—by fraud and force and bribery and purchase. It has to be remembered with satisfaction that some of the noblest Englishmen of the time were as strenuously opposed to such a measure as Grattan himself. Pitt had made liberal promises about Catholic Emancipation while he was striving to carry the Act of Union, but when the Act was passed he dropped all talk about Catholic Emancipation, and pleaded as his excuse that the king would not listen to any further proposals on the subject. O'Connell's first political speech was made in January, 1800, at a meeting of Catholics held in Dublin to protest against the Act of Union.

Something else had to be done, however, before it could be possible in Ireland to encounter the Act of Union with anything like a successful constitutional agitation. The right had to be obtained for a Catholic to sit in Parliament. The Catholic Association had been formed for the purpose, and O'Connell became its recognized leader, and, more than that, the recognized leader of the Irish people. Meanwhile there were constant efforts made in Parliament for the emancipation of the Catholics. Sir Robert Peel, who had begun his career as

Chief Secretary to the Lord Lieutenant of Ireland, had become Secretary of State for the Home Department—and it may be well to mention to American readers that the Irish Secretaryship is really a subordinate part of the Home Office. Peel, as Home Secretary, was necessarily kept in constant touch with everything going on in Ireland. He was greatly impressed by some of the debates in the House of Commons. He was especially impressed by an observation which Lord Brougham, then Mr. Brougham, made in a speech supporting Catholic Emancipation, to the effect that not one of those who spoke against emancipation had ventured even to suggest that things could remain as they then were. Something will have to be done, Peel said to himself. What is the something to be? The new king, George the Fourth, in whose succession to the throne O'Connell and Thomas Moore and the Irish people generally had had so much hope, was doggedly opposed to the political relief of the Catholics.

Accident helped to bring about a settlement of the question. A sudden vacancy occurred in the Parliamentary representation of the County of Clare, owing to the fact that the former representative had accepted office in the government, and had therefore to offer himself for re-election. The leaders of the Catholic Association determined on the bold policy of putting forward a candidate to contest the seat. O'Connell, of course, was recognized by everyone as the man to fight the battle. He willingly accepted the responsibility. Even moderate men, partly sympathetic, shook their heads when they heard of this determination. "O'Connell will end his life on the gallows" was the confident prediction of some who passed among their neighbors for sensible persons. The Viceroy of Ireland predicted that O'Connell would take care to maintain good order in Clare during the election. O'Connell's opponent predicted that O'Connell would not dare to come to Clare in person ; that he would not run the risk of confronting his enemies. O'Connell ran the risk—he was not a man likely to be afraid of risks. He went to Clare. The enthusiasm was wild, but the order was perfect. O'Connell, the excluded Catholic, was elected by a majority of more than two to one. The result set Peel thinking. What he thought we have in his own words. Was it possible to take no account of "that political and religious excitement which was quickening the pulse and fluttering the bosom of the whole Catholic population—which had inspired the serf of Clare with the resolution and the energy of a freeman?" No, it was not possible. Peel soon made up his mind.

O'Connell presented himself at the bar of the House of Commons later on, but not until after Peel and Wellington had crammed emancipation down the king's throat and compelled him to accept it. Wellington seems to have reasoned much in this way : "I know nothing about the question—Peel knows all about it ; Peel thinks it will be for the good of the king and the country to pass Catholic Emancipation ; the king, I am sure, does not know any more about the matter than I do, and I am prepared to go with Peel, and the king must come with us. Peel thinks there must be civil war if we don't pass Catholic Emancipation, and I have had too much of war in my time—and I don't propose to stand a civil war—not if I know it." The king had, of course, to give way in the end, and Catholic Emancipation was passed. It was passed rather ungraciously. It was accompanied by a quite superfluous measure suppressing the Catholic Association, which had in fact already dissolved itself, its work being done, and invalidating the election of O'Connell. Perhaps, without these sops to religious bigotry, an act for the emancipation of the Catholics could not then have been carried through the Houses of Parliament. O'Connell presented himself at the bar of the House of Commons and claimed a right to take his seat. He was called upon to swear the old oaths—what we may fairly call the anti-Catholic oaths. Of course he refused. A new writ was ordered for Clare, and O'Connell was triumphantly returned. The struggle was over.

The remainder of O'Connell's life was devoted mainly to the cause of Repeal of the Union—in other words, the cause of Home Rule. He organized the great system of monster meetings—vast out-of-door gatherings, which he swayed as he pleased by the magic of his eloquence, his humor, his passion, and the charm of his wonderful voice. No doubt he sometimes used very strong language ; no doubt some of the younger men fully believed that he meant rebellion—that he had rebellion up his sleeve if his demands were not conceded. The meetings were always held on the Sunday ; were indeed, regarded as, in a certain sense, religious celebrations. The meeting of October 8, 1843, was to be held on the historic ground of Clontarf, and it was expected to be the greatest of all the assemblages, although some of them had drawn together a crowd of nearly a quarter of a million of men. The Government issued a proclamation prohibiting the meeting, and O'Connell bowed to the prohibition. He sent messengers in every direction countermanding the assembling of men, in order to prevent any chance of that disorder and bloodshed which he had always shrunk from and abhorred. He and some of his friends, Sir Charles Gavan Duffy among the rest, were put on their trial on a charge of sedition. Most of them were found guilty and sentenced to fine and imprisonment. They were confined in Richmond Prison, Dublin. Their incarceration did not last long, and indeed, was what might be called " internment " rather than actual imprisonment. A majority of the law lords in the House of Peers, the final tribunal, annulled the sentences on the ground that the jury had been unfairly chosen—was packed, in fact. O'Connell and his colleagues were set free after a few months ; but the leader never recovered his former ascendency over the political movement of Ireland. He was growing old ; he had been reckless of his great physical resources, he had been unsparing of his strength ; and undoubtedly, the younger men in the agitation fell away from him when he had made it clear that he never meant, under any conditions, to lead them into revolution. A number of his young and brilliant followers set up a party of their own—the Young Ireland Confederation— which after his death drifted into a generous, but hopeless, rebellion. The Young Ireland movement, however, quickened and established a national literature which had an immense effect on subsequent political history in Ireland. The Irish famine of 1846 and 1847 was a terrible blow to O'Connell in his rapidly weakening health. His last speech in the House of Commons was an appeal for a generous help to Ireland, and a prediction, which proved only too true, that if generous help were not given, one-fourth of Ireland's population must perish by starvation. His physicians ordered him to the Continent, and he passionately longed to reach Rome and die under the shadow of the Vatican. He had during some of his years led a wild life, and he had killed a man in a duel—a duel which was literally forced upon him, but for which he always felt deeply penitent. His ultimate longing had come to be a quiet death in the papal city. He was not graced so far. He died in Genoa on May 15, 1847.

As a politician O'Connell was absolutely consistent. He was in favor of liberty for Ireland, but he was in favor of liberty for every other country. His definition of liberty was practical and not merely declamatory. He was in favor of equal rights for all men before the law; he was in favor of a free press, a free vote, and as nearly as possible a manhood suffrage. He was in many ways far in advance of the English liberals of his day. When the question of slavery in the West Indian colonies was under discussion in Parliament, he went farther for abolition than even the professed philanthropists and emancipationists, the Clarksons and the Buxtons, were inclined to go. He was almost fanatically opposed to the advocates of the slave system in the United States, and he refused to receive any help in money from them to carry on his Repeal agitation. He declined to endure any political dictation from the Vatican, although he was a most devoted Roman Catholic. He would take, he said, without question his religion from Rome, but not his politics. There was no great cause of freedom upheld all through the world in his time, but he clung to it and cleaved to it. The writer of this article once talked to Mr. Gladstone about O'Connell, well knowing that in early life Mr. Gladstone had been a great admirer of O'Connell's abilities. Mr. Gladstone told many anecdotes of O'Connell's personal energy in pursuit of any purpose which he believed to be just, and in illustration of his wonderful mastery over even a thoroughly hostile audience. When asked what he believed to be O'Connell's principal characteristic, Mr. Gladstone paused for a while and thought the question out, and then gravely and deliberately answered: "I should think his greatest characteristic was a passion of philanthropy" A passion of philanthropy! Is it possible to have a nobler epitaph pronounced on one than that— and pronounced by such a man? No man in our modern history was ever so bitterly and savagely denounced in England as O'Connell. No words were too rough for him. He was commonly called in English newspapers the "Big Beggarman." He was accused every day, of making a fortune out of the contributions of a half-starving people. The truth was that all and much more than all the money raised by the Irish people, was spent on the agitation for repeal of the Union. The truth was that O'Connell gave up his splendid practice at the bar, for the sake of advocating the Irish national cause. The truth was that he spent his own money and reduced his own property to all but pauperism, for the sake of advancing the same cause. The truth was that he died poor, leaving his children poor. But he had his reward. A man whom Mr. Gladstone could describe

20

as possessed above all other things by a passion of philanthropy, may leave his memory safely in the charge of those whose best interests he honestly strove to serve.

Justin McCarthy

SIMON BOLIVAR*

By Hon. John P. St. John

(1783–1830)

So far as the world knew, the birth of Simon Bolivar at Caracas, Venezuela, on July 24, 1783, was of no greater importance than that of any other child. Perhaps but one person entertained the slightest thought that he would ever be the hero of many battles and the liberator of his countrymen ; and that person was his mother. A mother, as a rule, always in her imagination anticipates a brilliant future for her boy. If Bolivar's mother was not an exception to this rule, surely her highest anticipations were fully realized in the wonderful career of her son.

His father, Juan Vincente Bolivar y Ponte, and his mother, Maria Concepcion Palacios y Sojo, were descendants of noble families in Venezuela. Nothing unusual occurred in his school-boy days to distinguish him from others of his age and rank. He was attentive to his studies, warm-hearted, generous, and always a favorite among his associates. When he had made sufficient advancement in his studies at home, and had arrived at the proper age, he was sent to Madrid, where he remained several years, during which time he completed his education.

Bolivar was now a full-grown man, and as a source of needed recreation after years of hard study, he spent some time in visiting places of special interest in the south of Europe. On his journey he stopped for a time at the French capital, where he witnessed the closing scenes of the French revolution. This was the hour of Napoleon's greatest glory. He was the acknowledged military hero of the age. All France bowed at his feet. Is it not probable that here was where Bolivar caught the inspiration that led him to make an effort to be to his own country, what Napoleon was to France? From Paris Bolivar returned to Madrid, where, in 1801, he married the daughter of Don N. Toro, uncle of the Marquis of Toro, in Caracas. He soon sailed with his young bride for his native country, but it was only a little while until she fell a victim to yellow fever. The sudden and unexpected death of his young wife, to whom he was intensely devoted, so shattered his health and frustrated his plans, that he wended his way back to Europe, where he remained until 1809, when he returned through the United States to his own country. His remembrance of the closing scenes of the French revolution, and the realization as he passed through the United States of the blessings of her free institutions, no doubt account in some measure for the fact that, as soon as he reached Venezuela, he joined the movement then crystallizing into an aggressive warfare for independence, and a larger degree of freedom for his own countrymen.

In 1810 he received a colonel's commission from the revolutionary junta, and was associated with Luis Lopez Mendez in a mission to the court of Great Britain, which was rendered fruitless by England announcing her position in relation to the troubles in Venezuela as one of strict neutrality. On July 5, 1811, Venezuela formally declared her independence from the mother-country. This brought on a clash of arms at once.

The Spanish troops under Monteverde, owing to a lack of concert of action on the part of the "patriots," forced Bolivar, with his little band of volunteers, to abandon the important post of Puerto Cabello, and flee to Curaçao, which was reached in safety, while Monteverde at the head of the Spanish troops gained control of Venezuela.

Chafing under defeat, Bolivar, in September, 1812, repaired to Carthagena, where a commission was given him to make war upon the Spanish troops along the Magdalena River. Although his army numbered but 500 men, he succeeded in driving the enemy, not only from the country along the Magdalena River, but entered Venezuela, and forced his way westward to the important towns of Merida and Truxillo, where the people gladly welcomed him and rallied to his support. Encouraged by his success, and embittered by the brutalities of the enemy, as he pressed forward he issued his noted proclamation of "War to the death."

He soon routed Monteverde's army at Lastoguanes, forcing him to take refuge in Puerto Cabello, while Bolivar pushed forward, entering Caracas in triumph August 4, 1813. But the tide of battle soon turned. The Royalists concentrated all their available force, and a number of bloody battles ensued, and finally Bolivar's men, inferior in numbers, were badly defeated near Cura. The fall of Caracas soon followed, and before the close of the year 1814 the Royalists were again in full possession of Venezuela. Though defeated, Bolivar was not dismayed. He had great faith in the righteousness of his cause, and his consciousness of this fact seemed to give him that courage which never knows defeat.

He next went to Tunja, where the revolutionary congress was in session, and notwithstanding the misfortunes of war and the bitter opposition of a few personal enemies, his enthusiastic reception showed that he still retained the confidence and respect of the people.   He was soon given command of an expedition against Santa Fé de Bogota, where Don Cundinamarca had refused official recognition of the new union of the provinces, which, without any conflict of arms, was crowned with success by the surrender of the rebellious leaders.   For this service Bolivar received the special thanks of Congress.   The Royalists having captured Santa Martha, Bolivar was ordered to retake it, but failed in his attempt.

In May, 1814, he resigned his commission, and went to Kingston, Jamaica, where an attempt was made to assassinate him, which resulted, by a mistake, in the murder of another.   Later on he went to Aux Cayes, in Hayti, where President Petion assisted him in organizing an expedition which, though it succeeded in reaching the main-land in May, 1816, eventually failed.   But Bolivar's past experience had taught him not to go wild over a victory, nor be discouraged by a defeat, so he returned to Aux Cayes, where he secured reinforcements, and in December landed his troops, first at Marguerite, and then at Barcelona.   At this point a provisional government was formed and all the available military force was promptly organized, and placed in readiness to resist the invasion of Morillo, who was at the head of a strong, well-disciplined army of Royalists. The opposing forces met on February 16, 1817, and a desperate battle, lasting three days, ensued, resulting in a complete rout of the Royalists, who, while retreating in great disorder, were assailed with such impetuosity by small bands of patriots, as to make their overthrow complete.

Being now the undisputed commander-in-chief, Bolivar seemed irresistible. Victory after victory crowned his efforts, until he established his headquarters at Angostura, on the Orinoco.   From this point, after a thorough reorganization of his forces, he pressed forward over the Cordilleras, and effected a junction with the army headed by General Santander, commander of the Republican forces in New Granada.   The armies thus united proved to be invincible.   The entire march was characterized by a succession of victories, ending in a complete overthrow of the enemy on August 7, 1819, at Bojaca, which gave him full possession, not only of Bogota, but of all New Granada.   This brilliant achievement attracted the attention of the civilized world then, and as we read about it now, it forcibly reminds us, in its conception, the skill and rapidity of its execution, and its results, of the wonderful march of Sherman from Atlanta to the sea. Taking advantage of the great prestige his marvellous victories had given him with the people, he procured the passage of a fundamental law, December 17, 1819, uniting Venezuela and New Granada under one government, to be known as the Republic of Colombia, of which Bolivar was made president.

Bolivar was now at the head of the grandest army he had ever commanded. The Royalists, under Morillo, having been beaten at several points, induced Bolivar, at Truxillo on November 20, 1820, to consent to an armistice for six months, which he did; no doubt with the hope that meantime a treaty of peace might be effected and the war thus brought to an end.

Subsequent events, however, gave strong reasons to believe that the armistice was a mere ruse to gain time while Morillo could be recalled and General Torre placed in command. Bolivar, no doubt incensed by this apparent trick, determined, upon the expiration of the armistice, to strike a blow that would not soon be forgotten ; which he did at Carabolo, by attacking and completely routing General Torre's command, compelling the fleeing fragments to seek shelter in Puerto Cabello, where two years after they surrendered to Paez. This practically closed the war in Venezuela. On August 30, 1821, the constitution of Colombia was adopted amid great rejoicing, with Bolivar as president and Santander as vice-president. But there was more work to do, and no one could do it so well as Bolivar. He determined that nowhere should the Royalists have a foothold in the whole country. He attacked them at Pichincha, in Ecuador, and after a desperate struggle they were forced to retreat in disorder, while victorious Bolivar with his enthusiastic followers triumphantly entered Quito, June 22, 1822. Next Lima was taken, but owing to the dissensions among the Republican factions in Peru, Bolivar was compelled to abandon the city, which was again occupied by the Royalists, while he withdrew to Truxillo.

Having thoroughly reorganized his forces, and gotten everything in good condition for an aggressive warfare, he again assaulted the Royalists with unrelenting vigor, driving them before him, and finally administering a crushing defeat on the plains of Junin, August 6th ; after which he returned to Lima, leaving Sucre, who had already displayed great military skill and bravery, to complete the work. This he did, by gaining a great victory at Ayacucho, which completely dispersed the Royalists, reducing their possessions in Peru to the Castles of Callao, which Rodil, after a little over a year's successful resistance, was compelled to surrender.

Upper Peru having detached itself from Buenos Ayres, was organized as a separate state under the name of Bolivia, in honor of the man who had accomplished so much for its freedom, and who by the first Congress of the new republic, which convened in August, 1825, was made perpetual Protector, and requested to prepare for it a constitution.

The country having been freed from armed resistance on the part of the Royalists, it next became Bolivar's duty to provide laws for the proper government of the people. Time proved this to be a more difficult task than meeting an open enemy on the field of battle. Many local leaders had been developed during the struggle for independence, among whom no little ill feeling was aroused by their scramble for recognition. Then there were some who were jealous of Bolivar's great popularity and influence with the people. They were busy in trying to turn public opinion against him by telling the people that he would use his power to add to, rather than lighten, their burdens. This feeling was intensified when he presented his plan of government for Bolivia to Congress on May 25, 1826, accompanied by an address in which he doubted the wisdom of extending the right of franchise indiscriminately to the people, and showed clearly his preference for a centralization of power, by proposing a president for life clothed with supreme executive powers, including the right to name his successor. It was charged by his enemies that this would be a monarchy in fact, and a republic only in name.

Meantime Paez, military commander in Venezuela, refused to recognize the constituted authorities, and assumed an attitude of open rebellion. But the presence in a short time of Bolivar, his old commander, followed by a personal interview and a decree of general amnesty, resulted in a complete restoration of peace and loyal adherence to the government. Bolivar and Santander having been re-elected to the respective offices of president and vice-president, Bolivar, before the time fixed by law for him to take the oath of office, resigned the presidency of the republic, with a view to retiring into private life, and thus refuting the charges made against him by personal enemies, that he was simply working in his own interest, and for his own personal aggrandizement.

But in response to Santander's earnest appeal, and a resolution of Congress urging him to resume his position as president, Bolivar went to Bogota, and there took upon himself the oath of office.

He soon issued three decrees: One granting general amnesty, another calling a national convention at Ocana, and a third for the establishment of constitutional order throughout Colombia. All eyes were now turned to the national convention at Ocana, which was to assemble in March, 1828. This was made the more important by the fact that it was to determine whether Bolivar's plan for a strong centralized government, backed up by ample military force, or a government controlled more directly by the great body of the people, should prevail. The events of the past year had served rather to strengthen Bolivar's position, and the action of the convention seems to have crystallized it into law, for a decree soon followed, dated August 27, 1828, giving to Bolivar supreme power over Colombia, which he continued to exercise until his death, which occurred at San Pedro, on December 17, 1830.

Thus closes the life of one of the most remarkable characters the world has ever known. He possessed the intrepid courage and dash of a Sherman, the unrelenting firmness of a Grant, and the tenderness of a Lincoln. Local revolts against lawful authority always yielded to his personal presence and counsel. We fail to find in his history a single act of cruelty recorded against him. His proclamation of " War to the death," was a military necessity. The Royalists had shown no mercy to his soldiers. They had refused to treat them as prisoners of war. They had fired upon his flag of truce. They gave no quarter to revolutionists, but put them to death wherever found. And there was but one alternative left, and that was, unpleasant as it must have been to a man of such kindly nature, to meet such brutalities by a threat of retaliation in kind. The proclamation was not prompted by a spirit of cruelty, but rather by a love for humanity. It had the effect which he no doubt intended it should, and that was to secure the same treatment for his soldiers when captured, that the civilized world acknowledged due to prisoners of war. He was in no sense mercenary. He expended nine-tenths of his fortune for his country's freedom, and when voted a million dollars by Congress he promptly declined it. He was always magnanimous, even to his bitterest enemies. He died comparatively poor. His remains sleep at Caracas, the place of his birth. His soul is with God. Monuments have been erected to his memory, one at Caracas and another at Lima. But his life-work has erected a monument in the hearts of his countrymen that will never perish. He sowed the seed for the harvest of a better government and higher civilization for all Spanish America. The influence of his example is not confined to his own country, but is felt throughout the civilized world. To-day, among the brightest and best of the world's good and great men, may justly be placed the name of Simon Bolivar.

John P St John

JEAN FRANÇOIS CHAMPOLLION *

By Georg Ebers

(1790–1832)

THE deciphering of hieroglyphics is one of the greatest achievements of the human race in this century. Jean François Champollion was the man who accomplished this great feat. He is surnamed "*le jeune*," the younger, to distinguish him from his elder brother, Champollion Figeac, whose life was one of paternal devotion and the most unselfish sacrifice for his younger brother. Both were born in Figeac, in the south of France, François on December 23, 1790. He made his home, however, in the beautiful little town of Grenoble, situated on the hills near the valley of the Isère. It was to this place that Champollion Figeac, who was here engaged as director of the town library, and later on as professor of Greek at the university, drew his twelve years younger brother François, who, at the age of nine, went to live with his elder brother, filled with the proudest hopes for the future, and grateful for the care and devotion bestowed upon him.

At that time, naturally, all eyes were turned toward Egypt, where the First Consul, Bonaparte, had led the army of the Republic, accompanied by a host of celebrated men of science. The newly opened world of monuments on the banks of the Nile excited the greatest interest in everybody ; but for few did it have as strong an attraction as for Champollion Figeac, who had occupied himself long previously with the study of the history and language of the ancient Egyptians. Furthermore, he and his brother François came, so to say, into indirect contact with the great expedition. For the famous mathematician Fourier, who had gone out with it, became afterward prefect of Grenoble, and one of Figeac's warmest and most intimate friends.

François, who, at the age of twelve, was already fully master of the classic languages, had, surrounded by the rich collection of books placed in his brother's care, drifted into a territory which is not embraced in the usual high-school curriculum, viz., the Oriental languages. While still at school, and during his leisure hours, he mastered with wonderful energy, aided as it was by an almost phenomenal power for acquiring knowledge, the Hebrew and most other Semitic languages, as also Sanscrit and Persian. As, however, Egypt had the greatest attraction for him, he also studied the Coptic dialect, the language of the Egyptians during the early centuries after Christ, which was written in Greek letters with some few others added. Withal, the remarkable youth was cheerful and companionable, finding time even to practise his poetic gifts ; nor did his physical development suffer through the severe exertion of his mind. His portrait, in the Louvre in Paris, represents him in manhood with bronzed skin, easily allowing him to be recognized as a native of the South of France. His nose is slightly bent, his forehead lofty, his hair black and of great abundance. The dark eyes, shaded by heavy brows, express serenity—earnest and profound sincerity—while his well-formed mouth gives evidence of winning manners and the friendliness of his nature.

At the age of seventeen he submitted his first work, a geography of ancient Egypt, to the Academy of Grenoble, which, notwithstanding his extreme youth, conferred upon him the degree of associate. Soon after he followed a course of lectures at the Oriental College of Paris. With youthful zeal he availed himself of the numerous educational advantages at his disposal in this great city, and gained even then the notice of the most prominent men of his profession. After two years' time, not quite twenty years of age, he was called to a position at the University of Grenoble.

When Napoleon rested in this town on his way from Elba to Paris, in 1815, he appointed the elder Champollion as his private secretary.

The close relationship into which this position brought Figeac to the emperor, and his republican ideas after Napoleon's downfall—which ideas were shared by his brother François—were circumstances which, in later years, became great obstacles to their further advancement. They were looked upon as characters dangerous to the state, and were deprived of their positions, while the Institute of France even withheld from François its protection.

The brothers were banished to their old homestead, Figeac, where they found leisure in abundance to complete several unfinished works ; and when in 1818, through the influence of the Duke of Decazes, their banishment was pronounced at an end, François had completed his great work, " L'Égypte sous les Pharaons."

This work, of the utmost importance at the time, in the preparation of which the Coptic sources were freely drawn upon, won François his lost chair at the Grenoble University. After he had secured this post he was encouraged to found a home of his own. Rose Blanc was the bride-elect, with whom he was united in a most happy marriage until his death.

Since many years François had occupied himself with the monument which gave promise to the possibility of deciphering hieroglyphics.

During the French expedition, as it happened, the talisman was found which was to become the key to disclose the mystery of the language and the written signs of the Ancient Egyptians—the tablet or the key of Rosetta, a stone-plate made of black granite. Three inscriptions, written in different signs, covered the originally rectangular surface of the tablet. The uppermost one, considerably injured, showed the hieroglyphics, which were familiar through the obelisks and other Egyptian monuments ; the second inscription was obscure ; while the third and lowest inscription, which had suffered but little injury, consisted of Greek letters clear to every philologist. It proclaimed that the tablet contained a decree of the Egyptian priesthood, in honor of the fifth king of the house of the Ptolemies, and that this was written in the holy language, in that of the people of Egypt, and in Greek, on the same tablet. Here was, therefore, a somewhat extensive text in two of the three modes of writing of the Egyptians of which Clemens of Alexandria makes mention, with a Greek translation of the same. The fortunes of war brought this extraordinary monument into the hands of the English. It was placed in the British Museum, and care was taken that copies of the three inscriptions should reach the various Egyptologists, among them Champollion.

The demotic inscription—that is to say, the text in the writing of the people, was one of the most inviting to decipher, because the signs composing it seemed to be letters representing sound. This was sedulously attempted by several scientists, and with the best results by the great French Orientalist, De Sacy, and by the Swede, Akerblad. But though the former by a mechanical method recognized correctly the meaning of several groups, and though Akerblad had even ascertained most of the signs of the demotic alphabet, still they were both incapable of discerning the elements of which the demotic writing is composed.

The great English physician and naturalist, Thomas Young, who also occupied himself with the three various texts, made better progress. Taking advantage and making use of the parts that had been revealed to him by demotic and hieroglyphic text, he succeeded, in a mechanical way, and by intelligent comparisons in deciphering the names Ptolemaios and Berenike, and in recognizing even the hieroglyphic signs for numbers. Still the true nature of the Egyptian writing was not revealed to him either. In their particulars his ascertainments are untrue, for in the names he had in no way discovered the alphabetic signs of which they were composed.

As to the remainder of the inscription he thought that it consisted of such drawn signs or forms with symbolical significance as might be found interpreted in the "Hieroglyphica of Horapollon."

That those groups of hieroglyphics surrounded by a frame (cartouche) are the names of kings, had been contended long before by the Dane Zoëge, Barthélemy, and others. The framed hieroglyphics on the tablet of Rosetta could, as the Greek text taught, signify but the name of Ptolemaios. Champollion also had originally held the same erroneous opinion as Young and his predecessors. Though he succeeded in defining several groups of characters of the people's writing, like Akerblad, by comparison, he, even as late as 1821, in his essay on hieroglyphics, entitled "De l'Écriture hiératique des Anciens Egyptiens," declares them to be symbolical signs and figures.

But he knew of Young's successful comparisons with Greek names; and when Mr. Bankes brought a small obelisk to England from the island of Philæ, on which the framed group of hieroglyphics were bound to contain the names of Ptolemaios and Cleopatra, because a Greek inscription at the foot of the obelisk mentioned these royal names, a firm starting-point was created by Champollion, from which he was to succeed in removing the mass of obstacles which had stood in the way of all previous explorations and researches.

He made his basis the supposition that the framed names were constructed of alphabetic signs. The name Ptolemaios was known through the tablet of Rosetta. If the second name on Bankes's obelisk were Cleopatra, a comparison of the two names should confirm this. The first letter in the name Ptolemaios being a " p " it should occur as fifth letter in Cleopatra. And this was actually the case. The third letter in Ptolemaios, the " o," was found again as the fourth one in Cleopatra. The fourth sign in Ptolemaios, "l," a lion, occurred correctly as the second one in Cleopatra. By further comparison every sign was correctly found, and when Champollion had deciphered a group of signs which he took to be Alexander, and again found every letter in its right place, he could assure himself that hieroglyphics also were based on the phonetic system.

He soon, with the aid of the letters discovered in the above-mentioned groups, deciphered other well-known names of kings, and in this way acquired a knowledge of the whole hieroglyphic alphabet. But the many hundred forms and signs, of which the holy scriptures of the Egyptians are composed, could not well be of an altogether alphabetic nature, and a further study of the subject brought the explorer to the conclusion that ideographs were interspersed among the alphabetical signs in order to make the alphabetic words more comprehensive. For instance, after a masculine proper name the picture of a man was drawn, and after every word connected with the motion of walking, the picture of two pacing legs.

Besides this, he found that some sounds could be represented by different hiero-glyphics. With this the most important elements of hieroglyphics were disclosed, and it was all accomplished in one year, from 1821–22. When François, after a period of extraordinary mental exertion, appeared before his brother one morning with all the proofs in his hands, calling to him, "*Je tiens l'affaire; vois!*" (I have found it; look here!) he fell to the floor fainting, worn out by the immense exertions of the last few months.

It required some time for him to recover his health; but Figeac read, on Sep-tember 17, 1822, his brother's pamphlet at the Academy in Paris. It appeared under the name of " Lettre à M. Dacier," and contained the details of his dis-covery.

That day decided Champollion's future career. As early as the year follow-ing he published his new work, " Précis du système hiéroglyphique," after which Louis Philippe of Orleans had the discovery officially announced before the Ori-ental Association, and Louis XVIII. made it his royal duty to lighten Champol-lion's future work.

The " Précis " embraces the foregoing results of his discovery, and consider-ing the short space of time in which all this was accomplished, it appears marvel-lous that François could thus early determine the most important elements of the hieroglyphic system in their minute details so correctly. In 1824 the king sent him to Italy, where he profited principally by the splendid collection of Egyptian antiquities in Turin. In 1826 Charles X. appointed him director of the Egyp-tian Museum in the Louvre, which Champollion founded by purchasing at Li-verno the celebrated " Salt Collection."

Soon after his return to France the king sent him on a mission to Egypt, where he remained from August, 1828, till the end of 1829. The Italian Rosel-lini joined him on the Nile.

His " Lettres écrites d'Égypte et de la Nubie" render his observations and im-pressions and describe his life and adventures in Egypt, in a most entertaining and instructive style. The many and various inscriptions, copied there by him, are all quoted in his great work on monuments, entitled, " Monuments de l'Égypte et de la Nubie," and in his posthumous work, " Notices descriptives conformes aux manuscrits autographes rédigés sur les lieux."

Soon after his return to Paris (in March, 1830), by which time his health had commenced to fail, he was elected a Member of the Academy, and in March, 1831, was appointed professor at the " College de France." The solidity and in-structiveness of his lectures brought the most celebrated leaders in science to hear him, but there were destined to be but few of the lectures, as he all too soon felt himself too weak to continue them. On March 4, 1832, at his old homestead Figeac, a stroke of apoplexy ended his active life of achieve-ment.

His great discovery was at first vigorously attacked. Erring minds declaring the system of the great Frenchman to be wrong, and submitting others of their own, as the Russian Klaproth and the German Seyffarth, disturbed Champollion's peace ; still more bitterly, however, was he pursued by the envy and hatred of his political opponents.

Even when the laurel already decorated his brow, they saw to it that the thorns were not wanting in the wreath. Especially in England various efforts were made to have, not him, but Thomas Young, recognized as the discoverer of the science of deciphering hieroglyphics. But though Young had succeeded previously to Champollion in deciphering some hieroglyphic names in a mechanical way, yet the genial Englishman mistook, during the whole course of his activity, the real character of hieroglyphic writing. To Champollion, on the other hand, it was left to recognize their nature and construction, so that science must acknowledge him to be the discoverer of the true nature of the system of hieroglyphical writing.

Shortly before his death it was vouchsafed him to proclaim to his loyal brother, " *Voici ma carte pour la postérité*," pointing to the manuscript of his " Egyptian Grammar," of which the last chapter was still missing. It contains the germs from which all similar works have sprung, which since have perfected and enlarged that of Champollion ; it showed the path in which all subsequent grammarians were to walk. The results of Young's discoveries remain without influence upon the progress of the science, and have found a place long since among old relics.

François Champollion's work is the seed, which even at the present day brings forth the richest fruits. When he died, at the age of forty-two, he left the world not only his " Egyptian Grammar," but also pioneer works in other branches of his science.

His " Panthéon Égyptien " (1823–25) dealt with Egyptian mythology ; his excellent knowledge of Coptic is clearly seen in many of his works ; and his " Egyptian Dictionary of Hieroglyphics " (1841–44) is, bearing in mind the time when it was written, a work of marvellous accomplishment.

This dictionary, with several other works and manuscripts of his literary estate, which the French Government had purchased for the sum of fifty thousand francs, were faithfully and lovingly edited and published after his death by his elder brother, Figeac. These posthumous works bear witness not only to the overwhelming industry of this great worker and explorer, but also to the loving unselfishness of his brother, who sacrificed a great part of his time and activity in editing and arranging the manuscripts of the departed. The " Grammar," the " Monuments," the " Dictionary," were all published by Figeac. At " Père Lachaise " Cemetery, in Paris, a weather-beaten obelisk and a broken stone tablet indicate the spot where the remains of François Champollion rest.

A monument which was erected in his honor at his native town, Figeac, bears the well-chosen inscription which so frequently occurs among the titles of the Pharaohs in hieroglyphics, " *'anch zete*," *i.e.*, " everlasting." A beautiful sentence, which Chateaubriand addressed to the faithful brother and co-worker of the great searcher, is also inscribed on the statue of François Champollion, le jeune.   It reads : "*Ses admirables travaux auront la durée des monuments qu'il nous a fait connaître.*"   (His admirable works will last as long as the monuments which he has taught us to understand.)

ANDREW JACKSON *
By Colonel Thomas Wentworth Higginson

(1767–1845)

Dr. Von Holst, the most philosophic of historians, when he passes from the period of John Quincy Adams to that of his successor, is reluctantly compelled to leave the realm of pure history for that of biography, and to entitle a chapter "The Reign of Andrew Jackson." This change of treatment could, indeed, hardly be helped. Under Adams all was impersonal, methodical, a government of laws and not of men.   With an individuality quite as strong as that of Jackson—as the whole nation learned ere his life ended—it had yet been the training of his earlier career to suppress himself, and be simply a perfect official. His policy aided the vast progress of the nation, but won no credit by the process.   Men saw with wonder the westward march of an expanding people, but forgot to notice the sedate, passionless, orderly administration that held the door open and kept the peace

* Reprinted from Harper's Magazine by permission.   Copyright, 1884, by Harper & Bros.

for all. In studying the time of Adams, we think of the nation; in observing that of Jackson, we think of Jackson himself. In him we see the first popular favorite of a nation now well out of leading-strings, and particularly bent on going alone. By so much as he differed from Adams, by so much the people liked him better. His conquests had been those of war, always more dazzling than those of peace; his temperament was of fire, always more attractive than one of marble. He was helped by what he had done, and by what he had not done. Even his absence of diplomatic training was almost counted for a virtue, because all this training was necessarily European, and the demand had ripened for a purely American product.

It had been quite essential to the self-respect of the new republic, at the outset, that it should have at its head men who had coped with European statesmen on their own soil and not been discomfited. This was the case with each of the early successors of Washington, and in view of his manifest superiority this advantage was not needed. Perhaps it was in a different way a sign of self-respect that the new republic should at last turn from this tradition, and take boldly from the ranks a strong and ill-trained leader, to whom all European precedent—and, indeed, all other precedent, counted for nothing. In Jackson, moreover, there first appeared upon our national stage the since familiar figure of the self-made man. Other presidents had sprung from a modest origin, but nobody had made an especial point of it. Nobody had urged Washington for office because he had been a surveyor's lad; nobody had voted for Adams because stately old ladies designated him as "that cobbler's son." But when Jackson came into office the people had just had almost a surfeit of regular training in their chief magistrates. There was a certain zest in the thought of a change, and the nation certainly had it.

It must be remembered that Jackson was in many ways far above the successive modern imitators who have posed in his image. He was narrow, ignorant, violent, unreasonable; he punished his enemies and rewarded his friends. But he was, on the other hand—and his worst opponents hardly denied it—chaste, honest, truthful, and sincere. It was not commonly charged upon him that he enriched himself at the public expense, or that he deliberately invented falsehoods. And as he was for a time more bitterly hated than anyone who ever occupied his high office, we may be very sure that these things would have been charged had it been possible. In this respect the contrast was enormous between Jackson and his imitators, and it explains his prolonged influence. He never was found out or exposed before the world, because there was nothing to detect or unveil; his merits and demerits were as visible as his long, narrow, firmly set features, or as the old military stock that encircled his neck. There he was, always fully revealed; everybody could see him; the people might take him or leave him—and they never left him.

Moreover, there was, after the eight years of Monroe and the four years of Adams, an immense popular demand for something piquant and even amusing, and this quality they always had from Jackson. There was nothing in the least melodramatic about him; he never posed or attitudinized—it would have required too much patience; but he was always piquant. There was formerly a good deal of discussion as to who wrote the once famous "Jack Downing's" letters, but we might almost say that they wrote themselves. Nobody was ever less of a humorist than Andrew Jackson, and it was therefore the more essential that he should be the cause of humor in others. It was simply inevitable that during his progresses through the country there should be some amusing shadow evoked, some Yankee parody of the man, such as came from two or three quarters under the name of Jack Downing. The various records of Monroe's famous tours are as tame as the speeches which these expeditions brought forth, and John Quincy Adams never made any popular demonstrations to chronicle; but wherever Jackson went there went the other Jack, the crude first-fruits of what is now known through the world as "American humor." Jack Downing was Mark Twain and Hosea Biglow and Artemus Ward in one. The impetuous President enraged many and delighted many, but it is something to know that under him a serious people first found that it knew how to laugh.

The very extreme, the perfectly needless extreme, of political foreboding that marked the advent of Jackson furnished a background of lurid solemnity for all this light comedy. Samuel Breck records in his diary that he conversed with Daniel Webster in Philadelphia, March 24, 1827, upon the prospects of the government. "Sir," said Mr. Webster, "if General Jackson is elected, the government of our country will be overthrown; the judiciary will be destroyed; Mr. Justice Johnson will be made Chief-Justice in the room of Mr. Marshall, who must soon retire, and then in half an hour Mr. Joseph Washington and Mr. Justice Story will resign. A majority will be left with Mr. Johnson, and every constitutional decision hitherto made will be reversed." As a matter of fact, none of these results followed. Mr. Justice Johnson never became Chief-Justice; Mr. Marshall retained that office till his death in 1835; Story and Washington also died in office; the judiciary was not overthrown, nor the government destroyed. But the very ecstasy of these fears stimulated the excitement of the public mind. No matter how extravagant the supporters of Jackson might be, they could hardly go farther in that direction than did the Websters in the other.

But it was not the fault of the Jackson party if anybody went beyond them in exaggeration. An English traveller, William E. Alexander, going in a stage-coach from Baltimore to Washington in 1831, records the exuberant conversation of six editors, with whom he was shut up for hours. "The gentlemen of the press," he says, "talked of 'going the whole hog' for one another, of being 'up to the hub' (nave) for General Jackson, 'who was all brimstone but the head, and that was aqua-fortis,' and swore if anyone abused him he ought to be 'set straddle on an iceberg, and shot through with a streak of lightning.'" Somewhere between the dignified despair of Daniel Webster, and the adulatory slang of these gentry we must look for the actual truth about Jackson's administration. The fears of the statesman were not wholly groundless, for it is always hard to count in advance upon the tendency of high office to make men more reasonable.

The enthusiasm of the editors had a certain foundation ; at any rate it was a part of their profession to like stirring times, and they had now the promise of them.   After four years of Adams, preceded by eight years of Monroe, any party of editors in America, assembled in a stage-coach, would have showered epithets of endearment on the man who gave such promise in the way of lively items. No acute journalist could help seeing that a man had a career before him who was called " Old Hickory " by three-quarters of the nation, and who made " Hurrah for Jackson ! " a cry so potent that it had the force of a popular decree.

There was, indeed, unbounded room for popular enthusiasm in the review of Jackson's early career.   Born in such obscurity that it is doubtful to this day whether he was born in South Carolina, as he himself claimed, or on the North Carolina side of the line, as Mr. Parton thinks, he had a childhood of poverty and ignorance.   He was taken prisoner as a mere boy during the Revolution, and could never forget that he had been wounded by a British officer whose boots he had refused to brush.   Afterward, in a frontier community, he was successively farmer, shopkeeper, law-student, lawyer, district attorney, judge, and Congressman, being first Representative from Tennessee, and then Senator, and all before the age of thirty-one.   In Congress Albert Gallatin describes him " as a tall, lank, uncouth-looking personage, with long locks of hair hanging over his brows and face, and a queue down his back tied in an eel-skin ; his dress singular, his manners and deportment those of a backwoodsman."   He remained, however, but a year or two in all at Philadelphia—then the seat of national government—and afterward became a planter in Tennessee, fought duels, subdued Tecumseh and the Creek Indians, winning finally the great opportunity of his life by being made a Major-General in the United States army on May 31, 1814. He now had his old captors, the British, with whom to deal, and entered into the work with a relish.   By way of preliminary he took Pensacola, without any definite authority, from the Spaniards, to whom it belonged, and the English whom they harbored ; and then turned, without orders, without support, and without supplies, to undertake the defence of New Orleans.

Important as was this city, and plain as it was that the British threatened it, the national authorities had done nothing to defend it.   The impression prevailed at Washington that it must already have been taken, but that the President would not let it be known.   The *Washington Republican* of January 17, 1815, said, " That Mr. Madison will find it convenient and will finally determine to abandon the State of Louisiana we have not a doubt."   A New York newspaper of January 30th, quoted in Mr. Andrew Stevenson's eulogy on Jackson, said, " It is a general opinion here that the city of New Orleans must fall."   Apparently but one thing averted its fall—the energy and will of Andrew Jackson. On his own responsibility he declared martial law, impressed soldiers, seized powder and supplies, built fortifications of cotton bales, if nothing else came to hand.   When the news of the battle of New Orleans came to the seat of government it was almost too bewildering for belief.   The British veterans of the Peninsular War, whose march wherever they had landed had heretofore seemed a holiday parade, were repulsed in a manner so astounding that their loss was more than two thousand, while that of the Americans was but thirteen. By a single stroke the national self-respect was restored; and Henry Clay, at Paris, said "Now I can go to England without mortification."

All these things must be taken into account in estimating what Dr. Von Holst calls "the reign of Andrew Jackson." After this climax of military success he was for a time employed on frontier service, again went to Florida to fight Englishmen and Spaniards, practically conquering that region in a few months, but this time with an overwhelming force. Already his impetuosity had proved to have a troublesome side to it; he had violated neutral territory, had hung two Indians without justification, and had put to death, with no authority, two Englishmen, Ambrister and Arbuthnot. These irregularities did not harm him in the judgment of his admirers; they seemed in the line of his character and helped more than they hurt him. In the winter of 1823–24 he was again chosen a Senator from Tennessee. Thenceforth he was in the field as a candidate for the Presidency, with two things to aid him—his own immense popularity and a friend. This friend was one William B. Lewis, a man in whom all the skilful arts of the modern wire-puller seemed to be born full-grown.

There was at that time (1824) no real division in parties. The Federalists had been effectually put down, and every man who aspired to office claimed to be Democratic-Republican. Nominations were irregularly made, sometimes by a Congressional caucus, sometimes by State legislatures. Tennessee, and afterward Pennsylvania, nominated Jackson. When it came to the vote, he proved to be by all odds the popular candidate. Professor W. G. Sumner, counting up the votes of the people, finds 155,800 votes for Jackson, 105,300 for Adams, 44,200 for Crawford, 46,000 for Clay. Even with this strong popular vote before it, the House of Representatives, balloting by States, elected on the first trial John Quincy Adams. Seldom in our history has the cup of power come so near to the lips of a candidate and been dashed away again. Yet nothing is surer in a republic than a certain swing of the pendulum afterward, in favor of any candidate to whom a special injustice has been done, and in the case of a popular favorite like Jackson, this might have been foreseen to be irresistible. His election four years later was almost a foregone conclusion, but, as if to make it wholly sure, there came up the rumor of a "corrupt bargain" between the successful candidate and Mr. Clay, whose forces had indeed joined with those of Mr. Adams to make a majority. For General Jackson there could be nothing more fortunate. The mere ghost of a corrupt bargain is worth many thousand votes to the lucky man who conjures up the ghost.

When it came the turn of the Adams party to be defeated, in 1828, they attributed this result partly to the depravity of the human heart, partly to the tricks of Jackson, and partly to the unfortunate temperament of Mr. Adams. The day after a candidate is beaten everybody knows why it was, and says it was just what anyone might have foreseen. Ezekiel Webster, writing from New Hampshire, laid the result chiefly on the candidate, whom everybody disliked, and who would

21

persist in leaving his bitter opponents in office. The people, he said, "always supported his cause from a cold sense of duty, and not from any liking of the man. We soon satisfy ourselves," he added, "that we have discharged our duty to the cause of any man when we do not entertain for him one personal kind feeling, nor cannot, unless we disembowel ourselves, like a trussed turkey, of all that is human within us." There is, indeed, no doubt that Mr. Adams helped on his own defeat, both by his defects and by what would now be considered his virtues. The trouble, however, lay further back. Ezekiel Webster thought that "if there had been at the head of affairs a man of popular character like Mr. Clay, or any man whom we were not compelled by our natures, instinct, and fixed fate to dislike, the result would have been different." But we can now see that all this would really have made no difference at all. Had Mr. Adams been personally the most attractive of men, instead of being a conscientious iceberg, the same result would have followed, the people would have felt that Jackson's turn had come, and the demand for the "old ticket" would have been irresistible.

Accordingly, the next election, that of 1828, was easily settled. Jackson had 178 electoral votes; Adams but 83—more than two to one. Adams had not an electoral vote south of the Potomac or west of the Alleghanies, though Daniel Webster, writing to Jeremiah Mason, had predicted that he would carry six Western and Southern States. In Georgia no Adams ticket was even nominated, he being there unpopular for one of his best acts—the protection of the Cherokees. On the other hand, but one Jackson elector was chosen from New England, and he by less than two hundred majority.

   .   .   .   .

On the day of his inauguration the president was received in Washington with an ardor that might have turned a more modest head. On the day when the new administration began (March 4, 1829), Daniel Webster wrote to his sister-in-law, with whom he had left his children that winter : "To-day we have had the inauguration. A monstrous crowd of people is in the city. I never saw anything like it before. Persons have come five hundred miles to see General Jackson, and they really seem to think that the country is rescued from some frightful danger." It is difficult now to see what this peril was supposed to be ; but we know that the charges of monarchical tendency made against John Adams had been renewed against his son—a renewal that seems absurd in case of a man so scrupulously republican that he would not use a seal ring, and so unambitious that he always sighed after the quieter walks of literature. Equally absurd was the charge of extravagance against a man who kept the White House in better order than his predecessors on less than half the appropriation—an economy wholly counterbalanced in some minds by the fact that he had put in a billiard-table. But however all this may have been, the fact is certain that no president had yet entered the White House amid such choruses of delight ; nor did it happen again until Jackson's pupil, Van Buren, yielded, amid equal popular enthusiasm, to another military hero, Harrison.

For the social life of Washington the President had one advantage which was altogether unexpected, and seemed difficult of explanation by anything in his earlier career. He had at his command the most courteous and agreeable manners. Even before the election of Adams, Daniel Webster had written to his brother: "General Jackson's manners are better than those of any of the candidates. He is grave, mild, and reserved. My wife is for him decidedly." And long after, when the president was to pass in review before those who were perhaps his most implacable opponents, the ladies of Boston, we have the testimony of the late Josiah Quincy, in his "Figures from the Past," that the personal bearing of this obnoxious official was most unwillingly approved. Mr. Quincy was detailed by Governor Lincoln, on whose military staff he was, to attend President Jackson everywhere when visiting Boston in 1833; and this narrator testifies that, with every prejudice against Jackson, he found him essentially "a knightly personage—prejudiced, narrow, mistaken on many points, it might be, but vigorously a gentleman in his high sense of honor, and in the natural, straightforward courtesies which are easily distinguished from the veneer of policy." Sitting erect on his horse, a thin, stiff type of military strength, he carried with him in the streets a bearing of such dignity that staid old Bostonians, who had refused even to look upon him from their windows, would finally be coaxed into taking one peep, and would then hurriedly bring forward their little daughters to wave their handkerchiefs. He wrought, Mr. Quincy declares, "a mysterious charm upon old and young;" showed, although in feeble health, a great consideration for others; and was in private a really agreeable companion. It appears from these reminiscences that the president was not merely the cause of wit in others, but now and then appreciated it himself, and that he used to listen with delight to the reading of the "Jack Downing" letters, laughing heartily sometimes, and declaring: "The Vice-President must have written that. Depend upon it Jack Downing is only Van Buren in masquerade." It is a curious fact that the satirist is already the better remembered of the two, although Van Buren was in his day so powerful as to preside over the official patronage of the nation and to be called the "Little Magician."

The two acts with which the administration of President Jackson will be longest identified are his dealings with South Carolina in respect to nullification, and his long warfare with the United States Bank. The first brought the New England States back to him, and the second took them away again. He perhaps won rather more applause than he merited by the one act, and more condemnation than was just for the other. Let us first consider the matter of nullification. When various Southern States—Georgia at first, not South Carolina, taking the lead—had quarrelled with the tariff of 1828, and openly threatened to set it aside, they evidently hoped for the co-operation of the President; or at least for that silent acquiescence he had shown when Georgia had been almost equally turbulent on the Indian question and he would not interfere, as his predecessor had done, to protect the treaty rights of the Indian tribes. The whole South was therefore startled when he gave, at a banquet on Jefferson's birthday (April 13, 1830), a toast that now seems commonplace—"The Federal Union; it must be preserved." But this was not all; when the time came he took vigorous, if not altogether consistent, steps to preserve it.

When, in November, 1832, South Carolina for the first time officially voted that certain tariff acts were null and void in that State, the gauntlet of defiance was fairly thrown down, and Jackson took it up. He sent General Scott to take command at Charleston, with troops near by, and two gunboats at hand; he issued a dignified proclamation, written by Livingston (December 10, 1832), which pronounced the act of South Carolina contradictory to the Constitution, unauthorized by it, and destructive of its aims. So far so good; but unfortunately the president had, the week before (December 4, 1832), sent a tariff message to Congress, of which John Quincy Adams wrote, "It goes far to dissolve the Union into its original elements, and is in substance a complete surrender into the hands of the nullifiers of South Carolina." Then came Mr. Clay's compromise tariff of 1833, following in part the line indicated by this message, and achieving, as Mr. Calhoun said, a victory for nullification, leaving the matter a drawn game at any rate.

The action of Jackson thus accompanied settled nothing; it was like valiantly ordering a burglar out of your house with a pistol, and adding a suggestion that he will find a portion of the family silver on the hall-table, ready packed for his use, as he goes out.

Nevertheless, the burglar was gone for the moment, and the president had the credit of it. He had already been re-elected by an overwhelming majority in November, 1832, receiving 219 electoral votes, and Clay 49, while Floyd had the 11 votes of South Carolina (which still chose electors by its Legislature—a practice now abandoned), and Wirt the 7 of Vermont. Van Buren was chosen vice-president, being nominated in place of Calhoun by the Democratic National Convention, which now for the first time came into operation. The president was now at his high-water mark of popularity—always a dangerous time for a public man. His vehement nature accepted his re-election as a proof that he was right in everything, and he grew more self-confident than ever. More imperiously than ever, he ordered about friends and opponents, and his friends repaid it by guiding his affairs, unconsciously to himself. Meantime he was encountering another enemy of greater power, because more silent, than Southern nullification, and he was drifting on to his final contest with the United States Bank.

Sydney Smith says that every Englishman feels himself able, without instruction, to drive a pony-chaise, conduct a small farm, and edit a newspaper. The average American assumes, in addition to all this, that he is competent to manage a bank. President Jackson claimed for himself in this respect no more than his fellows; the difference was in strength of will and in possession of power. A man so ignorant that a member of his own family, according to Mr. Trist, used to say that the general did not believe the world was round, might easily convince himself that he knew all about banking. As he had, besides all this, very keen observation and great intuitive judgment of character, he was probably right in his point of attack. There is little doubt that the Bank of the United States, under Nicholas Biddle, concentrated in itself an enormous power; and it spent in four years, by confession of its directors, $58,000 in what they called self-defence "against politicians." When on July 10, 1832, General Jackson, in a message supposed to have been inspired by Amos Kendall, vetoed the bill renewing the charter of the bank, he performed an act of courage, taking counsel with his instincts. But when in the year following he performed the act known as the " Removal of the Deposits," or, in other words, caused the public money to be no longer deposited in the National Bank and its twenty-five branches, but in a variety of State banks instead, then he took counsel of his ignorance.

The consequence, immediate or remote, was an immense galvanizing into existence of State banks, and ultimately a vast increase of paper money. The Sub-Treasury system had not then been thought of ; there was no proper place of deposit for the public funds ; their possession was a direct stimulus to speculation ; and the president's cure was worse than the disease. All the vast inflation of 1835 and 1836 and the business collapse of 1837 were due to the fact not merely that Andrew Jackson brought all his violent and persistent will to bear against the United States Bank, but that when he got the power into his own hands he did not know what to do with it. Not one of his biographers—-hardly even a bigoted admirer, so far as I know—now claims that his course in this respect was anything but a mistake. " No monster bank," says Professor W. G. Sumner, " under the most malicious management, could have produced as much havoc, either political or financial, as this system produced while it lasted." If the bank was, as is now generally admitted, a dangerous institution, Jackson was in the right to resist it ; he was right even in disregarding the enormous flood of petitions that poured in to its support. But to oppose a dangerous bank does not necessarily make one an expert in banking. The utmost that can be said in favor of his action is that the calamitous results showed the great power of the institution he overthrew, and that if he had let it alone the final result might have been as bad.

Two new States were added to the Union in President Jackson's time—Arkansas (1836) and Michigan (1837). The population of the United States in 1830 had risen to nearly thirteen millions (12,866,020). There was no foreign war during his administration, although one with France was barely averted; and no domestic contest except with the Florida Indians—a contest in which these combatants held their ground so well, under the half-breed chief Osceola, that he himself was only captured by the violation of a flag of truce, and that even to this day, as the Indian Commissioners tell us, some three hundred of the tribe remain in Florida. The war being equally carried on against fugitive slaves called Maroons, who had intermarried with the Indians, did something to prepare the public mind for a new agitation which was to remould American political parties, and to modify the Constitution of the nation.

It must be remembered that the very air began to be filled in Jackson's time with rumors of insurrections and uprisings in different parts of the world. The French revolution of the Three Days had roused all the American people to sympathy, and called forth especial enthusiasm in such cities as Baltimore, Richmond, and Charleston. The Polish revolution had excited universal interest, and John Randolph had said " The Greeks are at your doors." All these things were being discussed at every dinner-table, and the debates in Virginia as to the necessity of restricting the growing intelligence of the slaves had added to the agitation. In the session of 1829–30 a bill had passed the Virginia Assembly by one majority, and had failed in the Senate, prohibiting slaves being taught to read or write ; and the next year it had passed almost unanimously. There had been, about the same time, alarms of insurrection in North Carolina, so that a party of slaves were attacked and killed by the inhabitants of Newbern ; alarms in Maryland, so that fifty blacks had been imprisoned on the Eastern Shore ; alarms in Louisiana, so that reinforcements of troops had been ordered to Baton Rouge ; and a traveller had written even from Richmond, Va., on February 12th, that there were constant fears of insurrections, and special patrols. Then came the insurrection of Nat Turner in Virginia—an uprising described minutely by myself elsewhere ; the remarkable inflammatory pamphlet called "Walker's Appeal," by a Northern colored man—a piece of writing surpassed in lurid power by nothing in the literature of the French Revolution ; and more potent than either or both of these, the appearance of the first number of the *Liberator*, in Boston. When Garrison wrote, " I am in earnest, I will not equivocate, I will not excuse, I will not retreat a single inch, and I will be heard," Andrew Jackson for once met a will firmer than his own, because more steadfast and moved by a loftier purpose. Thenceforth, for nearly half a century, the history of the nation was the history of the great antislavery contest.

DANIEL WEBSTER

By Rev. Dr. Tweedie

(1782–1852)

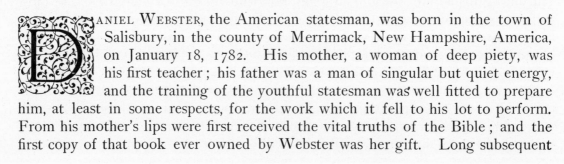

DANIEL WEBSTER, the American statesman, was born in the town of Salisbury, in the county of Merrimack, New Hampshire, America, on January 18, 1782. His mother, a woman of deep piety, was his first teacher ; his father was a man of singular but quiet energy, and the training of the youthful statesman was well fitted to prepare him, at least in some respects, for the work which it fell to his lot to perform. From his mother's lips were first received the vital truths of the Bible ; and the first copy of that book ever owned by Webster was her gift. Long subsequent to this period, and in the full blaze of his fame, he could say that he had never been able to recollect the time when he could not read the Bible, and supposed that his first schoolmistress began to teach him when he was three or four years of age. His first school-house was built of logs, and stood about half a mile from his father's house, not very far from the beautiful Merrimack. All was then humble enough with this great American statesman. He attended school only during the winter months, and assisted his father in the business of his farm and his mill as soon as he had strength for doing so. He was, however, the brightest boy at school ; and when the tempting reward of a knife was promised to the scholar who committed to memory the greatest number of verses from the Bible, Daniel came with whole chapters, which the master could not find time to hear him repeat in full. The boy secured the knife, and his delighted teacher subsequently told the father of that

child that "he would do God's work injustice" if gifts so promising were not nurtured at college.

But that consummation was not to be very soon realized. For some time Daniel had to assist his father at a saw-mill ; but so resolute was he in acquiring knowledge and training the mind while toiling with the body, that the operations at the mill were systematically interspersed with studies well fitted to form and to brace the embryo patriot for his great life-work. The saw took about ten minutes to cleave a log, and young Webster, after setting the mill in motion, learned to fill up these ten minutes with reading. As a patriot, a statesman, an orator, and a scholar, he became famous, and was called the greatest intellectual character of his country ; and we see where he laid the foundation of his greatness—by persistent and invincible ardor even in early boyhood. That magnanimous kindliness and tenderness of heart, which entered so largely into his character, was fostered amid such scenes ; and of all the men whose memories we are fain to embalm, he ranks among the least indebted to casualty, and the most to indefatigable earnestness, for the position to which he eventually rose. Amid the forest wilds of America his perseverance laid the foundation of power, of learning, of fame, and of goodness.

A simple incident which happened about this period decided his life-pursuit. He discovered a copy of the "Constitution of the United States," as drawn up by some of her ablest statesmen. It was printed upon a cotton handkerchief which he purchased in a country store with what was then his all, and which amounted to twenty-five cents. He was about eight years of age when that took place, and learned then, for the first time, either that there were United States, or that they had a Constitution.

From this date, or about the year 1790, his path through life was decided, not formally, but really, not by any avowal, but by a fostered predilection. Meanwhile other influences were at work. The father of this New Hampshire boy was strict in his religious opinions and observances, and the son had to conform, sometimes with a grudge at the restraint, but with effects of a vitally beneficial nature to the future patriot. His father then kept a place of entertainment, where teamsters halted to bait, and the attractions of the place were increased by the fact that young Webster often regaled those visitors by his readings. The Psalms of David were his favorite, and there, when only about seven years of age, he first imparted that pleasure by his oratory which he afterward carried up to the highest level which an American citizen can reach. To that humble abode Webster once returned in his declining years, and with streaming eyes descanted on the various events of the home of his youth.

The school which he attended during the winter months was about three miles from his father's house, and he had often to travel thither through deep snow. At the age of fourteen he attended a somewhat more advanced academy for a few months, and his first effort at public speaking there was a failure. He burst into tears; his antipathy to public declamation appeared insurmountable, and neither frowns nor smiles could overcome the reluctance. It *was* overcome, for when young Webster felt the power which was in him, he boldly employed it. At first, however, he was a failure as a public speaker. With all this, he went forward in the acquisition of knowledge and the bracing of his mind ; and in his fifteenth year he once undertook to repeat five hundred lines of Virgil, if his teacher would consent to listen.

About this time the elder Webster disclosed to his son his purpose to send him to college. The talents of the boy and the counsels of friends pointed out that as a proper path, and that son himself will describe the effects of his father's information. "I could not speak," he says. "How could my father, I thought, with so large a family, and in such narrow circumstances, think of incurring so great an expense for me, and I laid my head on his shoulder and wept." That boy, however, had further difficulties to surmount. He had to leave one of his schools to assist his father in the hay harvest ; he had, moreover, the hindrance of a slender and sickly constitution ; but the Bible, side by side with some standard authors, had now become his English classics, while Cicero, Virgil, Horace, Demosthenes, and others, were his manuals in ancient literature. It was knowledge pursued under unusual difficulties, but, in spite of all, acquired to an unusual extent. So indomitable and persistent was the boy that in a few months he mastered the difficulties of the Greek tongue, and finally graduated at Dartmouth when he was eighteen years of age. Incidents are recorded which show that during his residence at college he was determined to hold the first place or none.

It was at Dartmouth that Webster's patriotism first flashed forth with true American ardor, a harbinger to his whole future career. He had now mastered his boyish aversion to oratory, and on July 4, 1800, the twenty-fourth anniversary of American Independence, he delivered an oration full of patriotic sentiment, manifesting the decided bent of his mind, and deserving a place, in the opinion of some, among the works which he subsequently published. He was then only eighteen years of age.

To increase the straitened funds of the family, Daniel Webster for some time kept a school at Freyburg, in Maine. His income there, eked out by other means, which were the wages of indomitable industry, enabled him to send his brother, Ezekiel, to college—the grand object which he had in view in becoming a schoolmaster. He was, however, all the while prosecuting his studies in law, and in the year 1805 entered on the duties of a legal practitioner at Boston. His familiar title in the country where he resided was " All eyes," and he used them with singular advantage. In Boston, at Portsmouth, and elsewhere, he continued these pursuits, and he thus early adopted some of the maxims which guided him through life. " There are evils greater than poverty;" " What bread you eat, let it be the bread of independence;" " Live on no man's favor;" " Pursue your profession;" " Make yourself useful to the world. . . . You will have nothing to fear." Such were his convictions, and he embodied them in deeds. One instance of his generosity is recorded at this period. His father had become embarrassed; the devoted son hastened to liquidate his father's debt, and he did it with a decision like that which signalized him all his days. He resided as a lawyer at Portsmouth for about nine years.

It was in the year 1812 that Webster was first elected a member of Congress, and he reached that elevation by his masterly ability in the affairs of his profession. By persistent patience first, and then by resistless power, he took up the foremost position in the sphere in which he moved. He appeared in the majesty of intellectual grandeur, like one who was all might and soul, and poured forth the stores of an opulent mind in a manner which was entirely his own. His words had both weight and fire; and the contrast is now great between the boy who broke down and wept at his first declamation, and the man, bending opponents to his will by his energy and indomitable zeal. The laurel of victory, it has been fondly said, was proffered to him by all, and bound his brow for one exploit till he went forth to another. In his thirtieth year he entered the field of politics, like one who had made up his mind to be decided, firm, and straightforward; and such was the serenity of this great soul, amid wild commotions, that the enthusiast mistook it for apathy, the fierce for lukewarmness. It was the great calm of profound conviction, borne up by a thorough reliance on the right—the right as to time, as to degree, and as to resources for the battle of life. From the day on which he threw himself into the political arena, he belonged to the United States, and not to his native county alone. Crowds soon gathered round one who had mastered so many difficulties, and taken his place among the kingly men who rule the spirits whom they are born first to subdue, and then to bind to themselves by the spell of genius.

It is well known that this man, so humble in his origin, yet so masterly in his mind, passed through all the gradations of rank that are open to an American citizen, up to the right hand of the highest. We have seen when he entered Congress. In 1841 he became Secretary of State, and from that period bore the place in American politics which would be readily conceded, in this ardent country, to one who was deemed and called "the master mind of the world." In his love of freedom, Webster has been likened to Washington, or expressly called his equal in regard to patriotism and true greatness. It is not wonderful, therefore, that this patriot's friends proposed him as President of the United States. He failed, and felt the failure, but soothed his disappointment by the conviction that no man "could take away from him what he had done for his country." Those who loved and admired him thought that the word president would have dimmed the lustre of the name of Daniel Webster; and they add, in regard to his disappointment, "if we must sorrow that what men expected can never come to pass, let us not weep for him but for our country." Others, however, were of opinion that Webster was "rejected and lost"; while those who look deeper at the causes of events may see, in that disappointment, the needful antidote administered by the Supreme Wisdom to ward off the danger of too universal a success. This gifted and ambitious man was suffered to take an active part in the government of one of the greatest of the nations. By his bold and manly grasp of American interests, he did much to weld the different States more closely into one. He negotiated, on the part of his country, some of the most important treaties which promote the peace and the amity of nations, for example, what is called the Ashburton treaty with Great Britain; and it would have seemed too much for one mortal, successful as Webster had already been, to be lifted to an official level with princes. That was denied him; his empire was not countries — it was minds. He was to be trained for a nobler exaltation than a throne.

Little has yet been said regarding Webster as an orator. It was mainly in that respect, however, that he surpassed his fellows, and mainly by that means was he enabled to ascend to the high position which he held so long. The versatility of his powers was very great, and the mode in which he sometimes employed them was not a little remarkable. He had, on one occasion, spent several hours with his colleagues in adjusting some important questions involving the interests of kingdoms; and on returning home he sportively sallied forth and purchased some eggs, on the principle of seeing how extremes meet, in regard to occupation as well as in other respects. But there were serious things mixed with his jests; and as an orator, Webster stands in the first rank, if not foremost, in the New World. When it was known that he was to speak, the excitement sometimes amounted to a furor, and a hundred dollars have been paid for a ticket of admission to hear him. Meanwhile the avenues that led to his arena were blocked up by the crowds pressing for admittance; and when he did appear, it was to rouse, to agitate, and convulse. He felt what he said in his inmost soul, and his words were winged with fire, even while they were massively powerful, and connected with a logic which tolerated no breaks in the chain.

Webster reached the allotted term of mortal existence, and in his seventy-first year passed away alike from the frowns and the applause of mortals. On the morning of Sabbath, October 24, 1852, he was summoned away. Though much enfeebled, his mind was calm, and he died with the confidence of a little child, reposing on the mercy of his God as revealed in the Saviour. Among his last utterances was this, "Heavenly Father, forgive my sins, and welcome me to thyself through Christ Jesus." His very last words were, "I still live," and his loving, weeping friends took them up as a prediction of that immortality on which he was about to enter. Through life he had hallowed the Sabbath, and he died upon it. The autumn was his favorite season, and he passed away amid its mellow glories, after affectionately and solemnly taking leave of his weeping wife, children, kindred, and friends, down to the humblest members of his household. His death, it is supposed, was hastened by injuries received by the breaking down of his carriage; but it did not find him unprepared. Long years before he had erected his own tomb; and there, on a plain marble slab over the door, the visitor reads the simple inscription—DANIEL WEBSTER.

Some ten thousand friends, countrymen, and lovers, helped to lay him there, and one of the orations pronounced in connection with his departure was thus touchingly closed: "The clasped hands—the dying prayers—oh, my fellow-citizens, this is a consummation over which tears of pious sympathy will be shed, after the glories of the forum and the senate are forgotten."

The following letter to a friend on the choice of a profession, written by Webster when only twenty years of age, is reprinted from "The Life of Daniel Webster" by George Ticknor Curtis, through the courtesy of D. Appleton & Co., the publishers, and with the permission of the widow and heirs of the author.

"What shall I do? Shall I say, 'Yes, gentlemen,' and sit down here to spend my days in a kind of a comfortable privacy, or shall I relinquish these prospects, and enter into a profession, where my feelings will be constantly harrowed by objects either of dishonesty or misfortune, where my living must be squeezed from penury (for rich folks seldom go to law), and my moral principle continually be at hazard? I agree with you that the law is well calculated to draw forth the powers of the mind, but what are its effects on the heart? Are they equally propitious? Does it inspire benevolence, and awake tenderness; or does it, by a frequent repetition of wretched objects, blunt sensibility, and stifle the still small voice of mercy?

"The talent with which Heaven has intrusted me is small, very small, yet I feel responsible for the use of it, and am not willing to pervert it to purposes reproachful and unjust; nor to hide it, like the slothful servant, in a napkin.

"Now, I will enumerate the inducements that draw me toward the law: First, and principally, it is my father's wish. He does not dictate, it is true, but how much short of dictation is the mere wish of a parent, whose labors of life are wasted on favors to his children? Even the delicacy with which the wish is expressed gives it more effect than it would have in the form of a command. Secondly, my friends generally wish it. They are urgent and pressing. My father even offers me—I will sometime tell you what—and Mr. Thompson offers my tuition gratis, and to relinquish his stand to me.

"On the whole, I imagine I shall make one more trial in the ensuing autumn. If I prosecute the profession, I pray God to fortify me against its temptations. To the winds I dismiss those light hopes of eminence which ambition inspired, and vanity fostered. To be 'honest, to be capable, to be faithful' to my client and my conscience, I earnestly hope will be my first endeavor. I believe you, my worthy boy, when you tell me what are your intentions. I have long known and long loved the honesty of your heart. But let us not rely too much on ourselves; let us look to some less fallible guide to direct us among the temptations that surround us."

WILLIAM HENRY SEWARD*

By Hon. Charles E. Fitch

(1801-1872)

WILLIAM HENRY SEWARD, the American statesman, was born in Florida, Orange County, N. Y., May 16, 1801, and died at Auburn, in the same State, October 10, 1872. Precocious in his studies, he pursued his preliminary education in his native village, and, at the age of fifteen, entered, as a sophomore, Union College, then under the presidency of Eliphalet Nott, between whom and his pupil a life-long friendship, illustrated by mutual confidence and counsel, was early established. Seward's college course, especially brilliant in rhetoric and the classics, was interrupted in his senior year by a residence of six months, as a teacher, in Georgia, where previous impressions against African slavery were confirmed by observation of its workings. Returning to college, he was graduated with high honors in 1820, the subject of his Commencement oration being "The Integrity of the American Union."

He was admitted to the bar at Utica, in October, 1822, and in January, 1823, settled at Auburn as a partner of Judge Elijah Miller, whose daughter he married in October, 1824. Although certain features of the law—its technicalities and uncertainties—were repugnant to him, he was soon in the full tide of professional success, and, in the opening of the circuit courts to equity jurisprudence, found much that was in harmony with his sense of justice. He was also, from the first, interested in politics, for which he had decided genius. He came upon the stage in the closing days of " The Era of Good Feeling," under President Monroe, when parties were again dividing upon the issues that have mainly obtained throughout the constitutional era. He approved the principles of Hamilton, although his boyish training had been in the Jeffersonian school. Enunciating his views with precision and felicity of diction, his voice and pen were in constant request, and he rapidly rose to distinction until, in 1834, he was the acknowledged leader in the State of the Whig party and its candidate for governor.

Meanwhile he had supported De Witt Clinton, the champion of internal improvements, and in 1824 drafted, for the Republican Convention of his county, a trenchant address, detailing the history and criticising the aims of the " Albany Regency," which inspired the hostility to that famous clique that compassed its overthrow fourteen years later. Among his notable utterances of this period were an address on Grecian independence, at Auburn, in 1827; a Fourth-of-July oration, at Syracuse, in 1831, in which Calhoun's dogma of secession was denounced; and an eulogy on La Fayette, at Auburn, in 1834. In 1828 he presided over the Young Men's Convention, at Utica, in behalf of the renomination of President Adams, and declined a congressional nomination. In 1830 he was elected by the Anti-Masons to the State Senate, and was re-elected in 1832. He had a prominent and an influential part in the deliberations of that body, although its youngest member, and in the political minority, whose addresses to the people he wrote at the close of each session. His most notable speeches were those for the common-school and canal systems, the abolition of imprisonment for debt, the amelioration of prison discipline, and the reform of the militia law, and against corporate monopolies, increasing judicial salaries, Governor Marcy's loan law, and the removal of the deposits by President Jackson. The Senate was then a constituent portion of the Court of Errors, the tribunal of last resort, and Seward delivered many opinions which materially enhanced his legal reputation. In one instance he carried, with substantial unanimity, the court with him, against the views of the presiding judge, the eminent Chancellor Walworth. In 1833 he made a rapid tour of Europe, embodying his reflections in letters to the Albany *Evening Journal*, then edited by Thurlow Weed, between whom and Seward there was, for fifty years, an intimate and unbroken attachment, unique in political annals.

In 1838 he was again the Whig candidate for governor, and defeated Governor Marcy, his former rival, his victory being the precursor of the national Whig triumph in 1840, in which year he was re-elected. He was inaugurated, January 1, 1839, his message to the Legislature embracing, with a masterly exposition of Whig policies, certain suggestions of his own concerning immigration, education, and eleemosynary institutions that revealed the catholic spirit and the philosophical habit which, despite his party fealty, he consistently exhibited. This message outlined the conduct of the administration that succeeded—enlightened in its scope, liberal to all classes, distinctly loyal to the Union, yet jealously guarding against any infringement of the rights of the State. It widened educational privileges, urged the prosecution of the public works, including the enlargement of the Erie Canal, granted franchises to railways, removed imprisonment for debt and the remaining guarantees of slavery from the statute-books, composed the anti-rent troubles and executed the laws within the insurrectionary section, perfected the banking system, and proposed jury trials for fugitive slaves and a constitutional amendment abolishing the property qualification for the colored suffrage.

Governor Seward's regard for the dignity of the State was displayed by his refusal to discharge from custody, without trial, one Alexander McLeod, a citizen of Canada, held for the burning of the steamer Caroline, in New York waters, although the demand of the British government, to that effect, was supplemented by the request of Presidents Harrison and Tyler. His abhorrence of slavery was accentuated in his denial of the application of the Governor of Virginia for the rendition of seamen charged with the abduction of a slave, upon the ground that the offence, if defined as a crime in Virginia, was not so in New York, and he did not hesitate to add that his feelings coincided with his conception of his constitutional prerogative. When a Democratic Assembly subsequently passed resolutions disapproving his action, he declined to transmit them to the Virginia authorities, and he also failed to respond to a similar requisition from South Carolina. His proposition for the employment of Roman Catholic teachers in the common schools showed his independence of partisan behest and popular clamor.

Leaving office in 1843, he passed the next six years in professional labors, varied by occasional addresses of a literary or patriotic cast, and by many Whig speeches in the campaigns of 1844 and 1848. To his practice in the State courts was united that in patent cases, which not only brought him a lucrative clientage, but largely increased his acquaintance with public men at Washington. His gubernatorial service had given him national fame, and he was, although not in public life, esteemed as one of the national leaders of his party. In the courts he commanded respect for the clearness and strength of his arguments, but, even there, he was at his best when his heart inspired his speech with fervor, as in his pleas for Van Zandt and others charged with harboring fugitive slaves. The defence of Greeley, in the Cooper libel suit, and of the Michigan rioters, may be cited as instances of his persuasiveness before juries, but that in the case of William Freeman is celebrated both for its own quality and the intrepidity of its author. Gladstone has characterized it as the greatest forensic effort in the English language, not excluding the masterpieces of Erskine. It is a plea for the life of a brutalized negro who butchered a whole family under circumstances of peculiar atrocity. The deed was without excuse or palliation, save in the insanity of the perpetrator, of which Seward became convinced, and volunteered as counsel amid the surprise, imprecations, and threats of the Auburn community, where the case was at issue. The moment was a supreme one for him, but he did not hesitate. Without reward, or the hope of reward, even in the gratitude of the insensate wretch for whom he risked professional standing and public favor, he worked as indefatigably as though the weightiest honors and emoluments depended thereon, from the impanelling of the jury to the failure of executive clemency; but Freeman's death in prison and the autopsy that disclosed the morbid condition of his brain fully vindicated Seward's analysis and exalted him in public regard.

On March 4, 1849, coincident with the accession of General Taylor to the presidency, Seward entered the United States Senate, having been chosen thereto by a large majority of the Legislature of New York. When he took his seat, the Whig party was already divided upon the slavery question, and Seward, by virtue of his previous utterances and his skill as a politician, became the exponent of the free-soil element, as also the representative of the administration, an unprecedented trust to be confided to a senator in his first term. He thus found himself in opposition to Webster and Clay, and especially to the "Omnibus" bill of the latter, a measure intended to reconcile conflicting claims concerning the admission of new States, the status of slavery in the Territories, and the protection to be accorded it in the free States. On March 11, 1850, he made a speech, generally pronounced to be his ablest, as it is certainly his most noteworthy deliverance, in which he declared that there is a law higher than the Constitution, whose authority may be invoked in legislation for the national domain. The death of General Taylor brought him into collision with President Fillmore, who hailed from New York, and was largely indebted for his vice-presidential nomination to Seward's kindly offices. Fillmore urged the adoption of the compromise scheme and signed the separate bills therefor as they successively passed Congress, thereby incurring censure at the North, while Seward retained his ascendency with the anti-slavery masses throughout the country, as well as with the Whigs of New York.

He was re-elected to the Senate in 1855 by a combination of Whigs and Anti-Nebraska Americans, and on October 12th, of that year, at Albany, formally announced his adhesion to the new Republican party. In the Senate he easily ranked as one of its most polished and effective speakers who, while resolutely maintaining his own convictions, scrupulously preserved the amenities of debate. He especially distinguished himself by his earnest, yet unavailing, resistance to the repeal of the Missouri Compromise. Among his popular addresses of conspicuous merit are those on "The Elements of Empire in America," at Union College, 1843; "Daniel O'Connell," at New York, 1847; "John Quincy Adams," before the New York Legislature, 1848; "The Destiny of America," at Columbus, O., and "The True Basis of American Independence," at New York, 1853; "The Development of the American People," at Yale College, 1854, and "The Irrepressible Conflict"—i.e., between freedom and slavery—at Rochester, N. Y., 1858. He made an extended tour in Europe, Egypt, and Palestine, in 1859.

The Republicans met in National Convention at Chicago, in 1860, flushed with anticipated success. Northern opposition to the extension of slavery had combined, and the Democracy was being resolved into antagonistic factions. Seward's nomination for the presidency seemed assured. He was the foremost statesman in his party. He had crystallized its ideas, interpreted its creed, and marshalled its forces. He had an enthusiastic following who believed that the occasion had met the man; but there were others who objected that his very superiority would provoke assault against him, which might hurt the cause for which he stood. They reasoned against his availability, and their argument prevailed. He led on the first two ballots in the convention, but, on the third, Abraham Lincoln, then comparatively unknown, became the Republican standard-bearer. Seward met this reverse tranquilly, rebuked certain manifestations of disaffection, proffered the candidate his hearty support, and, in a series of remarkably able and eloquent speeches, extending from Massachusetts to Kansas, contributed materially to his election.

Seward accepted the portfolio of State in Lincoln's cabinet and immediately assumed the gravest reponsibilities. American relations with foreign governments during the Civil War were uniformly serious and sometimes perilous. The duties of the Secretary of State were exacting and delicate. Seward, by his tact and discretion, as well as his courage and wisdom, kept peace with the world, without debasing the honor or forfeiting the rights of the republic. One of the most intricate issues arose in the first year of the war. It is known as the Trent case. Mason and Slidell, Confederate envoys to England and France respectively, were forcibly taken by an American naval commander from a British vessel and lodged in Fort Warren. The American public was exultant over the capture and protested vigorously against their release; but Seward had to decide officially the question of their surrender to the British Government, and, when the demand was duly made, he yielded to it, basing his conclusion, with admirable adroitness, not only upon international comity, but also upon American precedents. The president, at first disposed to take the contrary view, conceded the force of Seward's argument, the people acquiesced, and a war with England was avoided. Seward's state papers and despatches are models of style, and by their frankness of statement and hopefulness of tone did much to sustain the Union cause abroad. In accord with Lincoln in holding that the paramount task of the Government was to subdue rebellion against it and discouraging precipitate movements for the abolition of slavery, he was also in accord with the president in the policy of emancipation, as ultimately formulated, and, on January 1, 1863, attested the proclamation which has made the name of Lincoln immortal. He proclaimed the adoption of the Thirteenth Amendment to the Constitution, by which slavery was abolished, December 18, 1865, and of the Fourteenth, conferring suffrage and civil rights upon the freedmen, July 26, 1868. On February 3, 1865, he attended, with the president, the so-called Peace Conference, in Hampton Roads, with Messrs. Stephens, Hunter, and Campbell, the Confederate commissioners. The conference was fruitless, owing to the inflexible determination of the president not to entertain any proposals that did not involve the complete restoration of the national authority as a condition precedent.

Lincoln began his second term March 4, 1865, Seward remaining in the cabinet. On April 5th, Seward was badly injured by being thrown from his carriage. Nine days thereafter Lincoln visited him in his sick chamber. It was their last meeting. On the same evening Lincoln was assassinated, and the murder of Seward was attempted. He was stabbed in several places in the head and throat, and for several days his life was despaired of, but he slowly recovered, and in June resumed his desk in the State Department, President Johnson having urged him to retain it. He continued in office throughout Johnson's administration, favoring the reconstruction policy of his chief, without, however, incurring the active hostility of his Republican friends. Distinctive events of his second term were his maintenance of the Monroe doctrine, in the refusal to recognize the French empire in Mexico, and the purchase of Alaska, which was in consonance with views long entertained by him as to the propriety of the expansion of the territory of the United States upon the continent of North America. In the best sense of the term he was an advocate of "Manifest Destiny," and was proud of the acquisition of the Russian territory at the Far North. A treaty which he negotiated for the cession of the Danish West India islands of St. Thomas and St. John failed of ratification by the Senate.

He retired to private life March 4, 1869, and within the next three years visited Alaska and Mexico, and made a journey around the world, being everywhere received with official welcome and popular acclaim. The last few months of his life were passed at his home, where he dictated the story of his travels and began his "Autobiography," which, even in its unfinished state, is a charming narrative.

Seward achieved greatness as an executive, a legislator, and a diplomatist; was one of the most accomplished writers of his time, and was second only to Lincoln, among civilians, in conserving American nationality and enlarging American liberties. There is a statue to his memory in Madison Square, New York, and, on November 15, 1888, another was unveiled in front of the Auburn homestead, William M. Evarts delivering the oration. Charles Francis Adams also paid his tribute, in an address at the Capitol, in Albany, 1873, upon invitation of the New York Legislature. Seward published a volume on the "Life and Public Services of John Quincy Adams," 1849. His "Essays, Speeches, and Extracts from his Diplomatic Correspondence," etc., edited by George E. Baker, with a memoir, embrace five volumes. His adopted daughter published his "Travels Around the World," 1873, and his "Autobiography," to 1834, has been supplemented by a "Memoir" by his son, Frederick W. Seward, with extracts from his letters and selections from his "Table Talk."

Chas. E. Fitch

ABRAHAM LINCOLN *

By Terence Vincent Powderly

(1809–1865)

EARLY HOME

ORN in obscurity and poverty, with health and a good disposition as a heritage from nature, and with Christian parents as teachers and guides, Abraham Lincoln—sixteenth president of the United States—entered upon life's journey through toil and vicissitude to fame and immortality.

Abraham Lincoln, grandfather of the president, was born in Union, Pa., and in 1759 removed with his parents to a point near Harrisonburg, Va. John Hanks and Squire Boone, father of Daniel Boone, were neighbors of the Lincolns at Union ; the former took up his residence at Harrisonburg, Va., and Squire Boone removed to Holman's Ford, on the Yadkin River, in North Carolina. When he was twenty-one years old, Abraham Lincoln went to North Carolina to visit his old neighbors, the Boones, and while there met and married Mary Shipley. He built a log cabin on the banks of the Yadkin and lived there several years. Here it was that Thomas Lincoln, father of the president, was born. Shortly after his birth his parents, in 1778, removed to Kentucky and settled near Elizabethtown, in Hardin County. In 1784, when Thomas was but six years old, his father was killed by the Indians. There were no schools in that neighborhood, and Thomas Lincoln grew to manhood without receiving an education. Joseph Hanks, son of John Hanks, removed to Kentucky about the time that Abraham Lincoln moved there from North Carolina. His daughter, Nancy Hanks, who was born and educated in Virginia, grew up a playmate of Thomas Lincoln, and in 1806 became his wife. Thomas Lincoln selected a farm near Hodgensville, now the county seat of Larue County, Ky., built a log cabin containing but one room, in which, on February 12, 1809, Abraham Lincoln, the future president, was born. A poor farmer, with no education and no capital other than his labor, Thomas Lincoln found little to encourage his stay in Kentucky. The institution of slavery, which lived on the toil of the black man, threw a dark shadow across the path of the " poor white " who could claim no title to property in human flesh and sinew, and in 1817 he removed from Kentucky to Spencer County, Ind., and settled in the forest at Pigeon Creek, near the town of Gentryville. On October 5, 1818, Mrs. Lincoln died and was laid to rest at the foot of a tree on the farm which her husband had hewed out of the forest with his axe.

Eighteen months after the death of his wife, Mr. Lincoln married Mrs. Sarah

Bush Johnston, a widow who had been a neighbor of his in Kentucky. To his stepmother Abraham became very much attached, and he always entertained the greatest respect and affection for her. His education was very simple, his school days few, and his books fewer still. Before leaving Kentucky he learned to read while listening to his mother as she gave lessons to his father. In 1814, a Catholic priest, Zachariah Riney, who travelled through the country, opened a school in an untenanted cabin at Hodgensville, and for a few weeks gave instructions to the youth of the neighborhood. Abraham attended this school during its brief existence. In 1822 Azel Dorsey was employed as teacher at Pigeon Creek, Ind., and during his short stay Abraham Lincoln was his most attentive pupil. Two years after, Abraham went to school for several months, and in 1824 his school days came to an end. His time at school did not exceed twelve months altogether. In the meantime he had read Defoe's " Robinson Crusoe," Bunyan's " Pilgrim's Progress," Æsop's " Fables," The Bible, and Weems's " Life of Washington." In 1824 his father, in need of his assistance as a bread-winner, began to instruct him in the carpenter trade. In 1825 he was employed at $6 a month to manage a ferry across the Ohio River at Gentry's Landing, near the mouth of Anderson Creek. His wages were paid to his father. The first money he earned for himself came in the shape of two half-dollars paid to him by two gentlemen whose trunks he transferred from the shore to a passing steamer. In 1828 Mr. Gentry engaged him to go to New Orleans on a flat-boat with a load of produce. In 1830 John Hanks, who had removed from Kentucky to Illinois, wrote to Thomas Lincoln, urging him to move to that State. Acting on the advice, Mr. Lincoln removed to Illinois and settled at a point some ten miles west of Decatur. Abraham Lincoln drove the ox team which hauled the household effects of the family, and wearing a coon-skin cap, jean jacket, and a pair of buckskin trousers, he entered the State poor, friendless, and unknown. Thirty years later he left Illinois the foremost man in the nation, and known to all the world. He assisted his father in clearing fifteen acres of land, and split the rails with which to build the fence. Although of age, he had no money, and having but a scant supply of clothing, made a bargain with Nancy Miller to make him a pair of trousers. For each yard of cloth required he split four hundred fence-rails, and as he was over six feet in height it took fourteen hundred rails to pay for his trousers. On April 19, 1831, he went to New Orleans with a flat-boat load of pigs, corn, pork, and beef ; the pigs refusing to walk, Lincoln carried them aboard in his arms. John Hanks and Lincoln's half-brother, John Johnston, accompanied him on the trip. While in New Orleans he first saw men and women sold as slaves, and as every instinct of his nature revolted at the spectacle, he said to John Hanks : " If ever I get a chance to hit that institution, I'll hit it hard." Returning from New Orleans, he went to New Salem to clerk in the store of Denton Offut. While waiting for a shipment of goods he acted as clerk on a local election board, and thus filled his first political position. During his stay in New Salem he was frequently called on to exercise his great strength in quelling disturbances, and inspired the turbulent element of the place with a wholesome respect for his powers of muscular persuasion. He was not quarrelsome, never engaged in contention, but never hesitated to take his own part or that of another who might need a helping hand. He subscribed for the Louisville *Journal*, and generously read its contents aloud to those who gathered in the store. During the Black Hawk war he enlisted as private in a company which was raised in the neighborhood, and was at once elected captain. In a short time the company was mustered out, and he re-enlisted in an "Independent Spy Battalion" which continued in service until the end of the war. On returning to New Salem he announced himself an independent candidate for the Legislature, and at a meeting held during the canvass made his first political speech in these words: "Fellow-citizens: I presume you know who I am; I am humble Abraham Lincoln. I have been solicited by many friends to become a candidate for the Legislature. My politics can be briefly stated. I am in favor of the internal improvement system, and a high protective tariff. These are my sentiments and political principles. If elected, I shall be thankful; if not, it will be all the same."

In the winter of 1832 he became a partner of a man named Berry, in the purchase and management of a store. They had no money, but gave their notes. Berry became dissipated, lost interest in the business, and the firm failed. In 1833 President Jackson appointed Lincoln postmaster of New Salem; he remained postmaster until 1836. While holding the office Lincoln voluntarily established the "free delivery" system in New Salem by carrying the letters around in his hat. He began the study of law, and was soon after appointed deputy surveyor. The note he gave on going into partnership with Berry had been sold to a man who wanted his money, and in the fall of 1834 the sheriff levied on and sold his instruments to satisfy the debt. In that year he was elected to the Legislature, and borrowed the money with which to purchase a suit of clothes to go to the State capital at Vandalia. He was re-elected to the Legislature in 1836, and during the canvass declared his principles as follows:

"I go for all sharing the privileges of the government who assist in bearing its burdens; consequently, I go for admitting all whites to the right of suffrage who pay taxes or bear arms, *by no means excluding females*."

A few years later, when questioned concerning that utterance, he said:

"All questions of social and moral reform find lodgement first with enlightened souls, who stamp them with their approval. In God's own time they will be organized into law, and thus woven into the fabric of our institutions."

In 1836 he met Stephen A. Douglas for the first time, at the State capital. In 1837 he was admitted to the bar, in 1838 re-elected to the Legislature, and again in 1840. The capital had been removed from Vandalia to Springfield, and in partnership with John T. Stuart he began the practice of law in that city in 1839. On November 4, 1842, he was married to Mary Todd, daughter of Hon. Robert S. Todd. In the presidential campaigns of 1840 and 1844 he canvassed the State as a presidential elector on the whig ticket, and in both campaigns was pitted, in joint debate, against Stephen A. Douglas. In 1846 he was elected to the thirtieth Congress, and was the only whig representative in that body from

A. Lincoln

Illinois. On January 12, 1848, he made his first speech in Congress, on a resolution which he offered calling on the president to provide a statement relating to the war with Mexico. On January 16, 1849, he introduced a bill to abolish slavery in the District of Columbia and to compensate the owners of the liberated slaves. He declined a re-election to Congress, and in 1849 was an unsuccessful candidate for United States senator. In 1850 he refused to accept the appointment as Governor of Oregon, tendered him by President Fillmore. For a few years he gave no attention to political matters, but the introduction in Congress of the bill to admit Nebraska and Kansas to the Union, and the agitation for the repeal of the " Missouri Compromise," aroused his interest, and in a short time he became the leader of a new party in the State. All who opposed the repeal of that compromise, of whatever party, were known as " Anti-Nebraska" in the beginning, but gradually they began to call themselves " Republicans," and as such they carried most of the "Free State" elections of 1854. Senator Douglas, in defending his course on the " Nebraska Bill," made speeches through Illinois. On October 1, 1854, Lincoln, in reply to one of these speeches, in speaking of slavery said:

" I hate it because it deprives our republican example of its just influence in the world ; it enables the enemies of free institutions to taunt us as hypocrites ; causes the real friends of freedom to doubt our sincerity ; is at war with the vital principles of civic liberty ; contrary to the Declaration of Independence ; and maintains that there is no right principle of action but self-interest. . . . No man is good enough to govern another man without the other's consent. . . . I object to the Nebraska Bill because it assumes there can be moral right in the enslaving of one man by another."

He was a candidate for United States Senator in 1855, but his withdrawal from the contest gave the election to Mr. Trumbull. In 1856 he received one hundred and ten votes for vice-president at the first Republican national convention, and canvassed the State as one of the presidential electors. During this canvass he said :

" Sometimes when I am speaking I feel that the time is soon coming when the sun shall shine and the rain fall on no man who shall go forth to unrequited toil. . . . How it will come about, when it will come, I cannot tell ; but that time will surely come."

The Supreme Court of the United States, on March 6, 1857, committed itself to the perpetuation of slavery in the " Dred Scott " decision, and that act, together with the question of admitting Kansas to the Union as a slave or free State, furnished the argument for the legislative campaign of 1858, in which Lincoln was a candidate for United States senator against Stephen A. Douglas. In his speech accepting the nomination he, in referring to the agitation for the abolition of slavery, said :

" In my opinion it will not cease until a crisis shall have been reached and passed. 'A house divided against itself cannot stand.' I believe this Government cannot endure permanently half slave and half free. I do not expect the Union to be dissolved, I do not expect the house to fall, but I do expect it will cease to be divided."

On May 16, 1860, the second Republican national convention met in Chicago, and on the third ballot nominated Lincoln for the presidency over William H. Seward, who was at that time the idol of the radical element of the party. Not many who listened to the clergyman who delivered the prayer at the opening of the convention, gave serious thought to these prophetic words as they fell from his lips :

" We entreat Thee that at some future, but no distant, day the evil which now invests the body politic shall not only have been arrested in its progress, but wholly eradicated from the system."

The Northern Democrats nominated Stephen A. Douglas ; the slave-holding, Southern Democrats nominated John C. Breckenridge, and a Constitutional Union party nominated John Bell. The Electoral College gave Lincoln 180 votes, Breckenridge 72, Bell 39, and Douglas 12. In his inaugural address Lincoln said :

" I have no purpose, directly or indirectly, to interfere with the institution of slavery in the States where it exists. I believe I have no lawful right to do so, and I have no inclination to do so."

Although his inaugural breathed peace and conciliation in every line, it had no effect on the hot-headed advocates of secession. The war began with the bombardment of Fort Sumter on April 12, 1861, and ended with his death. On April 15th, he issued his first call for troops, and during his administration the total number called for was 2,759,049. With the exception of Russia, the foreign powers exhibited evidences of hostility to the Union, and when urged to retaliation Lincoln said : " One war at a time, if you please, gentlemen." On May 20, 1862, he signed the Homestead Law, a boon of inestimable value to settlers on land. On January 1, 1863, he issued the " Emancipation Proclamation " which stamped the seal of eternal truth on the Declaration of Independence. On November 19, 1863, at the dedication of the Gettysburg Cemetery, he, in concluding a speech which should be committed to memory by every citizen of the nation, said :

" It is rather for us to be here dedicated to the great task remaining before us. . . . That we here highly resolve that the dead shall not have died in vain ; that the nation shall, under God, have a new birth of freedom ; and that government of the people, by the people, and for the people shall not perish from the earth."

On June 8, 1864, he was renominated by the Republican national convention, General McClellan was nominated by the Democrats, and at the election Lincoln received 212 of the 233 electoral votes cast. In concluding his inaugural address, March 4, 1865, he said :

" Both read the same Bible and pray to the same God, and each invokes His aid against the other. It may seem strange that any men should dare to ask God's assistance in wringing their bread from the sweat of other men's faces ; but let us judge not, that we be not judged. . . . Fondly do we hope, fervently do we pray, that this mighty scourge of war may speedily pass away. Yet if God wills that it continue until all the wealth piled by the bondsman's two hundred and fifty years of unrequited toil shall be sunk, and until every drop of blood drawn with the lash shall be paid by another drawn with the sword, as was said three thousand years ago, so, still, it must be said, that the judgments of the Lord are true and righteous altogether. With malice toward none, with charity for all, with firmness in the right as God gives us to see the right, let us finish the work we are in, to bind up the nation's wounds, to care for him who shall have borne the battle, and for his widow and his orphans, to do all which may achieve and cherish a just and a lasting peace among ourselves and with all nations."

On the evening of April 14, 1865, while seated in a box at Ford's Theatre, witnessing the play, "Our American Cousin," he was shot by an actor, J. Wilkes Booth, and at twenty-two minutes past seven on the morning of the 15th his life ended. His body was embalmed and taken, in funeral procession, from Washington through Baltimore, Harrisburg, Philadelphia, New York, Albany, Buffalo, Cleveland, and Chicago to Springfield, and was buried on May 4th at Oak Ridge Cemetery. On October 15, 1874, his remains were taken up and placed in a tomb beneath a magnificent and elegantly designed monument consisting of a statue of the martyred president and an obelisk of imposing appearance.

No pen can do justice to the character of Lincoln, for the world will never know of the trials, embarrassments, and misgivings which beset him from his infancy in the backwoods to his tomb in Springfield. During his administration he never knew a moment free from anxiety. Each day he faced a new problem, and finding no precedent to guide him in its solution, he acted in accordance with his own good common sense, and proved equal to every emergency. Frequently misunderstood by the nation and her foremost men, he removed all doubts by the touch of the statesman when the time was ripe. To fully estimate the statesman we must know the man, and as years go by the full nobility of his private character will be disclosed to the world in all its simple grandeur. His was "a spirit of the greatest size and divinest metal" which no temptation could allure from the course of right. His administration was the most trying that could fall to the lot of man, no other furnished so many opportunities to amass wealth through speculation and intrigue, but greed and avarice were strangers to his nature, and no stain rests upon his memory. He was slow to arrive at conclusions, but when deliberation gave birth to conviction he unfalteringly strove for the right. His education was practical, not theoretical, and was acquired in the school of nature and among men rather than among books. The basis of his life was earnestness. No rhetorical display marked his speech, but his oratory fastened the attention, appealed to reason and carried conviction to the hearts of his listeners. He valued public opinion, for he said:

"With public sentiment nothing can fail; without public sentiment nothing can succeed. Consequently he who moulds public sentiment goes deeper than he who enacts statutes or pronounces decisions."

He opposed the extension of slavery rather than its abolition; but as he divined the real sentiments of its advocates he realized that enduring peace would not bless the nation while the institution lived, a menace to free labor and industrial prosperity. He professed no religion, for his great heart throbbed in sympathy with all humanity, and he would not be separated from even the humblest among men by the artificial barriers of creed. He believed in the gospel of liberty and would guarantee it to all men through constitutional enactment. When he became president he found slavery intrenched behind the bulwarks of constitutional law and judicial decision; he found a united South, resolute in her determination to perpetuate slavery in the nation; a vacillating North, divided in its sentiment on the great question of property in man. He found the nation in the throes of civil war, and died in the triumphal hour of his country's deliverance, with the sceptre of slavery shattered, her fetters broken and in rust, and her power crumbled to ashes.

Public criticism never annoyed him, and he was not averse to taking counsel from the poorest among men. It was love of country, not selfish ambition, which turned his attention to public life, and toward the end of his administration he was rewarded by public confidence and a respect for his honesty and singleness of aim toward the good of the nation. He had a great relish for story-telling and used his fund of anecdote to good advantage in illustrating points in conversation.

His administration stands the guide-post of the centuries, set by the Eternal as the dividing line between the serfdom of the past and the freedom of the future. His monument stands the altar of a nation's fame, and his name will live to guide the world to enfranchisement.

HORACE GREELEY*

BY NOAH BROOKS

(1811–1872)

HORACE GREELEY was one of the few persons whose manhood fulfilled the precocious promise of his youth. He could read before he could speak plainly, and at the age of six he had declared that his purpose in life was to be a printer. At eleven he tried to be apprenticed at the village printing-office and was unsuccessful; at the age of fourteen he was taken on as an apprentice in the office of the *Northern Spectator*, at East Poultney, Vt.

His family were of Scotch-Irish origin, but had lived in the northern part of New Hampshire for several generations. Horace was born in Amherst, N. H., February 3, 1811. So quick of apprehension was he, and so active was his intellect, that the commonest of common-school education was for him sufficient. His schooling was only that which he could obtain during three or four months in winter; for at other seasons of the year he labored in the field with his father and brothers; and when he went to be an apprentice for five years in the printing-office, he was paid a very slender pittance, the greater part of which he gave to his father, whose income was probably next to nothing.

In June, 1830, the newspaper office in which young Greeley was learning his trade became insolvent, and Greeley, then in his twentieth year, was released from his indentures. He tramped from office to office as a journeyman printer, and his father having removed to the then "new country of western Pennsylvania," the youngster, with ten dollars in his pocket, walking part way and part way earning his passage on a tug-boat, entered the city of New York, August 18, 1831. For days he sought in vain for employment among the printing-offices of the metropolis. He was gawky, poorly clad, and doubtless presented a very grotesque appearance to the cityfied people to whom he vainly applied for employment. Finally he effected an entrance into one of the printing-offices of the city, and, much to the surprise of those who sneered at his ungainly and unpromising figure, he straightway proved himself to be a competent, careful, and skilful printer. For fourteen months or more, he picked up odd jobs in the offices of the newspapers, always making friends and always managing to save a little money.

Finally, at the beginning of 1833, in partnership with Francis V. Story, a printer, he established a penny paper called *The Morning Post*. This venture failed, but Greeley and Story saved from the wreck two-thirds of their capital, which was $150, all told, and still had on hand their type and materials. They now became master job-printers and made small contracts with persons who had newspaper printing to give out. In his New England boyhood Greeley had occasionally contributed to the columns of the newspapers on which he worked, and now he resumed that employment. He wrote for several of the feeble newspapers of the time, and on the death of his partner, Francis Story, he associated himself with Jonas Winchester. The firm prospered, and in 1834 was strong enough to establish a weekly literary newspaper called *The New Yorker*. The first number of this paper appeared on March 22, 1834, and it sold one hundred copies; for the three months next succeeding this was the average of its weekly circulation. The paper gradually increased in popularity, and the name of its Editor-in-Chief, Horace Greeley, was now known and respected. He furnished editorials also to the *Daily Whig* and to other journals, and was selected by William H. Seward and Thurlow Weed for the editorship of a campaign paper called *The Jeffersonian*, published in Albany. This was a Whig newspaper printed weekly, and the audacity, aggressiveness, and ability with which it was edited commanded the respect of its readers. *The Jeffersonian* was finally suspended in the spring of 1839, and during the presidential canvass of the following year, Greeley, foreseeing the activity of the campaign, seized upon the opportunity to establish a new campaign paper called *The Log Cabin*. This journal at once achieved the extraordinary circulation of twenty thousand copies for its first edition. It succeeded beyond the most sanguine expectations of its founders, H. Greeley & Company, and in a few weeks the circulation ran up to sixty thousand, eighty thousand, and even ninety thousand copies, a newspaper circulation in those days absolutely unprecedented. *The Log Cabin* was characterized by the homely wit, the unsparing logic, and the terseness and vigor of expression which were always Horace Greeley's most marked traits as a journalist.

After the campaign of 1840 *The Log Cabin* became a family political paper, and on April 10, 1841, its name was supplanted by that of *The New York Tribune*. Its home was at 30 Ann Street, and Horace Greeley, its editor, promised that it should be " worthy of the hearty approval of the virtuous and refined, and a welcome visitant to family firesides."

As an editor Mr. Greeley was eccentric, and his marked personal traits were perceptible in his management of his newspaper. He was severely temperate, although opposed to prohibition as impracticable; he was in favor of a high protective tariff, opposed to slavery, predisposed to vegetarian diet, and at times manifested a proclivity to the doctrines of Fourier and Prudhomme.

In his management of *The Tribune* Mr. Greeley made a wide acquaintance with the newspaper men, politicians, and the statesmen of the time. Among those associated with him in the management of his paper was Henry J. Raymond, who afterward became the founder of *The New York Times*. Those who rendered service to *The Tribune* were George William Curtis, Charles A. Dana, Margaret Fuller, Bayard Taylor, and others who subsequently achieved renown. Mr. Greeley himself has said that of his first issue of five thousand copies of the paper, nearly all " were with difficulty given away." *The Tribune* was first sold at one cent a copy ; in a month's time it reached a circulation of three thousand, and a month later it had reached the extraordinary circulation of eleven and twelve thousand. *The New Yorker* and *The Log Cabin* had all along been managed as weekly issues from the same office ; but in September of the first year of the establishment of *The Tribune* these were merged in what was now *The New York Weekly Tribune*, which at once leaped to a large circulation and became a great force throughout the country, especially in the rural districts.

In 1842 Mr. Greeley began to print in his paper one column daily of matter on Fourierite topics, written by Albert Brisbane, and occasionally these theories were defended in his editorial columns, and he thereby gained a certain amount of obloquy from which he did not readily recover. The paper had the reputation of being not only extremely radical in its political views, but also committed to many of the " isms " of the times. It paid much attention to the spirit-rappings of the Fox sisters, of Rochester, and investigated the curious phenomena with fearless open-mindedness. *The Tribune* prospered, though not greatly, and it was evident that Mr. Greeley's business management was never very successful ; and it may be said that his greatest success as the editor of a prosperous and profitable newspaper was always achieved by the co-operation of wiser managers than himself. His personal appearance was peculiar, and he very soon became a well-known figure in the public life of New York. He usually wore a broad-brimmed, soft white hat and a light-colored overcoat, and his appearance, although always spotlessly neat, was characterized by a certain disorderliness which instantly attracted attention. He had a shrill, high-keyed voice ; he was irascible in temper, and was never the " philosopher " which those who least knew him credited him with being. In an angry letter published in his own newspaper he referred to the editor of *The Daily Times* as " that little villain, Raymond ; " and replying to an offensive charge against him by *The Evening Post*, he began with, " You lie, villain, wilfully, wickedly, basely lie." Other passages at arms like these occasionally enlivened, if they did not disfigure, the editorial columns of *The Tribune*, over which Greeley exercised a personal censorship which, in later years, he found it necessary to relax. He was sincerely and ardently devoted to the cause of Protection, to the interests of the farmer and the laboring man, to sound money, and to all the ennobling and refining activities of social life. In spite of a careless personal manner, and a voice not at all agreeable to the ear, he became a popular and greatly sought public speaker. As a lecturer in the lyceums of towns and villages, then greatly in vogue, he was always an acceptable and greatly admired figure.

In 1848 he was elected to the United States House of Representatives to fill a vacancy for three months. With great vigor he charged upon several of the most prominent abuses of the time, and selecting the practice of paying mileage to Congressmen, he assaulted that with a vehemence which ultimately destroyed it. As a member of Congress he also introduced the first bill to give free homesteads to actual settlers on the public lands. He was a candidate in 1861 for United States Senator, but was defeated by Ira Harris, of Albany. In 1864 he was one of the Republican Presidential Electors, and in 1870 was nominated for Congress in a hopelessly Democratic district, and was defeated. He had always been an intense opponent of human slavery, and in 1848 his hostility to the war with Mexico was doubtless inspired by his dread of the extension of the slave system. He was an enthusiastic supporter of John C. Fremont, who was nominated for President by the Republicans in 1856 ; and he made his newspaper so dreaded and feared by the opposition that he was indicted in Virginia for circulating incendiary documents through its columns. During these years he was an incessant and untiring worker, and produced for the columns of his own and other newspapers a prodigious amount of matter. He had heretofore labored in politics in conjunction with William H. Seward, Governor, and afterward United States Senator. In 1854 the separation between Greeley, Seward, and Thurlow Weed became established, and Mr. Seward's friends prevented the election of Mr. Greeley as a delegate to the Republican Convention which nominated Abraham Lincoln in 1860. Greeley, however, obtained a seat as delegate in the Convention as a representative from the State of Oregon, and in that capacity he, more than any other man, doubtless turned the tide against Mr. Seward and in favor of Abraham Lincoln, who was nominated by the Convention.

At the breaking out of the Civil War Mr. Greeley manifested great trepidation and reluctance to face the issue. He even advised in *The Tribune* that the " Erring Sisters " be allowed to depart in peace ; but later he rallied manfully to the cause of the defence of the Union, and his newspaper rang with impassioned appeals for the freedom of the slaves held in bondage in the South. He incessantly urged a more vigorous prosecution of the war, and called upon President Lincoln to take every possible measure for the emancipation of the Southern bondmen.

In 1864, being convinced that the cause of the rebellion was gradually weakening, he urged upon the President the policy of negotiating with the leaders of the Confederate government for a surrender of their warlike policy, on conditions to be arrived at by commissioners from both sides. This proposition excited much indignation throughout the country, and when, in answer to repeated demands from Mr. Greeley, President Lincoln authorized him to undertake such a conference at Niagara Falls, the people generally applauded the wisdom of the President, as well as the disappointment of Mr. Greeley, when the conference came to naught.

After the final surrender at Appomattox and the capture of the Confederate President, Mr. Greeley visited Richmond and signed the bail bond of Jefferson Davis. This action raised a storm of public censure, and he was for a time overwhelmed by the wrath and indignation of those who had been formerly associated with him in political affairs. He defended himself with great vigor, and fearlessly assailed those who stigmatized him as a sympathizer with the fallen rebel chieftain. He was not friendly to the nomination of General Grant in 1868, and disapproved of many of the schemes that marked his administration. Returning from a visit through the Southern States in the early years of President Grant's term, he brought to his newspaper some vigorous and outspoken denunciations of the "carpet-bag" governments of the formerly rebel States, and denunciations of the "scalawags" who, he said, "were the pests of the reconstructed States of the South." These and similar outgivings attracted the attention of a large element of the Republican party, and he was nominated for the Presidency, against General Grant, in 1872. Mr. Greeley's canvass was one of great picturesqueness and industry. He made a series of speeches extending over a tour from New England to the West, and returning to New York, which were marked by a most wonderful originality, freshness, and brilliance ; but nothing could avail to stem the tide of prejudice which rose against him and in favor of General Grant. He had been nominated by the so-called Liberal Republicans and by the Democrats, but he failed to carry any one of the Northern States, and of the other States he carried only Georgia, Kentucky, Maryland, Missouri, Tennessee, and Texas. He was assailed during this canvass in the bitterest terms by those who regarded him as a turncoat and a traitor, and undoubtedly the vituperation and abuse showered upon him had the effect of disheartening him and destroying the zest with which he had theretofore undertaken the multifarious duties of life. He returned to New York from an exhausting campaign, depressed in spirit and weary in body and in mind. The death of his devoted wife added to his sorrows, and on November 29, 1872, only a few weeks after the Presidential election, he died at Pleasantville, N. Y., of mental and nervous prostration. His body lay in state in the City Hall, and his funeral was attended by the notables of the land—President Grant, who had just been re-elected by the people, being numbered among those who mourned at his bier.

In addition to his editorial labors Mr. Greeley was the author of a number of works, among which were " Hints toward Reforms," " Glances at Europe," " History of the Struggle for Slavery Extension," " Overland Journey to San Francisco," " The American Conflict," and " Recollections of a Busy Life." He was also the founder of " The Whig Almanac," a manual of politics, which in later years became known as " The Tribune Almanac," and survived his demise.

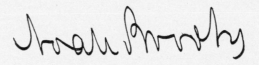

LOUIS AGASSIZ *

By Asa Gray

(1807–1873)

THERE is no need to give an abstract of the contents of these fascinating volumes, for everybody is reading them. Most are probably wishing for more personal details, especially of the American life; but the editorial work is so deftly and delicately done, and "the story of an intellectual life marked by rare coherence and unity" is so well arranged to tell itself and make its impression, that we may thankfully accept what has been given us, though the desired "fulness of personal narrative" be wanting.

Twelve years have passed since Agassiz was taken from us. Yet to some of us it seems not very long ago that the already celebrated Swiss naturalist came over, in the bloom of his manly beauty, to charm us with his winning ways, and inspire us with his overflowing enthusiasm, as he entered upon the American half of that career which has been so beneficial to the interests of natural science. There are not many left of those who attended those first Lowell Lectures in the autumn of 1846—perhaps all the more taking for the broken English in which they were delivered—and who shared in the delight with which, in a supplementary lecture, he more fluently addressed his audience in his mother-tongue.

In these earliest lectures he sounded the note of which his last public utterance was the dying cadence. For, as this biography rightly intimates, his scientific life was singularly entire and homogeneous—if not uninfluenced, yet quite unchanged, by the transitions which have marked the period. In a small circle of naturalists, almost the first that was assembled to greet him on his coming to this country, and of which the writer is the sole survivor, when Agassiz was inquired of as to his conception of "species," he sententiously replied : " A species is a thought of the Creator." To this thoroughly theistic conception he joined the scientific deduction which he had already been led to draw, that the animal species of each geological age, or even stratum, were different from those preceding and following, and also unconnected by natural derivation. And his very last published works reiterated his steadfast conviction that " there is no evidence

* Written in 1886, on the publication of "Louis Agassiz, His Life and Correspondence." Reprinted, by permission of Messrs. Houghton, Mifflin & Co., from "The Scientific Papers of Asa Gray."

of a direct descent of later from earlier species in the geological succession of animals." Indeed, so far as we know, he would not even admit that such "thoughts of the Creator" as these might have been actualized in the natural course of events. If he had accepted such a view, and if he had himself apprehended and developed in his own way the now well-nigh assured significance of some of his early and pregnant generalizations, the history of the doctrine of development would have been different from what it is, a different spirit and another name would have been prominent in it, and Agassiz would not have passed away while fighting what he felt to be—at least for the present—a losing battle. It is possible that the "whirligig of time" may still "bring in his revenges," but not very probable.

Much to his credit, it may be said that a good share of Agassiz's invincible aversion to evolution may be traced to the spirit in which it was taken up by his early associate, Vogt, and, indeed, by most of the German school then and since, which justly offended both his scientific and his religious sense. Agassiz always "thought nobly of the soul," and could in no way approve either materialistic or agnostic opinions. The idealistic turn of his mind was doubtless confirmed in his student days at Munich, whither he and his friend Braun resorted after one session at Heidelberg, and where both devotedly attended the lectures of Schelling —then in his later glory—and of Oken, whose "Natur-Philosophie" was then in the ascendant. Although fascinated and inspired by Oken's *à priori* biology (built upon morphological ideas which had not yet been established, but had, in part, been rightly divined) the two young naturalists were not carried away by it, probably because they were such keen and conscientious observers, and were kept in close communion with work-a-day nature. As Agassiz intimates, they had to resist "the temptation to impose one's own ideas upon nature, to explain her mysteries by brilliant theories rather than by patient study of the facts as we find them," and that "overbearing confidence in the abstract conceptions of the human mind as applied to the study of nature; although, indeed," he adds, "the young naturalist of that day who did not share in some degree the intellectual stimulus given to scientific pursuits by physio-philosophy would have missed a part of his training." That training was not lost upon Agassiz. Although the adage in his last published article, "A physical fact is as sacred as a moral principle," was well lived up to, yet ideal prepossessions often had much to do with his marshalling of the facts.

Another professor at Munich, from whom Agassiz learned much, and had nothing to unlearn, was the anatomist and physiologist Döllinger. He published little, but he seems to have been the founder of modern embryological investigation, and to have initiated his two famous pupils, first Von Baer, and then Agassiz, into at least the rudiments of the doctrine of the correspondence between the stages of the development of the individual animal with that of its rank in the scale of being, and the succession in geological time of the forms and types to which the species belongs : a principle very fertile for scientific zoölogy in the hands of both these naturalists, and one of the foundations of that theory of evolution which the former, we believe, partially accepted, and the other wholly rejected.

The botanical professor, the genial Von Martius, should also be mentioned here. He found Agassiz a student, barely of age ; he directly made him an author, and an authority, in the subject of his predilection. Dr. Spix, the zoölogical companion of Martius in Brazilian exploration, died in 1826 ; the fishes of the collection were left untouched. Martius recognized the genius of Agassiz, and offered him, and indeed pressed him, to undertake their elaboration. Agassiz brought out the first part of the quarto volume on the " Fishes of the Brazilian Expedition of Spix and Martius" before he took his degree of doctor of philosophy, and completed it before he proceeded to that of doctor in medicine, in 1830. The work opened his way to fame, but brought no money. Still, as Martius defrayed all the expenses, the net result compared quite favorably with that of later publications. Moreover, out of it possibly issued his own voyage to Brazil in later years, under auspices such as his early patron never dreamed of.

This early work also made him known to Cuvier ; so that, when he went to Paris, a year afterward, to continue his medical and scientific studies—the one, as he deemed, from necessity, the other from choice—he was received as a fellow-savant ; yet at first with a certain reserve, probably no more than was natural in view of the relative age and position of the two men ; but Agassiz, writing to his sister, says : " This extreme but formal politeness chills you instead of putting you at your ease ; it lacks cordiality, and, to tell the truth, I would gladly go away if I were not held fast by the wealth of material of which I can avail myself." But only a month later he writes—this time to his uncle—that, while he was anxious lest he " might not be allowed to examine, and still less to describe, the fossil fishes and their skeletons in the Museum, . . . knowing that Cuvier intended to write a work on this subject," and might naturally wish to reserve the materials for his own use ; and when the young naturalist, as he showed his own sketches and notes to the veteran, was faintly venturing to hope that, on seeing his work so far advanced, he might perhaps be invited to share in a joint publication, Cuvier relieved his anxiety and more than fulfilled his half-formed desires.

"He desired his secretary to bring him a certain portfolio of drawings. He showed me the contents : they were drawings of fossil fishes, and notes which he had taken in the British Museum and elsewhere. After looking it through with me, he said he had seen with satisfaction the manner in which I had treated this subject ; that I had, indeed, anticipated him, since he had intended at some future time to do the same thing ; but that as I had given it so much attention, and had done my work so well, he had decided to renounce his project, and to place at my disposition all the materials he had collected and all the preliminary notes he had taken."

Within three months Cuvier fell under a stroke of paralysis, and shortly died. The day before the attack he had said to Agassiz, " Be careful, and remember that work kills." We doubt if it often kills naturalists, unless when, like Cuvier, they also become statesmen.

But to live and work, the naturalist must be fed. It was a perplexing problem how possibly to remain a while longer in Paris, which was essential to the carrying on of his work, and to find the means of supplying his very simple wants. And here the most charming letters in these volumes are, first, the one from his mother, full of tender thoughtfulness, and making the first suggestion about Neuchâtel and its museum, as a place where the aspiring naturalist might secure something more substantial than "brilliant hopes" to live upon; next, that from Agassiz to his father, who begs to be told as much as he can be supposed to understand of the nature of this work upon fossil fishes, which called for so much time, labor, and expense; and, almost immediately, Agassiz's letter to his parents, telling them that Humboldt had, quite spontaneously and unexpectedly, relieved his present anxieties by a credit of a thousand francs, to be increased, if necessary. Humboldt had shown a friendly interest in him from the first, and had undertaken to negotiate with Cotta, the publisher, in his behalf; but, becoming uneasy by the delay, and feeling that "a man so laborious, so gifted, and so deserving of affection . . . should not be left in a position where lack of serenity disturbs his power of work," he delicately pressed the acceptance of this aid as a confidential transaction between two friends of unequal age.

Indeed, the relations between the "two friends," one at that time sixty-three, and the other twenty-five, were very beautiful, and so continued, as the correspondence shows. Humboldt's letters (we wish there were more of them) are particularly delightful, are full of wit and wisdom, of almost paternal solicitude, and of excellent counsel. He enjoins upon Agassiz to finish what he has in hand before taking up new tasks (this is in 1837), not to spread his intellect over too many subjects at once, nor to go on enlarging the works he had undertaken; he predicts the pecuniary difficulties in which expansion would be sure to land him, bewails the glacier investigations, and closes with "a touch of fun, in order that my letter may seem a little less like preaching. A thousand affectionate remembrances. No more ice, not much of echinoderms, plenty of fish, recall of ambassadors *in partibus*, and great severity toward booksellers, an infernal race, two or three of which have been killed under me."

The ambassadors *in partibus* were the artists Agassiz employed and sent to England or elsewhere to draw fossil fishes for him in various museums, at a cost which Humboldt knew would be embarrassing. The ice, which he would have no more of, refers to the glacier researches upon which Agassiz was entering with ardor, laying one of the solid foundations of his fame. Curiously enough, both Humboldt and Von Buch, with all their interest in Agassiz, were quite unable to comprehend the importance of an inquiry which was directly in their line, and, indeed, they scorned it; while the young naturalist, without training in physics or geology, but with the insight of genius, at once developed the whole idea of the glacial period, with its wonderful consequences, upon his first inspection of the phenomena shown him by Charpentier in the valley of the Rhône.

It is well that Humboldt's advice was not heeded in this regard. Nevertheless he was a wise counsellor. He saw the danger into which his young friend's

23

enthusiasm and boundless appetite for work was likely to lead him.   For Agassiz it might be said, with a variation of the well-known adage, that there was nothing he touched that he did not aggrandize.   Everything he laid hold of grew larger under his hand—grew into a mountain threatening to overwhelm him, and would have overwhelmed anyone whose powers were not proportionate to his aspirations.   Established at Neuchâtel, and giving himself with ardor to the duties of his professorship, it was surely enough if he could do the author's share in the production of his great works on the fossil and the fresh-water fishes, without assuming the responsibilities and cares of publication as well, and even of a lithographic establishment which he set up mainly for his own use.   But he carried *pari passu*, or nearly so, his work on fossil mollusca—a quarto volume with nearly a hundred plates—his monographs of echinoderms, living and fossil, his investigations of the embryological development of fishes, and that laborious work, the " Nomenclator Zoologicus," with the " Bibliographia," later published in England by the Ray Society.   Moreover, of scattered papers, those of the Royal Society's Catalogue, which antedate his arrival in this country, are more than threescore and ten.   He had help, indeed ; but the more he had, the more he enlarged and diversified his tasks ; Humboldt's sound advice about his zoölogical undertakings being no more heeded than his fulminations against the glacial theory.

In the midst of all this, Agassiz turned his glance upon the glaciers, and the " local phenomenon " became at once a cosmic one.   So far a happy divination ; but he seems to have believed quite to the last that, not only the temperate zones, but whole intertropical continents—at least the American—had been sheeted with ice.   The narrative in the first volume will give the general reader a vivid but insufficient conception of the stupendous work upon which he so brilliantly labored for nearly a decade of years.

Cœlum, non animum, mutant who come with such a spirit to a wider and, scientifically, less developed continent.   First as visitor, soon as denizen, and at length as citizen of the American republic, Agassiz rose with every occasion to larger and more various activities.   What with the Lowell Institute, the college in Charleston, S. C., and Cornell University, in addition to Harvard, he may be said to have held three or four professorships at once, none of them sinecures. He had not been two months in the country before a staff of assistants was gathered around him, and a marine zoölogical laboratory was in operation.   The rude shed on the shore, and the small wooden building at Cambridge, developed under his hand into the Museum of Zoölogy—if not as we see it now, yet into one of the foremost collections.   Who can say what it would have been if his plans and ideas had obtained full recognition, and "expenditure" had seemed to the trustees, as it seemed to him, "the best investment ;" or if efficient filial aid, not then to be dreamed of, had not given solid realization to the high paternal aspirations?   In like manner grew large under his hand the Brazilian exploration, so generously provided for by a Boston citizen and fostered by an enlightened emperor ; and on a similar scale was planned, and partly carried out, the " Contributions to the Natural History of the United States," as the imperial quarto work was modestly entitled, which was to be published " at the rate of one volume a year, each volume to contain about three hundred pages and twenty plates," with simple reliance upon a popular subscription ; and so, indeed, of everything which this large-minded man undertook.

While Agassiz thus was a magnanimous man, in the literal as well as the accepted meaning of the word, he was also, as we have seen, a truly fortunate one.   Honorable assistance came to him at critical moments, such as the delicate gift from Humboldt at Paris, which perhaps saved him to science ; such as the Wollaston prize from the Geological Society in 1834, when he was struggling for the means of carrying on the " Fossil Fishes."   The remainder of the deficit of this undertaking he was able to make up from his earliest earnings in America. For the rest, we all know how almost everything he desired—and he wanted nothing except for science—was cheerfully supplied to his hand by admiring givers.   Those who knew the man during the twenty-seven years of his American life, can quite understand the contagious enthusiasm and confidence which he evoked.   The impression will in some degree be transmitted by these pleasant and timely volumes, which should make the leading lines of the life of Agassiz clear to the newer generation, and deepen them in the memory of an older one.

CHARLES DARWIN

Extracts from " Life and Letters of Charles Darwin," BY ARCH. GEIKIE, LL.D., F.R.S.

(1809–1882)

B Y the universal consent of mankind, the name of Charles Darwin was, even during his lifetime, among those of the few great leaders who stand forth for all time as the creative spirits who have founded and legislated for the realm of science. It is too soon to estimate with precision the full value and effect of his work. The din of controversy that rose around him has hardly yet died down, and the influence of the doctrines he propounded is extending into so many remote departments of human inquiry, that a generation or two may require to pass away before his true place in the history of thought can be definitely fixed. But the judgment of his contemporaries as to his proud pre-eminence is not likely ever to be called in question. He is enrolled among Dii majorum gentium, and there he will remain to the end of the ages. When he was laid beside the illustrious dead in Westminster Abbey, there arose far and wide a lamentation as of personal bereavement. Thousands of mourners who had never seen him, who knew only his writings, and judged of the gentleness and courtesy of his nature from these, and from such hearsay reports as passed outward from the privacy of his country home, grieved as for the loss of a friend. It is remarkable that probably no scientific man of his day was personally less familiar to the mass of his fellow-countrymen. He seemed to shun all the usual modes of contact with them. His weak health, domestic habits, and absorbing work kept him in the seclusion of his own quiet home. His face was seldom to be seen at the meetings of scientific societies, or at those gatherings where the discoveries of science are expounded to more popular audiences. He shrank from public controversy, although no man was ever more vigorously attacked and more completely mis-represented. Nevertheless, when he died the affectionate regret that followed him to the grave, came not alone from his own personal friends, but from thousands of sympathetic mourners in all parts of the world, who had never seen or known him. Men had ample material for judging of his work, and in the end had given judgment with general acclaim. Of the man himself, however, they could know but little, yet enough of his character shone forth in his work to indicate its tenderness and goodness. Men instinctively felt him to be in every way one of the great ones of the earth, whose removal from the living world leaves mankind poorer in moral worth as well as in intellect.

Charles Darwin came of a family which from the beginning of the sixteenth century had been settled on the northern borders of Lincolnshire. Several of his ancestors had been men of literary taste and scientific culture, the most noted of them being his grandfather, Erasmus Darwin, the poet and philosopher. His father was a medical man in large practice at Shrewsbury, and his mother a daughter of Josiah Wedgwood, of Etruria. Some interesting reminiscences are given of the father, who must have been a man of uncommon strength of character. He left a large fortune, and thus provided for the career his son was destined to fulfil. Of his own early life and later years, Darwin has left a slight but most interesting sketch in an autobiographical fragment, written late in life for his children, and without any idea of its ever being published. Shortly before his mother's death, in 1817, he was sent, when eight years old, to a day-school in his native town. But even in the period of childhood he had chosen the favorite occupation of his life : "My taste for natural history," he says, "and more especially for collecting, was well developed. I tried to make out the names of plants, and collected all sorts of things—shells, seals, franks, coins, and minerals. The passion for collecting which leads a man to be a systematic naturalist, a virtuoso, or a miser, was very strong in me, and was clearly innate, as none of my sisters and brothers ever had this taste."

Some of the incidents of his Cambridge life which he records are full of interest in their bearing on his future career. Foremost among them stands the friendship which he formed with Professor Henslow, whose lectures on botany he attended. He joined in the class excursions and found them delightful. But still more profitable to him were the long and almost daily walks which he enjoyed with his teacher, during the latter half of his time at Cambridge. Henslow's wide range of acquirement, modesty, unselfishness, courtesy, gentleness, and piety, fascinated him and exerted on him an influence which, more than anything else, tended to shape his whole future life. The love of travel which had been kindled by his boyish reading, now took a deeper hold of him as he read Humboldt's " Personal Narrative " and Herschel's " Introduction to the Study of Natural Philosophy." He determined to visit Teneriffe, and even went so far as to inquire about ships. But his desire was soon to be gratified in a far other and more comprehensive voyage. At the close of his college life he was fortunate enough, through Henslow's good offices, to accompany Sedgwick in a geological excursion in North Wales. There can be little doubt that this short trip sufficed to efface the dislike of geology which he had conceived at Edinburgh, and to show him how much it was in his own power to increase the sum of geological knowledge. To use his own phrase, he began to " work like a tiger " at geology.

But he now had reached the main turning-point of his career. On returning home from his ramble with Sedgwick he found a letter from Henslow, telling him that Captain Fitz-Roy, who was about to start on the memorable voyage of the Beagle, was willing to give up part of his own cabin to any competent young man who would volunteer to go with him, without pay, as a naturalist. The post was offered to Darwin and, after some natural objections on the part of his father, accepted.

The Beagle weighed anchor from Plymouth on December 27, 1831, and returned on October 2, 1836.

On his return to England, Darwin at once took his place among the acknowledged men of science of his country. For a time his health continued to be such as to allow him to get through a large amount of work. The next two years, which in his own opinion were the most active of his life, were spent, partly at Cambridge, and partly in London, in the preparation of his " Journal of Researches," of the zoölogical and geological results of the voyage, and of various papers for the Geological and Zoölogical Societies. So keen was his geological zeal that, almost against his better judgment, he was prevailed upon to undertake the duties of honorary secretary of the Geological Society, an office which he continued to hold for three years. And at each period of enforced holiday, for his health had already begun to give way, he occupied himself with geological work in the field. In the Midlands he watched the operations of earthworms, and began those inquiries which formed the subject of his last research, and of the volume on " Vegetable Mould " which he published not long before his death. In the Highlands he studied the famous Parallel Roads of Glen Roy ; and his work there, though in after-years he acknowledged it to be "a great failure," he felt at the time to have been "one of the most difficult and instructive tasks " he had ever undertaken.

In the beginning of 1839 Darwin married his cousin, daughter of Josiah Wedgwood, and grand-daughter of the founder of the Etruria Works, and took a house in London. But the entries of ill-health in his diary grow more frequent. For a time he and his wife went into society, and took their share of the scientific life and work of the metropolis. But he was compelled gradually to withdraw from this kind of existence, which suited neither of them, and eventually they determined to live in the country. Accordingly, he purchased a house and grounds at Down, in a sequestered part of Kent, some twenty miles from London, and moved thither in the autumn of 1842. In that quiet home he passed the remaining forty years of his life. It was there that his children were born and grew up around him; that he carried on the researches and worked out the generalizations that have changed the whole realm of science; that he received his friends and the strangers who came from every country to see him; and it was there that, after a long and laborious life, full of ardor and work to the last, he died, at the age of seventy-three, on April 19, 1882.

The story of his life at Down is almost wholly coincident with the history of the development of his views on evolution, and the growth and appearance of the successive volumes which he gave to the world. For the first four years his geological tastes continued in the ascendant. During that interval there appeared three remarkable works, his volume on "Coral Islands," that on "Volcanic Islands," and his "Geological Observations on South America."

After working up the geological results of the long voyage in the Beagle, he set himself with great determination to more purely geological details. While on the coast of Chili he had found a curious new cirripede, to understand the structure of which he had to examine and dissect many of the common forms. The memoir, which was originally designed to describe only his new type, gradually expanded into an elaborate monograph on the Cirripedes (barnacles) as a whole group. For eight years he continued this self-imposed task, getting at last so weary of it as to feel at times as if the labor had been in some sense wasted which he had spent over it; and this suspicion seems to have remained with him in maturer years. But when at last the two bulky volumes, of more than one thousand pages of text, with forty detailed plates, made their appearance, they were hailed as an admirable contribution to the knowledge of a comparatively little known department of the animal kingdom. In the interests of science, perhaps, their chief value is to be recognized, not so much in their own high merit, as in the practical training which their preparation gave the author in anatomical detail and classification. He spoke of it himself afterward as a valuable discipline, and Professor Huxley truly affirms that the influence of this discipline was visible in everything which he afterward wrote.

It was after Darwin had got rid of his herculean labors over the "Cirripede" book, that he began to settle down seriously to the great work of his life—the investigation of the origin of the species, of plants and animals. Briefly, it may be stated here that he seems to have been first led to ponder over the question of the transmutation of species, by facts that had come under his notice during the

South American part of the voyage in the Beagle—such as the discovery of the fossil remains of huge animals akin to, but yet very distinct from, the living armadillos of the same regions ; the manner in which closely allied animals were found to replace one another, as he followed them over the continent ; and the remarkable character of the flora and fauna of the Galapagos Archipelago. " It was evident," he says, " that such facts as these, as well as many others, could only be explained on the supposition that species gradually become modified ; and the subject haunted me." His first note-book for the accumulation of facts bearing on the question was opened in July, 1837, and from that date he continued to gather them "on a wholesale scale, more especially with respect to domesticated productions, by printed inquiries, by conversation with skilful breeders and gardeners, and by extensive reading."

.   .   .   .

He now set to work upon that epitome of his observations and deductions which appeared in November, 1859, as the immortal "Origin of Species."

Those who are old enough to remember the publication of this work, cannot but marvel at the change, which, since that day, not yet thirty years ago, has come alike upon the non-scientific and the scientific part of the community in their estimation of it. Professor Huxley has furnished to the biography a graphic chapter on the reception of the book, and in his vigorous and witty style recalls the furious and fatuous objections that were urged against it. A much longer chapter will be required to describe the change which the advent of the "Origin of Species" has wrought in every department of science, and not of science only, but of philosophy. The principle of evolution, so early broached and so long discredited, has now at last been proclaimed and accepted as the guiding idea in the investigation of nature.

One of the most marvellous aspects of Darwin's work was the way in which he seemed always to throw a new light upon every department of inquiry into which the course of his researches led him to look. The specialists who, in their own narrow domains, had been toiling for years, patiently gathering facts and timidly drawing inferences from them, were astonished to find that one who, in their eyes, was a kind of outsider, could point out to them the plain meaning of things which, though entirely familiar to them, they had never adequately understood. The central idea of the "Origin of Species" is an example of this in the biological sciences. The chapter on the imperfection of the geological record is another.

After the publication of the "Origin" Darwin gave to the world, during a succession of years, a series of volumes in which some of his observations and conclusions were worked out in fuller detail. His books on the fertilization of orchids, on the movements and habits of climbing plants, on the variation of animals and plants under domestication, on the effects of cross- and self-fertilization in the vegetable kingdom, on the different forms of flowers on plants of the same species, were mainly based on his own quiet work in the greenhouse and garden at Down. His volumes on the descent of man and on the expression of the emotions in man and animals, completed his contributions to the biological argument. His last volume, published the year before his death, treated of the formation of vegetable mould and the habits of earthworms, and the preparation of it enabled him to revive some of the geological enthusiasm which so marked the earlier years of his life.

Such, in briefest outline, was the work accomplished by Charles Darwin. The admirable biography prepared by his son enables us to follow its progress from the beginning to its close. But higher even than the intellect which achieved the work, was the moral character which shone through it all.

LOUIS ADOLPHE THIERS

(1797–1877)

LOUIS ADOLPHE THIERS, French historian, politician, and patriot, was born at Marseilles on April 16, 1797. His father, who seems to have belonged to a family in decayed circumstances, was a locksmith. Through the influence of his mother, who was a Chenier, he received a good education, first at the *Lycée* in his native city, and subsequently (1815) at Aix, whither he was sent to study law. At Aix he made the acquaintance of Mignet, cultivated literature rather than the law, and won a prize for a dissertation on Vauvenargues. Called to the bar at the age of twenty-three, he set off for Paris in the company of Mignet. His prospects did not seem brilliant, and his almost ludicrously squat figure and plain face were not recommendations to Parisian society. His industry and belief in himself were, however, unbounded, and an introduction to Lafitte, of the *Constitutionnel*, then the leading organ of the French liberals, gave him the chance of showing his capacity as a public writer. His articles in the *Constitutionnel*, chiefly on political and literary subjects, gained him the entry into the most influential salons of the opposition. At this time he made the acquaintance of Talleyrand, Casimir Périer, the Comte de Flahault, and Baron Louis, the financier. Meanwhile he was rapidly—indeed too rapidly—preparing his " Histoire de la Révolution Française." The first two volumes—there were ten in all—appeared in 1823. This work, although it has been demonstrated to be very untrustworthy and inaccurate, more especially in its estimates of persons, gave its author a prominent place among French politicians and men of letters. About this time, too, the gift by his admirer, Cotta, the German publisher, of a share in the *Constitutionnel* raised him to comparative affluence. In January, 1830, he, along with Armand Carrel, Mignet, and other friends, started the *National*, and in its columns waged relentless war on the Polignac administration. The ministry met the opposition it had provoked by the Ordonnances of July. Among the other repressive measures that were taken was the sending of a commissary of police to the office of the *National*, interdicting its publication. Its conductors, with Thiers at their head, defied the ministry, and the result was the revolution which drove Charles X. into exile.

Thiers now entered on an active career as a politician. He was elected deputy for the town of Aix, and was appointed secretary-general to the minister of finance. His first appearance in the Chamber of Deputies gave no promise of his subsequent distinction. His diminutive person, his small face, encumbered with a pair of huge spectacles, and his whole exterior presenting something of the ludicrous, the new deputy, full of the impassioned eloquence of the revolutionary orators, attempted to impart the thrilling emotions affected by Mirabeau. The attempt provoked derision ; but soon subsiding into the oratory natural to him—simple, easy, rapid, anecdotic—he became one of the most formidable of parliamentary speakers. Almost from the moment of his entrance into public life he and Guizot stood forth in opposition to each other as the champions of radicalism and conservatism, respectively. But he was a stanch monarchist, and for a time a favorite with Louis Philippe. In 1832 he accepted the post of minister of the interior under Soult, exchanging it subsequently for the ministry of commerce and public affairs, and that in turn for the foreign office. He was universally regarded as a stronger man than any of his chiefs during this period ; but his public and private actions alike were always marked by a certain fussy quarrelsomeness which prevented him from being ever accounted a statesman of the first rank. The spirited foreign policy, calculated above all things to precipitate a quarrel between France and Great Britain, of which for many years he was the chief advocate, is now allowed to have been a great, and might have been a fatal, mistake. In 1836 he became president of the council, but in August of the same year he resigned office, and became the leader of the opposition. In 1840 he was again summoned to office as president of the council and foreign minister. In a few months he was a terror to the peace of Europe. He refused Lord Palmerston's invitation to enter into an alliance with Britain, Austria, and Prussia for the preservation of the integrity of the Ottoman empire, from a sympathy with the principles which dictated the first Napoleon's invasion of Egypt and Syria, and a desire to accomplish by diplomacy with Mehemet Ali what Bonaparte had endeavored to effect by force of arms—the supremacy of France in these regions. He talked menacingly of setting aside the treaties of 1815, and of extending the French frontier to the Rhine, and is said to have actually spent £8,000,000 on military and naval demonstrations. Then followed the seizure of the Society Islands, and a well-founded protest by the British government against the ill-treatment by the French of Mr. Pritchard, their consul at Tahiti.   In consequence of this Thiers was forced to resign office, and retire into private life. He now returned to the study of French history.   The first volume of his " Histoire du Consulat et de l'Empire" appeared in 1845 ; it was not completed till 1860.   This, the most ambitious of all Thiers's literary enterprises, must be considered a large rather than a great work.   It is a monument to its author's industry in reading, and rises here and there to rhetorical brilliance.   But that it is inaccurate and unfair has been admitted even by French critics.   Thiers greatly overrated Napoleon, and probably to his own hurt.

Thiers was not one of the promoters of the revolution which in 1848 drove Louis Philippe from the throne.   On the contrary, he would, as prime minister summoned at the eleventh hour, have prevented it if he could.   He accepted its consequences in the form of the Republic.   He voted for the election of Prince Louis Napoleon as its president.   This action brought him much vituperation and ridicule from former political friends.   But whatever may have been the motive that inspired it, it certainly did not help him at the time of the coup-d'état of 1851 ; he was arrested, imprisoned in Mazas, and banished.   Next year, however, he was allowed to return from Switzerland to France.   For eight years he was occupied with his " History of the Consulate and Empire."   He re-entered the Chamber in 1863, having been elected liberal deputy for the Department of the Seine in opposition to the imperialist candidate.   Till the fall of the Second Empire he was regarded as the ablest and most formidable of its more moderate and parliamentary opponents.   His speeches in the years between 1863 and 1870 were filled with taunts of the Empire on account of the loss of prestige which had marked its history, and these must not be left out of account when blame has to be apportioned among the authors of the war of 1870, although he opposed it when declared by the Ollivier ministry, and predicted defeat.

The collapse of the Second Empire, however, enabled Thiers to play the greatest of all his parts, that of " liberator of the territory."   He declined, after Sedan, to become a member of the Government of National Defence ; but he voluntarily undertook diplomatic journeys to Great Britain, Russia, Austria, and Italy, on behalf of France—a self-imposed mission in which he was unsuccessful, but by which he obtained the gratitude of his countrymen.   He was largely instrumental in securing for his country that armistice which permitted the holding of a national assembly with a view to the negotiation of a peace.   Twenty constituencies chose him as their deputy.   Electing to sit for Paris, he was made head of the provisional government.   He had great difficulty in persuading the colleagues of the Assembly, and his countrymen generally, to agree to peace on terms that were practically dictated by Germany.   But he succeeded ; peace was voted March 1, 1871.   No sooner had he accomplished this task than he was face to face with the sanguinary madness of the Commune.   But this difficulty also he set himself to surmount with characteristic energy, and succeeded.   When the seat of government was once more removed from Versailles to Paris, Thiers was formally elected (August 30) President of the French Republic.   He held office only till 1873, but during this brief period he was probably of greater service to his country than at any previous time in his life.   He was mainly instrumental in securing the withdrawal of the Germans from France and the payment of the war indemnity, and in placing both the army and the civil service on a more satisfactory footing.   But in course of time the gratitude of the country exhausted itself, and Thiers, who was old-fashioned in many of his opinions, and as opinionative as he was old-fashioned, did not make any new friends.   He was specially detested by the Extreme Left, whose chief, Gambetta, he styled a *fou furieux*.   As a result, a coalition of Reactionaries and Radicals was formed expressly, as it seemed, to harass him, and even in the beginning of 1872 he tendered his resignation.   It was not accepted ; and his opponents for a time suspended their intrigues.   They were revived, however, in 1873, and resolved themselves into a resolute effort to limit the powers of the president. This Thiers stoutly resisted.   He made an appeal to the country, but this course did not increase the strength of his following.   Finally, what he interpreted as a vote of no confidence was carried (May 24) by a majority of sixteen.   He resigned, and his place was taken by Marshal MacMahon.   He lived four years longer, and never ceased to take an interest in politics.   In 1877 he took an active part in bringing about the fall of the ministry presided over by the Duc de Broglie.   He now leaned to the side of the Left, and was reconciled to Gambetta, and he might once again have played a prominent part in politics had he not died of apoplexy on September 3, 1877, at St. Germain en Laye.   He has not left behind him the memory either of a very great statesman, or of a very great historian.   But he was a man of indomitable courage, and his patriotism, if narrow and marred with Chauvinism, was deep and genuine.   He was, perhaps, the most successful of the large class of journalist-politicians that France has produced, and that he was at least a personal power in literature was evidenced by the great influence which he wielded in the Academy, of which he became a member in 1834.

LÉON GAMBETTA

(1838–1882)

LÉON MICHEL GAMBETTA was born at Cahors on April 3, 1838.   His father was a tradesman dealing in crockery ; his mother's maiden name was Massabie.   Léon's grandfather was a Genoese, who emigrated to France at the beginning of this century ; and as his name signifies, in the dialect of Genoa, a liquid measure of two quarts capacity, it has been supposed that it was conferred upon one of his forefathers as a sobriquet.   Léon Gambetta's grandfather was a poor man of no education, and his only son, Léon's father, thought he had done very well for himself when he set up a shop with the small dowry brought him by his wife, Mlle. Massabie. The mother of Léon died while he was a child, and he was indebted for

his early teaching to his maternal aunt and to her brother, a priest, who held a small benefice in a village near Cahors. It was at first intended that Léon should follow his father's trade; but, as he was a boy very apt at learning and fond of books, his uncle and aunt decided that it would be better to put him at the seminary, with a view to his ultimately taking holy orders. Léon's father does not seem to have much liked this scheme, for he had no second son who could succeed to his business; but he had a great love for his bright-witted boy, and having conceived a high respect for his talents, yielded to the pleasing idea that he would some day become an ornament to the Church. This belief may be explained by the fact that Léon was, as a child, ardently religious. When twelve years old he wrote an ode dedicated to his "patron, St. Léon, and to all the popes called Léon," and this composition was printed in the Catholic journal of the diocese. In after-years some of his political enemies tried to get hold of a copy, but failed, and published a spurious one which they gave out for his.

The career of Léon Gambetta must continue to exercise over young advocates and journalists the same kind of fascination as that of Napoleon I. does over young officers; and, indeed, the fact that Bonaparte and Gambetta were both of Italian origin, and came to sudden and great power while they were very young, was often quoted to draw a parallel between the two. But there is this difference between Bonaparte and Gambetta, that whereas the latter made his mark in life later by some three or four years than the former, brilliant destinies were prophesied for him by others besides his relations, when he was still a child. While Bonaparte was a pupil at the school of Brienne, his masters predicted that he would make a poor officer, because he had no aptitude for mathematics; when Gambetta was at the seminary, his tutors foretold that he would make a great figure in life, "but never," they regretfully added, "as a churchman." The boy began well, but he had evidently no vocation for the strict discipline of the Church; he was too disputatious, not meek enough about taking blows without returning them, and in short, too headstrong, Anticipating the judgment which M. Grévy passed upon him when he was thirty-three years old, his ecclesiastical masters reported of him that he was *un esprit rebelle*, *turbulent*, and they advised his removal to another school.

Young Gambetta was accordingly sent to the *lycée*—that is, the lay public

school—of Cahors, and here he immediately won golden opinions by his clever-
ness, his industry, and the happy vivacity of his character.   One of the half-yearly
bulletins of the *lycée*, which has been preserved in his family, records that he
was "passionate without being vindictive, and proud without arrogance."   In
time he became the best Latin scholar at the school, and the most proficient in
French composition.   When he was in his sixteenth year, however, an accident,
which destroyed his left eye, quelled for a time the exuberance of his character
and suddenly gave a new direction to his studies.   Fearing lest he should lose his
sight altogether, he set himself to learn the alphabet for the blind, in order that
he might read in books with raised letters; he also applied himself to the study
of music and the violin.   During a whole year he was forbidden to open a book.

From Cahors Gambetta went to Paris to study law, and he quickly drew the
attention of the Imperial police upon himself by acting as ringleader in those demonstrations which the students of the Latin Quarter were accustomed to make
in time of public excitement.   Peaceful demonstrations they always were, because
the police would stand nothing like rioting, but it was something to march at the
head of a procession carrying wreaths to the tomb of a Republican, or to lead
cabals for hissing off the stage of the Théâtre Français or the Odéon pieces by
unpopular writers, like M. Edmond About (for in those days M. About was a
Bonapartist).

Gambetta's first public speech was delivered in 1861, in defence of the Marquis Le Guillois, a nobleman of facetious humor, who edited a comic newspaper
called *Le Hanneton*.   He was seized with unexpected nervousness as he began,
but before he had stammered out a dozen sentences he was stopped by the presiding judge, who told him mildly that no big words were required in a cause
which only involved a fine of 100 francs—"all the less so," added he, "as your
client is acquitted."

Gambetta used to say after this that it took him years to recover from the effect of the judge's quiet snub.   Like many other young men of talent, he had
gone into court expecting to carry everything before him, and had found that
the art of forensic pleading is not to be acquired without practice.   He did practise most diligently, and the speeches—some thirty in all—which he delivered in
unimportant cases during the next seven years, were conspicuous for their avoid-
ance of rhetorical flourish.   Adolphe Crémieux had cautioned him that the secret of oratory lies in mastering the subject of one's discourse.   " Don't try gym-
nastic feats until you have a firm platform to spring from "—a maxim which a
conceited young man, impatient of results, might have despised, but which com-
mended itself to an ambitious man who felt that, although a chance comes to
all, it is an important point to be prepared for the chance when it does come.
A plutocrat once asked Horace Vernet to " do him a little thing in pencil " for
his album.   Vernet did the little thing and asked 1,000 francs for it.   " But it
only took you five minutes to draw," exclaimed the man of wealth.   " Yes, but
it took me thirty years to learn to do it in five minutes," replied Vernet.   And
so Gambetta, when someone remarked that he was very lucky in having con-

quered renown by a single speech, broke out impetuously, " I was years preparing that speech—twenty times I wanted to deliver it, but did not feel that I had it here (touching his head), though it palpitated here (thumping his breast) as if it would break my heart."

The speech in question was delivered on November 17, 1868, before the notorious Judge Delesvaux (who has been called the Jeffreys of the Second Empire), in defence of Louis Charles Delescluze, editor of the *Réveil*. The *Réveil* had started a subscription for erecting a monument to the memory of the Representative Baudin, who was killed at the *coup-d'état* of 1851, and the Government unwisely instituted a prosecution against the editor. It was late in the afternoon when the case was called on after a number of others, but the sixth chamber was crowded with journalists and barristers, as it always was on Fridays, when Delesvaux—a man with hawk-like features and a flaming complexion—would sit "tearing up newspaper articles with beak and talons," as Émile de Girardin said of him. Just before Gambetta rose, Delesvaux observed, " I suppose you have not much to say ; so it will hardly be worth while to have the gas lighted." " Never mind the gas, sir, I will throw light enough on this affair," answered Gambetta ; and it was amid the laughter produced by this joke that he began. His genius found vent that day, and he spoke from first to last without a halt. Reviewing his client's case, he brought Napoleon III. himself to book, and recalled the circumstances under which Baudin had died, " defending that Republican Constitution which President Louis Bonaparte, in contempt of his oath, had violated." At this, Judge Delesvaux half rose in his seat and endeavored to stop the speaker, but a positive roar from the whole crowd in court forced him to sit down. It was a sign of the approaching political earthquake that Delesvaux should have sat down in that way, for he was a man of great resolution ; but he must have felt then as if the earth were trembling under him. So Gambetta continued to speak, denouncing with unimaginable energy the tyrannies and turpitudes of the reign which had confiscated all the liberties of France, till at last he concluded with this magnificent peroration, which was rendered most solemn by the increasing darkness of the court and the intense attentive silence of the audience : " In every country but this you see the people commemorate as a holiday the date which brought the reigning dynasty to the throne. You alone are ashamed of the day which gave you a blood-stained crown—the December 2d when Baudin died ! Well, that day which you reject, we Republicans will keep holy. It shall be the day of mourning for our martyrs and the festival of our hopes ! "

When Gambetta left the court after this, it was felt by all who had heard him that he was the coming man of the Republican party ; and next day opposition journals of every shade of opinion, from one end of France to the other, acclaimed him as a future leader.

Within the next two years the Republican party made such rapid strides that to regain his prestige the French emperor felt that a glorious war was necessary. The leader of the moderate reformers, M. Ollivier, was won over, and war forced upon Prussia. Gambetta and the Republicans felt that they had every cause for fear when matters had taken this turn. Relying upon Marshal Lebœuf's assurances that "everything was ready," they saw the prospect of a short sensational campaign like that against Austria in 1859, to be followed by some high-handed stroke of home policy that would sweep most of them into prison or exile. Gambetta could not refrain from bitterly upbraiding Ollivier. "You will find that you have been fooled in all this," he said; "for when the war is over you will be thrown aside like a squeezed orange." "I think my fate will be a happier one than yours, unless you mend you manners," answered Ollivier dryly. Three weeks after this, however, everything was changed. The imperial armies had been beaten at Woerth and Forbach; the Ollivier cabinet had fallen amid popular execration (hardly deserved); and Gambetta, forced by circumstances into a position of great influence, received a private visit from Madame Bazaine, who prayed him to agitate that her husband might be appointed as the commander-in-chief of the armies. Gambetta was too sincerely patriotic to feel any partisan satisfaction at the reverse which Napoleon III.'s armies had suffered; and in stirring up the Republicans in the Chamber and in the press to clamor for the appointment of Bazaine, he believed he was urging the claims of a competent soldier who was being kept from the chief command solely by dynastic jealousies. He was to learn, a couple of months later, how much he had been mistaken in his estimate of Bazaine's talents and rectitude of purpose; and, indeed, Bazaine's conduct toward Gambetta and the Republicans from first to last was the more inexplicable, as it was unquestionably owing to their agitation that he was placed in the high position which he had coveted.

During the three weeks between Forbach and Sedan, Gambetta had to take rather exciting precautions to insure his own safety. He was aware that the Empress-Regent's advisers were urging her to have the leaders of the opposition arrested, and he felt pretty certain that this course would be adopted if the news of a victory arrived. He used to sleep in a different house every night, and never ventured abroad unattended or without firearms. His position was one of great difficulty, for agents of the Internationale made overtures to him with a view to promote an insurrection in Paris, and he forfeited the confidence of these fanatics by declining to abet their plans. Gambetta was so little desirous of establishing a republic by revolution that, even when the tidings arrived on the night of September 3d of the emperor's surrender at Sedan, his chief concern was as to how he could get the deposition of Napoleon III. and the Empress-Regent effected by lawful methods. He hastened to M. Thiers's house, and asked him whether he would accept the presidency of a provisional government? Thiers, sitting up in bed, said he was willing, provided that this office was conferred upon him by the Corps Législatif.

Accordingly, Gambetta spent all the morning of Sunday, September 4th, whipping up members of the majority, and trying to persuade them to go down to the Palais Bourbon and elect a new government. But he found most of these gentlemen anxious to get off to the different railway stations as soon as possible in cabs. Going to the Chamber himself toward one o'clock, he was carried through the doors by the surging mob which invaded the palace, and in half an hour he shouted himself quite hoarse in adjuring the crowds from the tribune to let the Assembly deliberate in peace.   But while he was literally croaking in his attempts to make the people hear reason, news was brought to him that M. Blanqui and some other adventurous spirits, taking time by the forelock, had repaired to the Hôtel de Ville, and were setting up a government of their own.   Upon this, Gambetta precipitately left the palace, jumped into a victoria, and drove to the Hôtel de Ville, amid a mob of several thousands of persons who escorted him, cheering all the way.   Before five o'clock the deputies for Paris, with the exception of M. Thiers, had constituted themselves into a government, which, at the suggestion of M. Rochefort, took the name of Government of the National Defence ; and M. Gambetta received the appointment of Minister of the Interior.   It may be remarked in passing that on the day after these events, Judge Delesvaux, fearing, perhaps needlessly, that some of the triumphant Republicans whom he had so often punished would wreak vengeance upon him, committed suicide.   On the other hand, Gambetta's client in the Baudin affair—L. C. Delescluze—came to him on the morning of September 5th, and reproached him with much asperity for not having caused the empress to be arrested.   "We want no rose-water Republicans to rule us," said this honest, but gloomy, zealot, who was shot a few months later during the extermination of the Commune.

The siege of Paris brought M. Gambetta to the most romantic part of his career.   The National Defence Government had delegated two of their members, MM. Crémieux and Glaiz-Bizoin, to go to Tours and govern the provinces ; but being both elderly men of weak health, they were hardly up to their work ; and early in October M. Gambetta was ordered by his colleagues to join them. He had to leave Paris in a balloon, and in going over the German lines nearly met with misadventure, through the balloon sinking till it came within range of some marksmen's rifles.   He reached Tours in safety, however, and set to work at once with marvellous activity to organize resistance against the invasion.   He was ably seconded by M. de Freycinet, and between them these two did all that was humanly possible to perform ; but from the first their task was one of formidable difficulty, and all chances of repelling the Germans from French soil vanished after the shameful capitulation of Bazaine at Metz.

Nevertheless, all who saw M. Gambetta during his proconsulate at Tours will remember with what a splendid energy he worked, how sincerely hopeful he was, and—this must not be forgotten—how uniformly generous and genial.   Invested with despotic powers, he never once abused them to molest an opponent.

In his public harangues, both at Tours and Bordeaux (whither the Provisional Government repaired in December, being driven southward by the German advance), he somehow always managed to electrify his hearers.   He spoke from balconies, railway carriages, curb-stones ; wherever he went the people demanded a speech of him, and his words never failed to cheer, while they conquered for him a wide popularity.   Indeed, Gambetta so deluded himself while diffusing

THE ENROLLMENT OF VOLUNTEERS, 1870

BY

ALFRED PAUL DE RICHEMONT

LA PATRIE EST EN DANGER

RICHEMONT

Photogravure Ludovic Baschet

hope and combativeness into others, that when, after a five months' siege, Paris capitulated, he still persisted in thinking that resistance was possible, and rather than take any part in the national surrender he gave in his resignation. He was by that time fairly worn out, and had to go to St. Sebastian to recruit his health. It was alleged that he went there so as to avoid taking any side in the civil war between the Parliament of Versailles and the Commune; but after the Communist Government had been at work a fortnight, and when the impracticability of its aims was fully disclosed, he took care to let it be known that he was on the side of the National Assembly.

M. Thiers did not understand Gambetta as Gambetta understood him, or he would not have resigned in 1873, saying that the Republicans were making his work too difficult. When Marshal MacMahon succeeded to the Presidency it looked as if the Republic were doomed, and nothing but M. Gambetta's wonderful suppleness and tact during the sessions of 1874–75 could have saved it. He had to keep himself in the background, to use an Italian astuteness in explaining away the blunders of his followers; and when this would not do he had to use violent language, which should frighten timid doctrinaire Orleanists with prospects of popular risings in which he would take the lead. His greatest triumphs were earned when, by dint of superhuman coaxing in the lobbies, he got the Republic proclaimed as the Government of France (in 1875, on M. Wallon's motion) by a majority of one vote; and again when, at the first election for life senators, he concluded a treaty with the Legitimists, and by giving them a dozen seats, secured fifty for the Republicans and ousted the Orleanists altogether.

From this time the Republic was founded with at least temporary security, and although a coalition of all the reactionary parties rallied against it in 1877, when M. Jules Simon's ministry was dismissed, and when the Duc de Broglie was induced to try to destroy the new form of government by Cæsarist methods, yet there was never any real danger that the Republic would succumb. From the day when M. Thiers died, M. Gambetta stood guarding it like a sentinel. Just before the general election of 1877, an emissary was sent to him from the De Broglie-Fourtou Ministry, requesting him for his own sake not to make a speech against Marshal MacMahon. He laughed when he heard that he would be prosecuted if he made the speech. He was twirling a cigarette, and laid down a copy of the *Revue des Deux Mondes* in which he had been reading an essay on Mr. Gladstone's speeches about the Irish Church. "Tell the Prime Minister," he said, "that I will speak from a pedestal if I can, but if not, from a housetop. In one way or another, my voice shall reach further than his, and so long as I have a drop of blood to shed the Republic shall not fall." M. Gambetta was sentenced to four months' imprisonment for the speech in which he said that Marshal MacMahon would have to yield to the popular will or resign, but before he could be put into jail the De Broglie cabinet had ceased to exist. Marshal MacMahon's resignation in 1879 was the obviously natural consequence of the complete victory which the Republicans gained in 1877; but it was greatly to M. Gambetta's credit that he quietly tolerated during fifteen months the presi-

24

dency of the gallant soldier who had never been his friend. When urged to agitate for the marshal's overthrow, he always said, "It will do the Republic good if its first president serves his term of office quietly to the end."

Had Gambetta lived till 1885 he would probably have been the next president of the Republic he had established and preserved; but it was not to be. His work was done. He died December 31, 1882.

BENJAMIN DISRAELI*

By Harriet Prescott Spofford

(1804–1881)

Since the days of Richelieu, there has been no such picturesque figure in the history of civilization as that of Benjamin Disraeli.

Although his father, Isaac Disraeli, was in much more than easy circumstances and had made a literary reputation, he was under the social disadvantage that was the portion of a Jew, and his mother, Maria Basevi, was of the same despised race.

Their son was born in London, December 21, 1804, and his birth was attended by the usual Jewish ceremonies in the Spanish synagogue. When he was thirteen years old his father formally withdrew from the Jewish congregation, and the children were baptized into the Christian faith, Benjamin's godfather being Sharon Turner. The boy was early seen to have rare talents, and he was already an immense reader in his father's vast library. It was decided to give him an exact education and send him to one of the large schools, where he should have the advantage of discipline and the opportunity of desirable friendships; but the prejudice against his birth was an obstacle—life would have been made impossible by the indelicacy and cruelty of the high-born and Christian lads. He was finally sent to a school where he found himself the superior of his masters; even there he was taunted with his birth; and he was taken home to work with his father and with tutors, where, conscious of his powers and full of lively ambition, he studied twelve hours a day, and made himself the master of a vast and varied information. At seventeen he entered a solicitor's office, and while working there for three years, entered at Lincoln's Inn, he evinced an ability that promised him great eminence. It was not, however, precisely the sort of eminence that he desired, the strifes and achievements of political life being more to his taste.

He had the qualities which fitted him for that life, the "taking arts" and accomplishments; he was a fine linguist; he had a wonderfully well-stored memory, great self-confidence, self-respect, and assurance; his manners were easy, and he had all social graces and refinements; his face was singularly handsome, and remarkable through its pallor, the depth of its black eyes, and delicacy of its chiselled features framed in night-dark curls; he was a master of the art of self-defence, a hard and fine rider, and he was equipped with wit, sarcasm, poetical perception, keen reason, unbounded ambition, and undaunted courage.

He dressed in his early years in a manner that has been described as extraordinary, but which was the manner of the young men of the period, of D'Orsay and of Bulwer, at the time when Tennyson called the latter a band-box. Later his dress was more negligent, although always neat and fine.

He was on pleasant terms with the distinguished people whom he met at his father's table, and was everywhere sought in society, when, at twenty, he began his career by the publication of "Vivian Grey," a novel, unlike anything that had been written, bristling with point and sally, and full of daring portraiture, and which made him immediately famous.

His health, however, now gave way, a trouble in his head making it necessary to suspend work; and after a tour of Europe he remained for two or three years at Bradenham, near High Wycombe, his father's country-house, happy in the companionship of his father and mother, and his thoroughly congenial sister Sarah; passionately fond of country life, and during the time producing a novel, "The Young Duke," and three shorter works, "Popanilla," "The Infernal Marriage," and "Ixion in Heaven," gay and brilliant satires, sparkling with epigram and with beauty, and destined to live with the English language and English history.

In company with Mr. Meredith, to whom his sister was promised in marriage, he journeyed for the next two years through the south of Europe and the East. Spain was among the first of his objective points, in the proud memory of his descent from the Spanish nobles who, driven out of Spain in the fifteenth century, went over to Venice, and changed the name belonging to the House of Dara to that of D'Israeli, the sons of Israel—a cognomen never borne by any other family—and remained there for two hundred years, going to England only when, Venice falling into decay, it was necessary to go where they could live in safety. He wrote the account of his travels to his sister in a series of affectionate and light-hearted letters, which charmingly betray his own personality, and which are full of the most vivid pictures of Malta, Corfu, Albania, the Plains of Troy, Turkey—which was kind to his race when a cruel and unreasoning world showed it only malignant hate, and which he regarded with the gratitude that never forsakes a Jew; Cyprus, the advantage of whose possession he early recognized; Egypt, whose destinies were afterward in his hand; and Jerusalem, the holy city of his people, his impressions of which "Tancred" afterward embodied, together with a foreshadowing of much of his policy in the East. The journey made him acquainted with the theatre of his intentions, and with the prepossessions which it gave or fostered, doubtless had a great influence upon his life and action. The close of the journey was darkened by the death of his companion, for whom his sister mourned as long as she lived.

After his return home he wrote a new novel, " Contarini Fleming," a wonderful and poetical study of temperament, which Milman pronounced the equal of " Childe Harold," which Goethe and Heine and Beckford, the author of " Vathek," praised with delighted warmth. The " Wondrous Tale of Alroy," also, published a little later, with " The Rise of Iskander," Beckford found stirring and full of intensity and charm.

In 1832 Disraeli offered himself as an independent candidate for the borough of High Wycombe. The Government of course defeated him ; and not until after several hot contests during the next few years, did he gain his end, taking his seat, then at the age of thirty-three, in Queen Victoria's first Parliament. The character of the struggle at these elections may be inferred from O'Connell's declaration in one of them, that in all probability this " Disraeli was the heir-at-law of the blasphemous thief that died on the cross." Disraeli challenged O'Connell's son, who failed to accept the challenge. But Disraeli never cherished a grudge ; and only three weeks after he entered Parliament he risked his seat there by a pointed statement of the misgovernment of Ireland. Neither did O'Connell bear malice, and he said of one of Disraeli's speeches, somewhat later, that "it was all excellent except the peroration, and that was matchless." Not only in O'Connell's case was this impossibility in Disraeli's nature of doing anything ignoble shown ; he secured, when in power, a life-pension to the widow and children of the artist Leech, who had for half a lifetime showered him with the cruel ridicule of the caricaturist ; and he offered the Grand Cross of the Bath, and a life-income suitable to the maintenance of its dignity, to Carlyle, who had pursued him now with contempt and now with malignity. In the intervals of the electoral contests a series of letters to *The Times*, filled with biting sarcasm, under the signature of " Runnymede ;" a novel —" Henrietta Temple ;" a "Vindication of the British Constitution," dedicated to Lord Lyndhurst ; a contrasting presentation of the characters of Byron and Shelley, in the form of romance, under the title of " Venetia," sufficiently occupied Disraeli's time. He was, meanwhile, in the vortex of gay social life, a member of the Carlton Club, the friend of Count D'Orsay, Lady Blessington, Mrs. Norton, Lady Dufferin, Bulwer, Tom Moore, Lady Morgan, of Lyndhurst, of the public men and of the men of fashion, and he was courted by princes and pretty women. He had come to Parliament prepared as few or none before him, with coolness, courage, wit, and eloquence, and with a far-seeing sagacity that enabled him to make the most of something like the gift of prophecy. But he was handicapped with the fact of his race, with his debts, which, although he was not personally extravagant or at all self-indulgent, had become heavy, with the absence of a constituency or a popular cause ; and having no landed property, nor belonging even remotely to any great family, he was looked upon both by Whig and Tory as more or less of an adventurer.

Like almost all young men, his first preferences and professions were for reform. But brought face to face with responsibility he modified his opinions; and the great power and place that he ultimately won, were won through the originality, the thought, the force, and the independence that dared act without reference to his own advantage, and the splendid courage that was undismayed by any odds. Although he could have acquired office in the earlier years by withholding open expression of his opinions, he preferred his freedom; and although always in want of money, he never made a penny by means of the place or the power that he won, or even through the legitimate opportunities which these offered.

His first speech in Parliament was attended by peculiar circumstances. A number of the ruder members of the opposition were determined that he should not be heard, and they drowned every sentence in derisive cheers and mocking yells. Disraeli bore it with dignity, but as it was impossible to proceed in the noisy and barbarous din, he closed by saying that he had begun several times many things, and had succeeded at last; and then in a tone that resounded even above the clamor, for he had at all times a sonorous and impressive voice, he cried, " I will sit down now. But the time will come when you will hear me !" Of this speech Peel said it was anything but failure; and Sir John Campbell, the Attorney-General, assured him that there was a lively desire in the opposing party to hear him, but they were hindered by a coterie over whom they had no control. In describing the scene, in a letter to his sister that night, with great frankness, as disastrous, Disraeli signed himself, " Yours in very good spirits." When he spoke, a week afterward, he commanded the attention of the House.

Disraeli had always declared that no government should have his support which did not seek to improve the condition of the poor; and as he looked at the British constitution and social construction, he believed that the Conservatives were the best able to accomplish this end. Because he was a Jew he was none the less an Englishman, and he had the true interests of the United Kingdom at heart. He held that the strength of England lay in the land, and he supported the corn laws from stern principle. " It will be an exception to the principles which seem hitherto to have ruled society," he exclaimed, " if you can maintain the success at which you aim, without the possession of that permanence and stability which the territorial principle alone can afford. Although you may for a moment flourish after their destruction, although your ports may be filled with shipping, your factories smoke on every plain, and your forges flame in every city, I see no reason why you should form an exception to that which the page of history has mournfully recorded, that you should not fade like Tyrian dye, and moulder like the Venetian palaces."

He was already, in 1839, to a certain extent, a power in Parliament, launching the shafts of his sarcasm alike at the Chancellor of the Exchequer or an Under Secretary; and in this year he published his tragedy of "Count Alarcos," and married Mrs. Wyndham Lewis, the wealthy widow of his friend and colleague, several years his senior, but through thirty years his invaluable friend and *confidante*. In dedicating "Sybil" to her, he said, "I would inscribe this work to one whose noble spirit and gentle nature ever prompt her to sympathize with the suffering; to one whose sweet voice has often encouraged and whose taste and judgment have ever guided its pages, the most severe of critics, but a perfect wife." Her devotion to him was illustrated by her behavior one night when, on the eve of an exciting session, she drove with him to Palace Yard, and her hand being crushed in the carriage-door, she gave no sign, lest it should disturb his train of thought and lessen his power in the approaching debate, and endured her agony without blenching till he had left her. He rewarded such devotion in kind, his happiest hours were those spent in her society, and perhaps the proudest moment of his life was that when, the Queen having offered him a peerage, he declined it for himself but accepted it for his wife, and made her Viscountess Beaconsfield in her own right.

Immediately upon their marriage Mr. Disraeli travelled with his wife for a couple of months on the continent; and returning to London he received the congratulations of Peel, Wellington, and others, and began to entertain the party chiefs; he dined privately with Louis Philippe in Paris, shook hands with the King of Hanover in London, and in every way took his social and personal position firmly. In Parliament he crossed swords with Palmerston, refused his support to Peel's Coercion Bill in relation to Ireland, characterizing it as one of those measures which to introduce was degrading, and to oppose disgraceful; later he maintained that as revolution was the only remedy for the wrongs of Ireland, and as her connection with England prevented revolution, therefore it was the duty of England to effect by policy what revolution would effect by force; and as he had defended the Chartist petition, so in turn, when the Eastern Question came up, he defended Turkey; in all this making it supremely plain that he never was the one to truckle to rank or authority. He was the head of the small party of Young Englanders; he was feared and respected by both the larger parties; and the Commons, whose assemblage he had scornfully proclaimed a thing of past history, if they did not choose, had presently to accept him for their leader.

Henry Hope, entertaining a number of their friends at Deepdene, urged Disraeli to treat the questions of common interest in a literary form, and the powerful works—rather treatises than novels—"Coningsby" and "Sybil," appeared; and these were followed by "Tancred," in which the curious reader will find much of Disraeli's Eastern policy indicated. These three books the author regarded as a trilogy upon English politics, principles, and possibilities.

As a debater, then and always, Disraeli was keen, ready, and unanswerable; as a satirist, swift, subtle, and finished. His epigrams were among the "jewels that on the stretched forefinger of all time sparkle forever." It was he that said "Destiny is our will, and our will is nature." At another time he said, "The critics—they are those who have failed in literature and in art." When Prince

Napoleon was slain he exclaimed, "A very remarkable people the Zulus: they defeat our generals, they convert our bishops, they have settled the fate of a great European dynasty." Every one remembers the startling sentence in which he condemned Mr. Gladstone's Irish policy of 1868: "We have legalized confiscation; we have consecrated sacrilege; we have condoned treason." And his power of picturesque mockery appears in a speech made, in 1872, immediately before the downfall of the Gladstone ministry: "As I sat opposite the Treasury bench the ministers reminded me of those marine landscapes not unusual on the coasts of South America. You behold a range of exhausted volcanoes. Not a flame flickers on a single pallid crest. But the situation is still dangerous. There are occasional earthquakes, and ever and anon the dark rumbling of the sea." His attacks on Peel have been pronounced to be among the most remarkable speeches in the annals of the British Legislature. In 1849, at which period also he wrote the biography of his father and the memoir of his friend Lord George Bentinck, he was the recognized leader of the Conservatives. When Peel was overthrown, Disraeli, who had overthrown him, after a brief period, succeeded to his place.

It was not with cordiality that the Conservatives submitted to Disraeli's direction. He had carried himself in relation to them with an unsurpassed independence. He was of a people whom they held in contempt, and whose admission to Parliament he had enforced. In his speeches he had spared none of them. He had no friend at court, and he was still very young. But there was no help for it—he was master of the situation, and master of them. He was now thrice Chancellor of the Exchequer; and for a quarter of a century he led the opposition in the House of Commons, except in the brief intervals when he was identified with the Government. In leading the opposition he was never an obstructionist; and he lent his aid to every generous measure, such as the reduction of the hours of labor, the protection of factory children, the improvement of the homes of the poor, the extension of the suffrage. He refused English interference on the side of the South during the Civil War in the United States of America; he hindered disastrous hostilities with France at the time of Louis Napoleon's *coup-d'état;* he would have prevented the Crimean War had it been possible; and he would not allow retaliation in kind for the Sepoy atrocities. He did the most and the best with his opportunities. His policy was always to develop and sustain English character. "There is no country," he said in a remarkable warning to the House, "at the present moment that exists under the same circumstances and under the same conditions as the people of this realm. You have an ancient, powerful, and richly endowed Church, and perfect religious liberty. You have unbroken order and complete freedom. You have landed estates as large as the Romans, combined with a commercial enterprise such as Carthage and Venice united never equalled. And you must remember that this peculiar country, with these strong contrasts, is not governed by force. It is governed by a most singular series of traditionary influences, which generation after generation cherishes and preserves, because it knows that they embalm custom and represent law.   And with this you have created the greatest empire of modern times.   You have amassed a capital of fabulous amount.   You have devised and sustained a system of credit still more marvellous, and you have established a scheme so vast and complicated of labor and industry that the history of the world affords no parallel to it.   And these mighty creations are out of all proportion to the essential and indigenous elements and resources of the country.   If you destroy that state of society, remember this : *England cannot begin again.*"

In religion Disraeli accepted Christianity fully—but as a completion of the Hebrew revelation.   He coupled in thought and word "the sacred heights of Sinai and of Calvary."   He was proud of his great people, and never hesitated to declare his pride.   "All the north of Europe worship a Jew," he said, "and all the south of Europe worship a Jew's mother."   In spite of the fact that he was an Asiatic by nature, he despised what he called the pagan ceremonies of the ritualists, and distrusted what he felt to be the atheistic tendency of science.

Shortly after his father's death, Mr. Disraeli had purchased with his paternal inheritance the manor of Hughenden, near Bradenham, in whose park his wife erected a monument to his father ; and there, in the intervals of public business, he found quiet and enjoyment with his peacocks and swans and owls, his gardening, his tenantry.   His books brought him in great sums of money ; a friend, Mrs. Brydges Willyams, of Torquay, after twelve years of romantic intimacy with him and his wife, bequeathed him a fortune, and lies buried by the side of himself and Lady Beaconsfield at Hughenden.   His circumstances were easy, his fame was assured, and when he went down to Parliament for the first time after he became Prime Minister, the crowds outside cheered him to the echo, the crowds within took up the acclaim, and the House that once had silenced him with derisive mockery, hailed with wild welcome this man who, without money, without birth, without support, had made himself, by force of will, courage, genius, loyalty, and truth, the ruler of the British Empire.

While he was again in opposition Mr. Disraeli took occasion to write "Lothair," a precise portraiture of the British aristocracy and a clear presentation of its relation to the Church, the spirit of revolution, the intrigues of the ultramontanes, the simplicity of true religion ; every page splendid with wit and with picturesque charm.   During another period of enforced leisure he wrote "Endymion," in which there are some slight autobiographical features.

Succeeded by Mr. Gladstone as prime minister, a half-dozen years later Disraeli was again at the helm.   The Eastern question was then one of passionate interest ; and when Russia was dictating terms of peace with the Ottoman, Mr. Disraeli insisted on their revision at a Conference of all the Powers, held at Berlin, which he attended in person, and where he obliged Russia to yield, and won a great diplomatic victory.*   He returned to London, said Mr. Froude, "in a

---

* In the painting of the Berlin Conference by Werner, Prince Gortschakoff is seated at the left with his hand on Disraeli's arm.   Prince Bismarck in the foreground is shaking hands with Count Schuvaloff, while Count Andrassy stands beside them.   Lord Russell is seated a little farther to the right ; behind him on the other side of the table is Lord Salisbury.   The figure on the extreme right is Mehemet Ali.

blaze of glory, bearing peace with honor." He was made Earl of Beaconsfield, and given the Garter ; and before he went into retirement again, after the nation had revived its interest in imperialism, he had acquired the mastery of the Suez Canal, and he had annexed Cyprus, and, by giving the queen the additional title of Empress of India, this child of the Orient had made of Great Britain an Oriental empire. He had ruled the country for six consecutive years when he next went into retirement. He died shortly afterward, from the effect of a severe cold, aggravating an attack of gout, on April 19, 1881.

In public or in private Disraeli never did a dishonorable action. He never attacked the weak or the defenceless, but singled out the proudest adversary. He never held malice. His impulses were always the most generous, his ideas and his purposes of the largest. He desired in all things the good of his country, and he sought it by what seemed to him, whether or not he was mistaken, the surest and loftiest ways.

Harriet P. Spofford.

WILLIAM EWART GLADSTONE

By Justin McCarthy

(BORN 1809)

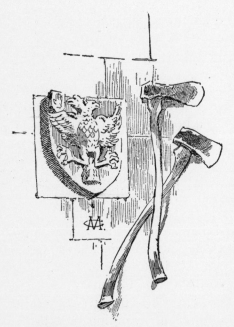

WILLIAM EWART GLADSTONE, statesman, orator, and author, was born in Rodney Street, Liverpool, on December 29, 1809. He is the fourth son of Sir John Gladstone (1764–1851), a well-known, and it might almost be said a famous, Liverpool merchant, who sat for some years in Parliament, and was a devoted friend and supporter of George Canning. Mr. Gladstone is of Scotch descent, on both sides, and has declared more than once in a public speech that the blood that runs in his veins is exclusively Scottish. He was educated at Eton and at Christ Church, Oxford. He became a student at Oxford in 1829, and graduated as a double first-class, in 1831. He had distinguished himself greatly as a speaker in the Oxford Union Debating Society, and had before that time written much in the *Eton Miscellany*, which indeed he helped to found. He appears to have begun his career as a strong opponent of all advanced measures of political reform. In the Oxford Union he proposed a vote of censure on the government of Lord Grey for introducing the great Reform Bill which was carried in 1832, and on the Duke of Wellington, because of his having yielded to the claims for Catholic emancipation. He also opposed a motion in favor of immediate emancipation of the slaves in the West Indian islands. He soon became known as a young man of promise, who would be able to render good service to the Conservative party in the great struggle which seemed likely to be forced upon them—a struggle, as many thought, for their very existence. It was a time of intense political emotion. Passion and panic alike prevailed. The first great "leap in the dark" had been taken; the Reform Bill was carried, the sceptre of power had passed away from the aristocracy and the privileged ranks to the middle and lower middle classes. The Conservative party were looking eagerly out for young men of promise to stiffen their ranks in the new parliament, the first elected under the Reform Bill, the first which the middle class had their due share in creating; the first in which such cities as Manchester and Liverpool and Birmingham were allowed to have representation.

Mr. Gladstone was invited to contest the burgh of Newark in the Conservative interest, and he had the support of the great Newcastle family. He stood for Newark, and he was elected. He delivered his maiden speech on a subject connected with the great movement for the emancipation of the West Indian slaves; but he seems to have confined himself mainly to a defence of the manner in which his father's estates were managed, the course of the debate having brought out some charge against the management of the elder Gladstone's possessions in one of the West Indian islands. The new orator appears to have made a decided impression on the House of Commons. His manner, his voice, his diction, his fluency were alike the subject of praise. Mr. Gladstone evidently continued to impress the House of Commons with a sense of his great parliamentary capacity. We get at this fact rather obliquely; for we do not hear of his creating any great sensation in debate; and to this day some very old members of the House insist that for a long time he was generally regarded as merely a fluent speaker, who talked like one reading from a book. But on the other hand, we find that he is described by Macaulay, in 1839, as "the rising hope" of the "stern and unbending Tories," and the whole tone of Macaulay's essay—a criticism of Gladstone's first serious attempt at authorship, his book on the relations between church and state—shows that the critic treats the author as a young man of undoubted mark and position in the House of Commons.

In December, 1834, Sir Robert Peel appointed Gladstone to the office of a Junior Lord of the Treasury. In the next year Peel, who was quick to appreciate the great abilities and the sound commercial knowledge of his new recruit, gave to him the more important post of Under-secretary for the Colonies. Gladstone looked up to Peel with intense admiration. There was much to draw the two men together. Knowledge of finance, thorough understanding and firm grasp of the principles on which a nation's business must be conducted—perhaps, it may be added, a common origin in the middle class—these points of resem-

MONTBARD PINXIT.

HAWARDEN CASTLE, THE HOME OF GLADSTONE.

blance might well have become points of attraction. But there were other and still higher sympathies to bring them close. The elder and the younger man were alike earnest, profoundly earnest; filled with conscience in every movement of their political and private lives; a good deal too earnest and serious, perhaps, for most of the parliamentary colleagues by whom they were surrounded. Mr. Gladstone always remained devoted to Peel, and knew him perhaps more thoroughly and intimately than any other man was privileged to do. Peel went out of office very soon after he had made Mr. Gladstone Under-secretary for the Colonies. Lord John Russell had brought forward a series of motions on the ominous subject of the Irish Church, and Peel was defeated and resigned. It is almost needless to say that Gladstone went with him. Peel came back again in office in 1841, on the fall of the Melbourne administration, and Mr. Gladstone became Vice-president of the Board of Trade and Master of the Mint, and was at the same time sworn in a member of the Privy Council. In 1843 he became President of the Board of Trade. Early in 1845 he resigned his office because he could not approve of the policy of the government with regard to the Maynooth grant.

The great struggle on the question of the repeal of the Corn Laws was now coming on. It would be impossible that a man with Mr. Gladstone's turn of mind and early training could have continued a protectionist, when once he applied his intellect and his experience to a practical examination of the subject. Once again he went with his leader. Peel saw that there was nothing for it but to accept the principles of the Free Trade party, who had been bearing the fiery cross of their peaceful and noble agitation all through the country, and were gathering adherents wherever they went.

It is a somewhat curious fact that Mr. Gladstone was not in the House of Commons during the eventful session when the great battle of free trade was fought and won. In thorough sympathy with Peel, he had joined the government again as Colonial Secretary. Knowing that he could no longer be in political sympathy with the Duke of Newcastle, whose influence had obtained for him the representation of Newark, he had given up his seat, and did not come into Parliament again until the struggle was over. At the general elections in 1847, Mr. Gladstone, still accepted as a Tory, was chosen one of the representatives for the University of Oxford.

Up to the time of the abolition of the Corn Laws, or at least of the movement which led to their abolition, Mr. Gladstone had been a Tory of a rather old-fashioned school. The corn-law agitation probably first set him thinking over the possible defects of the social and legislative system, and showed him the necessity for reform at least in one direction. The interests of religion itself at one time seemed to him to be bound up with the principles of the Tory party; and no doubt there was a period of his career when the principle of protection would have seemed to him as sacred as any other part of the creed. With a mind like his, inquiry once started, must go on. There was always something impetuous in the workings of his intellect, as well as the rush of his sympathy. He startled

Europe, and indeed the whole civilized world, by the terrible and only too truthful description which he gave, in 1851, of the condition of the prisons of Naples under the king who was known by the nickname of "Bomba," and the cruelties which were inflicted on political prisoners in particular. Again and again, in Mr. Gladstone's public life we shall see him carried away by the same generous and passionate emotion on behalf of the victims of despotic cruelty in any part of the world. Burke himself could not be more sympathetic, more earnest, or more strong.

By the death of Sir Robert Peel, in 1850, Mr. Gladstone had lost a trusted leader, and a dear friend. But the loss of his leader had brought Gladstone himself more directly to the front. It was not till after Peel's death that he compelled the House of Commons and the country to recognize in him a supreme master of parliamentary debate. The first really great speech made by Mr. Gladstone in Parliament—the first speech which would fairly challenge comparison with any of the finest speeches of a past day—was made in the debate on Mr. Disraeli's budget in the winter of 1852, the first session of the new Parliament. Mr. Disraeli knew well that his government was doomed to fall. He knew that it could not survive that debate. It was always one of Mr. Disraeli's peculiarities that he could fight most brilliantly when he knew that his cause was already lost. That which would have disheartened and disarmed other men, seemed only to animate him with all Macbeth's wild courage of despair. Never did his gift of satire, of invective, and of epithet show to more splendid effect than in the speech with which he closed his part of the debate, and mercilessly assailed his opponents. Mr. Disraeli sat down at two o'clock in the morning, and then Mr. Gladstone rose to reply to him. Most men in the House, even on the opposition side, were filled with the belief that it would be impossible to make any real impression on the House after such a speech as that of Mr. Disraeli. Long before Mr. Gladstone had concluded, everyone admitted that the effect of Mr. Disraeli's speech had been outdone and outshone. From that hour Mr. Gladstone was recognized as one of the great historic orators of the English Parliament—a man to rank with Bolingbroke and Chatham and Pitt and Fox. With that speech began the long parliamentary duel between these two great masters of debate, Mr. Gladstone and Mr. Disraeli, which was carried on for four and twenty years.

On the fall of the short-lived Tory administration, Lord Aberdeen came into office. He formed the famous Coalition Ministry. Lord Palmerston took what most people would have thought the uncongenial office of Home Secretary. Lord John Russell became Secretary of Foreign Affairs. Mr. Gladstone, who with others of the "Peelites," as they were called, had joined the new administration, was Chancellor of the Exchequer. His speech on the introduction of his first budget was waited for with great expectation, but it distanced all expectation. It occupied several hours in delivery, but none of those who listened to it would have wished it to be shortened by a sentence. It may be questioned whether even the younger Pitt, with all his magic of voice, and style, and phrase, could lend such charm to each successive budget as Mr. Gladstone was able to do. A budget speech from Mr. Gladstone came to be expected with the same kind of keen, artistic longing as waits the first performance of a new opera by some great composer. A budget speech by Mr. Gladstone was a triumph in the realm of the fine arts.

The Crimean War broke up the Coalition Ministry; but the year 1859 saw Lord Palmerston back again in office, and Mr. Gladstone in his old place as Chancellor of the Exchequer. The budget of 1860 was remarkable, as it contained the provisions for the reduction of the wine duties and the whole simplified system of taxation intended to apply to the commercial treaty which Mr. Cobden had succeeded in persuading the Emperor of the French to accept. Mr. Gladstone also introduced a provision for the abolition of the duty on paper—a duty which was simply a tax upon reading, a tax upon popular education. The House of Lords struck out this clause; a somewhat impassioned popular agitation followed; and in the next session the Lords passed the measure for the repeal of the duty without offering any further opposition. The death of Lord Palmerston, in 1865, called Lord Russell to the position of prime-minister, and made Mr. Gladstone leader of the House of Commons. Mr. Gladstone's mind had long been turning in the direction of an extension, or rather expansion, of the suffrage. It was assumed by everyone that Lord Russell and Mr. Gladstone being now at the head of affairs, a reform bill would be sure to come. It did come; a very moderate and cautious bill, enlarging the area of the franchise in boroughs and counties. The Conservative party opposed it, and were supported in their opposition by a considerable section of the Liberals, who thought the measure was going too far on the road to universal suffrage and the rule of the democracy. The bill was defeated, and the Liberal statesman went out of office (1866). Mr. Gladstone had carried his point, however, for when Mr. Disraeli came into office he saw that a reform bill was inevitable, and he prepared his party, or most of them, for the course which would have to be taken. In the very next session Mr. Disraeli introduced a reform bill of his own, which was enlarged and expanded until it became practically a measure of household suffrage for cities and boroughs.

Somewhere about this time the attention of Mr. Gladstone began to be attracted to the condition of Ireland. The distressed and distracted state of Ireland, the unceasing popular agitation and discontent, the Fenian insurrection, brought under England's very eyes by the schemes for an attack on Chester Castle—all these evidences of malady in Ireland's system led Mr. Gladstone to the conviction that the time had come when statesmanship must seek through Parliament for some process of remedy. Mr. Gladstone came after a while to the conclusion that the Protestant State Church in Ireland must be disestablished and disendowed, that the Irish land tenure system must be reformed, and that better provision must be made for the higher education of the Catholics of Ireland. He made short work with the Irish State Church. He defeated the government on a series of resolutions foreshadowing his policy; the government appealed to the country, the Liberals returned to power, and Mr. Gladstone became prime minister (1868). In his first session of government he disestablished and disendowed the State Church in Ireland. In the next session he passed a measure which for the first time recognized the right of the Irish tenant to the value of the improvements he had himself made at his own cost and labor. Never probably was there such a period of energetic reform in almost every direction as that which set in when Mr. Gladstone became prime-minister. For the first time in English history a system of national education was established. The Ballot Act was passed for the protection of voters. The system of purchase in the army was abolished by something, it must be owned, a little in the nature of a *coup-d'état*. Then Mr. Gladstone introduced a measure to improve the condition of university education in Ireland. This bill was intended almost altogether for the benefit of Irish Catholics; but it did not go far enough to satisfy the demands of the Catholics, and in some of its provisions was declared incompatible with the principles of their Church. The Catholic members of the House of Commons voted against it, and with that help the Conservatives were able to throw out the bill (1873). Mr. Gladstone tendered his resignation of office. But Mr. Disraeli declined just then to take any responsibility, and Mr. Gladstone had to remain at the head of affairs. The great wave of reforming energy had, however, subsided in the country. The period of reaction had come The by-elections began to tell against the Liberals. Mr. Gladstone suddenly dissolved Parliament and appealed to the country, and the answer to his appeal was the election of a Conservative majority. Mr. Disraeli came back to power, and Mr. Gladstone retired from the leadership of the House of Commons (1874).

For a while Mr. Gladstone occupied himself in literary and historical studies, and he published essays and pamphlets. But even in his literary career Mr. Gladstone would appear to have always kept glancing at the House of Commons, as Charles V. in his monastery kept his eyes on the world of politics outside. The atrocious conduct of the Turkish officials in Bulgaria aroused his generous anger, and he flung down his books and rushed out from his study to preach a crusade against the Ottoman power in Europe. The waters rose and lifted him, whether he would or no, into power. The Parliament which had gone on from the spring of 1874 was dissolved in the spring of 1880, and the Liberals came in with an overwhelming majority. The period of reaction had gone, and the period of action was come again. Mr. Gladstone had to become prime-minister once more. His name was, to adopt the phraseology of continental politics, the only name that had come out of the voting urns.

It was an unpropitious hour at which to return to office. There were troubles in Egypt; there was impending war in the Soudan and in South Africa. There was something very like an agrarian revolution going on in Ireland; and the Home Rule party in the House of Commons was under new, resolute, and uncompromising leadership. Mr. Gladstone succeeded, nevertheless, in carrying what might be called a vast scheme of parliamentary reform, a scheme which established something very near to universal suffrage, arranged the constituencies into proportionate divisions, extinguished several small boroughs, leaving their electors

GLADSTONE'S FIRST HOME RULE BILL.

to vote in their county division, and in general completed the work begun in 1832, and carried further in 1867. It is to the credit of the Conservative party that after a while they co-operated cordially with Mr. Gladstone in his reforming work of 1885. This was a triumph for Mr. Gladstone of an entirely satisfactory character; but he had sore trials to counterbalance it. He found himself drawn into a series of wars in North and South Africa; and he, whose generous sympathy had of late been so much given to Ireland, and who had introduced and carried another land bill for Ireland, found that in endeavoring to pass the measures of coercion, which the authorities in Dublin Castle deemed advisable, he had to encounter the fiercest opposition from the Irish members of Parliament and the vast bulk of the Irish population. That time must have been, for a man of Mr. Gladstone's nature, a time of darkness and of pain. Lord Frederick Cavendish and Mr. Burke were assassinated in Dublin; General Gordon perished at Khartoum. In the end the Irish members coalesced with the Conservatives in a vote on a clause in the budget, and Mr. Gladstone's government was defeated. Lord Salisbury came back into office, but not just then into power. He was in a most precarious position, depending on the course which might be taken by the Irish members. He was out of office in a few months, and then the general elections came on. These elections were to give the first opportunity to the newly made voters under Mr. Gladstone's latest reform act; and these voters sent him back into office and apparently into power once again. The use Mr. Gladstone made of office and of power astonished his enemies, and startled and shocked not a few of his friends. His government had had, in the years between 1881 and 1884, to fight a fierce battle against the policy of obstruction organized by Mr. Parnell, the leader of the Home Rule party. The obstruction was organized to prevent or delay the passing of coercion measures, and to force the attention of the British public to the claims of Ireland. The struggles that were carried on will be always memorable in the history of Parliament. The fiercest passions were aroused on both sides, and at one time Ireland seemed to have come to regard Mr. Gladstone as her worst enemy. Many a statesman in his place might have allowed himself to be governed by a feeling of disappointment and resentment. But when the elections under the new and extended Reform Bill were held, and the Irish Nationalist party came back 87 members out of the whole Irish representation of 103, Mr. Gladstone made up his mind that the voice of the Irish people was in favor of Home Rule, and he resolved to stake power and popularity on an acceptance of their demand. In March, 1886, he brought in a measure to give a statutory Parliament to Ireland. A sudden and serious split took place in his party; some of his most influential colleagues declared against him; the bill was rejected on the second reading, and Mr. Gladstone appealed to the country, only to be defeated at the general elections.

Opinion is still divided—may be divided forever—as to the wisdom of his policy; but no impartial man can deny him the credit of his sacrifice and the sincerity of his intentions. Then the Conservative party came back into office, and with the help of Liberals who had declined to follow Mr. Gladstone, came back with a powerful majority, Mr. Gladstone leading the opposition.   At the general election of 1892, his party, including both sections of Irish Nationalists, secured a majority of above forty over the combined Conservatives and Liberal Unionists.   Under his leadership a home-rule bill for Ireland was passed by the Commons in spite of the most bitter opposition.   It was rejected almost unanimously by the House of Lords; and for a time it seemed probable that the Liberals would attack the very existence of that body.   Perhaps this was Mr. Gladstone's intention for he introduced several popular radical bills.   But time was beginning to tell upon the Grand Old Man; he was now eighty-four years old, and he felt himself unequal to the gigantic struggle.   He resigned his offices and retired into private life in March, 1894.

Mr. Gladstone will find his fame as a statesman and an orator.   We have taken little account here of his contributions to literature; his Homeric studies, his various essays in political and literary, in ecclesiastical, and even theological, criticism. For another man these in themselves would have made a not inconsiderable reputation; but to the world they are interesting chiefly as illustrating a marvellous mental activity stretching itself out in every direction; unresting in the best sense of the word; incapable of settling down into even momentary idleness. " Repos ailleurs" seems to have been the motto of Mr. Gladstone's career—let rest come elsewhere—this is the world of activity and of labor.   His work as a statesman has been almost unique; probably there is no other English minister who leaves behind him so long and so successful a record of practical legislation; and, as we have seen, some of the best legislation accomplished by his political opponents was initiated by him, was his own work taken out of his hands.   As a parliamentary debater he never had a superior—it is doubtful whether he ever had an equal—in the whole of the political history of the British Empire.   There have been, even in our time, orators who now and then shot their arrows higher; but so ready, so skilful, and so unerring an archer as he, taken all around, never drew bow on modern parliamentary battle-ground.   Nature had given him an exquisite voice, sweet, powerful, easily penetrating, capable of filling without effort any public building however large, vibrating to every emotion.   The incessant training of the House of Commons turned nature's gifts to their fullest account. He was almost too fluent; his eloquence sometimes carried him away on its impassioned tide; but his listeners were seldom inclined to find fault with this magnificent exuberance.   We should be inclined to rank him as one of the greatest orators, and the very greatest debater, of the House of Commons.

PRINCE VON BISMARCK*

BY PRINCE OUTISKY

(BORN 1815)

THE "aureole of unpopularity" which encircled Bismarck's brow during four short years of inaugural premiership has, to all appearance, vanished under the influence of unbroken success, making room throughout the world for a confiding deference to his capacity and forethought, that every year seems to intensify. It is he, in the belief of most governments, who has preserved to them what never was more indispensable for their very existence—peace in Europe. With supreme adroitness, he avoids entanglements for himself and his country, bears many an affront patiently before retorting, keeps up the appearance of a good understanding after its substance has long passed away, but, when fairly engaged in diplomatic contention, lays out his field in a manner that insures success. People agree, therefore, that it is best to take him as he is. And it is in the nature of man when he has once accorded that favor to a fellow-creature, to "take him as he is," that he ends by liking him. Thus Bismarck, of all living men the most unlikely to succeed in the race after a world-wide popularity, is probably at this moment the best-liked man in either hemisphere.

His own countrymen have shown a decided indisposition to admit him among their household gods. To them he was, from the commencement of his political career, the very embodiment of what had gradually become the most objectionable type of Teuton existence—the unmitigated squireen or Junker, with

---

* This sketch was written by Prince Outisky in 1885. The Emperor William I. died in March, 1888, and his son a few months later. The views of the young Emperor William II., thus advanced to the throne, did not at all coincide with those of Bismarck, and he retired into private life in 1890. Four years later a somewhat ostentatious reconciliation took place between him and the emperor; but Bismarck did not return to power, his great age perhaps incapacitating him for active work.

As regards his early life, he was born at Schönhausen, April 1, 1815, educated at Göttingen, Berlin, and Griefswald, and at first entered the army. He became a member of the General Diet in 1847, was successively ambassador to Austria, Russia, and France, and in 1862 became Minister of the King's House and Foreign Affairs in Prussia. He was created a count in 1865; and in 1871, having achieved his great aim in the coronation of his king as Emperor of United Germany at Versailles, he became Chancellor of the Empire and Prince von Bismarck-Schönhausen.

his poverty and arrogance, with his hunger and thirst after position and good living, with his hatred for the upstart liberal burgher class. "Away with the cities! I hope I may yet live to see them levelled to the ground." Is there not a ring of many centuries of social strife, so laboriously kept down by the reigning dynasty, in these stupendous words, which were pronounced by Bismarck in 1847, when among the leaders of the conservatives in the first embryo parliament of the Prussian monarchy? And if uncongenial to the generation of Prussians among whom he had grown up, how infinitely greater was the dislike against him of South Germans, more gifted, as a rule, by nature, to whom the name of Prussian is synonymous of all that is strait-laced and overweening and unnatural and—generally inconvenient.

Little of that sentiment remains among the Germans of the present day. Such strangers as have had the opportunity of observing the attitude of the nation during the late celebration of his seventieth birthday, agree in declaring them to have been spontaneous, enthusiastic, and at times almost aggressive. Some tell us, to be sure, that the farther from Berlin the more gushing has been the ecstasy. The electors of Professor Virchow and of Herr Löwe, in whose electoral districts a torchlight procession on the eve of Bismarck's birthday had to elbow its way through immense crowds, must have kept at home. The municipality of Berlin, a model body of civic administrators, sent a birthday letter to their "honorary citizen," but abstained, with proper self-respect, from tendering their congratulations through a deputation. No Berlin citizen of any importance had a hand in the management of the procession. Yet, if thousands kept aloof, tens of thousands shared the national enthusiasm—students of universities chiefly, but older men too, even in distrustful, radical Berlin. And as for South Germany, where the gospel of protection seems, perhaps, to be more firmly believed in than any other, we read of trains to Berlin taken by storm, banquets, processions, chorus-singing—of real, heartfelt, rapturous effervescence.

There cannot be a shadow of doubt that, to numberless non-Prussians at any rate, the new era of German unity has brought a symbol of greatness not before known, and that they worship in Bismarck the hero who has given them a country to love, who has delivered them from the pettiness and self-satisfaction of Philistinism.

Now, if this be so—if, indeed, the countries of the world at large, and Germany in particular, acknowledge him almost affectionately as the leading statesman of the day, would it not be an interesting study to examine the degree of merit due to him personally, the character of the present administration, and what lasting good or lasting evil may be expected from this new phase of European politics? The subject, through its weight and its bulk alike, excludes full treatment within the limits of an essay. Nevertheless, since it intertwines itself with nearly every other question of moment, a few remarks by an outsider may be acceptable.

None but the incorrigibly childish can be inclined to ascribe to good luck a prosperous career extending over near twenty-three years, spent under the fiercest

VON WERNER PINXIT.

PROCLAMATION OF THE GERMAN EMPIRE AT VERSAILLES.

glare of the world's sunshine. No minister of any age was more bitterly assailed or opposed, even at the court of which he is now the acknowledged major domus in the manner of the Pepins and other Thum-Meiers of the Frankish monarchy. The king's brother, Prince Charles, detested the innovator whose opinions on the necessity of Austria being removed from membership in a remodelled German confederation, had for years leaked out from the despatch-boxes of the Foreign Office. Even the Junkers, whose dauntless leader he had been before and after the revolutionary events of 1848, shrank instinctively from a man who could not be credited with veneration for the Holy Alliance. It is remembered in Berlin that, on the nomination of one of them, well at court, a diplomatist of some standing, to the post of under-secretary of state for foreign affairs, the new member of the government confessed to his friends that he accepted the post *in spite* of Bismarck's "foreign" policy, and only in consideration of his contempt for parliamentarism. The queen, on the other hand, brought up in principles of constitutional government, and strongly attached to the English alliance, viewed with horror the bold pugilist who was daily assailing, not the persons only of the people's representatives, but some of the very foundations of every parliamentary edifice. Yet fiercer was the animosity shown him on every occasion by the Princess Royal of England, whose father had early taught her that a throne, to be safe, requires absolute solidity of institutions and agreement with the people, and who seriously trembled for the preservation of her children's future. Her husband expressed himself forcibly on a public occasion against some reactionary measures of the government. As the court, so were the liberal parties, so the people in general. When a fanatic, of the name of Kohn, attempted Bismarck's life in May, 1866, there were few persons who did not regret his failure. It may be said with truth that, for years, two men only understood a portion at least of his political views, and shared them. One was King William. Isolated as Herr von Bismarck was, he learned to rely implicitly on his sovereign's faithfulness, and has had no reason to regret his trust; for the king, though greatly his inferior in intellect, and far from unblest with legitimist predilections, was as firmly convinced as his minister that the confederation of German states, and Prussia herself, might be swept away unless placed upon a new footing, in one of those tornadoes which used periodically to blow across the continent of Europe. Thus, the new departure was as much his own programme as Bismarck's, and although he started (in 1861) with a hankering after "moral" rather than material conquests, he gradually understood the necessity for war, and has of a certainty "taken kindly," as the saying is, to material conquests of no inconsiderable magnitude.

None, even among Bismarck's modern sycophants, would pretend that their hero was the inventor of German unity. Passionately, though not over-wisely, had that ideal been striven after and suffered for by the best patriots in various parts of Fatherland, their vision becoming hazy just as often as they attempted to combine two opposite claims, that of a national texture, and that of a headship of Austria, which is non-German in a majority of its subjects, and alien in nearly

all its interests. The Frankfort Parliament of 1848 marks the transition to a
clear insight, inasmuch as its final performance, the constitution of 1849, placed
the new crown on the King of Prussia's head. When offered, it was haughtily
declined under the applause of Bismarck and his friends. The king refused because its origin lay in a popular assembly; in Bismarck's eyes its chief defect was
that Prussia would be dictated to by the minor states. It was not until later, in
1851, when appointed Prussian ambassador to the Germanic Diet, chiefly because
of his defence of the Treaty of Olmütz, which placed Prussia at the mercy of
Austria, that he recognized the central point to be the necessity of thrusting
Austria out of the confederation. It is proved now that he was sagacious
enough also to perceive that such a wrench would not lead to a permanent
estrangement, but that Austria, removed once and for all from her incubus-
like and dog-in-the-manger position within the federate body, would become,
in her own interest and that of European peace, New Germany's permanent
ally.

These, then, became the two purposes of his active life ever since the day
when, at the age of thirty-six, he obtained a share of the responsibility in the
management of affairs as ambassador in Frankfort; first, to transfer *Austria to a
position in the East*, and then to bestow upon the Fatherland *political unity under Prussia, the royal prerogative in the latter remaining uncurtailed*, so far as
circumstances would allow. Thirty-four years have now elapsed. His opponents, in his own country or out of it, are at liberty to reiterate that he was born
under a lucky star; that he merely took up the thread of German unification
where the Frankfort Parliament of 1849 had let it drop; that anybody could
have utilized such mighty armaments as those of Prussia with the same effect;
that, given total disregard of principle or moral obligations, the result, in the
hands of any political gamester, must have been what it was. There is something to be set against each of these assertions. For it was not the goddess of
Fortune which pursued Bismarck in the ungainly shape of his former friend, that
spiteful Prince Gortschakoff. The Frankfort assembly had left the Austrian
riddle unsolved, and apparently insoluble. There was no hand in the country
firm or skilful enough, no brain sufficiently hard or enlightened as to the needs
of the day—not the king's, not Count Arnim's, nor certainly that of any other
known to his contemporaries. And finally, when a public man so deftly gauges
the mental capacities or extent of power of his antagonists—such as Count Beust,
or Napoleon, or Earl Russell—that he knows exactly how far he can step with
safety; then such a " gamester," however terrible the risks to which he may have
exposed his country, is a great man. Complete unity of aims throughout, power
given to carry them out, a wonderful absence of very serious mistakes, and finally
a life sufficiently prolonged to admit of retrospection; in each of these respects
the career of Bismarck resembles that of Mr. Disraeli.

The oft-told story of his diplomatic adventures at Frankfort, at Vienna, at
Petersburg, and at Paris, and still more of his rulership in Prussia since 1862,
and in Germany since 1866, has been uniform under two aspects. First, as al-

ready mentioned, in the stern continuity of his purposes.   And secondly, in the mistaken view entertained regarding him at each successive period of his public life.   Passing under review the whole career of this political phenomenon, you naturally pause before its strangest and its most humorous feature, viz., that, although living under the closest inspection, he was misunderstood year after year. Who would, consequently, deny the possibility at least, of Bismarck's being so misunderstood, by friend and foe, at this present moment ?

While those despatches were written by him from Frankfort which Poschinger's researches have now exhumed, their writer was thought, by his partisans just as much as by his enemies, to be occupied solely with strengthening the " solidarity of conservative interests " and the supremacy of Austria, or with spinning the rope of steel which was to strangle all parliaments in Germany. And yet we know positively at present that, with increasing vigor day by day, did he warn his government against the scarcely concealed intention of Austria to " *avilir la Prusse d'abord et puis l'anéantir* " (Prince Schwartzenberg's famous saying in 1851) ; we observe with surprise how quickly legitimist leanings disappear behind his own country's interests ; we stand aghast at the iron sway obtained by so young a man over the self-conceit of a vacillating, yet dogmatic and wilful, king (Frederick William IV.).   It was he whose advice, given in direct opposition to Bunsen's, led to the refusal by Prussia of the Western alliance during the Crimean war.   But he did not give this advice, as German liberals then believed, out of subservience to the autocrat of the North, whose assistance his party humbly solicited in order to exterminate liberalism.   He persistently gave it to thwart Austria and to preserve Prussia (then in no brilliant military condition) from having to bear the brunt of Muscovite wrath, which he cunningly judged to be of more lasting importance in the coming struggles than the friendship of Western Europe.   At a time when European politicians considered that he was the mouthpiece of schemers for a Russo-French alliance in his repeated and successful endeavors to gain Napoleon's good-will, he was adroitly sounding the French emperor's mind and character.   He soon convinced himself that it was shallow and fantastic, and he built upon this conviction one of the most hazardous designs which ever originated in a brain observant of realities —that identical design which eventually led Prussia, some years later, first to Schleswig and then to Sadowa, with the " arbiter of Europe," as Napoleon was then called, stolidly looking on !   And what is one to say of the four years of parliamentary conflicts (1862 to 1866), during which no one doubted but that his object in life and his *raison d'être* consisted in a reinstatement of the Prussian king on the absolute throne of his ancestors—a reaction from all that was progressive to the grossest abuses of despotism ?   All this time he was fighting a desperate battle against backstairs influences, which with true instinct were deprecating and counteracting his schemes of aggrandizement and national reorganization.   It is clear, on looking back to that period which has left such indelible marks on the judgment of many well-meaning liberals, that his exaggerated tone of aggressive defence in the Prussian Landtag, the furious onslaught of his harangues, were intended to silence the tongues at court which denounced him as a demagogue and a radical. Paradoxical as it may sound, one may safely assert that nothing more effectually helped King William in his later foreign policy, than the opinion pervading all Europe in 1864 and 1866, that, having lost all hold upon the minds of his people, weakened and crippled in every sense of the word by Bismarckian folly, his Majesty could never strike a blow.

There was peace and concord in Germany between 1866 and 1877. Without becoming a liberal, and while opposing every attempt to outstep certain limits, Bismarck created and rather enjoyed an alliance with the majority formed in his favor by the national liberals and a moderate section of the conservatives. The German Empire, proclaimed by the German sovereigns at Versailles in January, 1871, was of his creation; and while established upon somewhat novel principles of federation by a parliamentary statute, it looked to outsiders like a home for progress and liberty. There were dangers lurking, it is true, beneath many a provision of the new constitution, such as the absence of an upper house, and the substitution in its stead of delegates from the separate governments, acting in each case according to instructions received, authorized to speak whenever they chose before the Reichstag, but deliberating separately and secretly both upon bills to propose, and upon replies to give to resolutions of the Reichstag. In fact, this Bundesrath, or federal council, represents the governing element under the emperor, with functions both administrative and legislative. By an artificial method of counting, Prussia, although she would command three-fifths of all the voters by virtue of her population, has less than one-third. Thus the possibility of an imbroglio between the governments is ever present, as well as that of a hasty vote in the popular assembly.

It will never, probably, be quite understood why Prince Bismarck broke loose from a political alliance which, it would seem, had given no trouble whatever. In foreign affairs the house, in its immense majority, abstained from even the faintest attempt at interference. As for patronage, it has been said that no appointment was ever solicited for anyone by a member of the liberal party. From ministerial down to menial posts no claim was raised, no request preferred. If the section of moderate conservatives above mentioned has furnished a few ambassadors like Prince Hohenlohe, Count Münster, Baron Keudell, and Count Stolberg, that was by the chief's free will. Why, then, it has been asked, a change so absolute as the one the world has witnessed, from the saying of the chancellor in 1877, that his ideal was to have high financial duties on half a dozen objects and free trade on all others, to one of the most comprehensive tariffs in the world two years later? His own and his friends' explanations are lamentably deficient—"growing anæmia and impoverishment of the country," "drowning of native industry by foreign manufacturers," "corn imported cheaper than produced," and what not. The present writer, looking from afar, has always thought two motives to have been paramount in the chancellor's mind when he separated from the liberals and became, not a convinced, but a thorough-going protectionist. It is not said that these were his only motives. Chess-players

Photogravure. Hanfstaengl

know that each important move affects not only the figures primarily attacked, but changes the whole texture of the play.

First, then, and foremost, fresh sources of income were wanted to make the finances of the empire independent from the several exchequers of the states bound by statute to make up for any deficiency *pro rata parte* of their population. Two or three objects would have provided the needful, viz., spirits and beetroot sugar, and (with due caution) tobacco; or an "imperial" income tax, changing according to each year's necessities; or both systems combined. Tobacco, it is true, was tried, and the attempt failed. Spirits would bear almost any taxation, but the chancellor does not choose to tread upon the tender toe of the great owners of land who are potato-growers, and consequently distillers on a large scale. And another important class of agriculturists, the beetroot growers and sugar-producers, were not to be trifled with either. But how about direct taxation, the manly sacrifice of free peoples, the plummet by which to sound the enlightenment of a nation? The chancellor instinctively felt, I believe, that there he would be going beyond his depth; that under such a *régime* the free will of citizens must have the fullest swing; the "prerogative" would suffer, if not immediately, yet as a necessary sequence. And so he deliberately abandoned free trade and espoused indirect taxation and protection.

Success, let free traders say what they please on the subject, success has accompanied Bismarck's genius on this novel field, as well as on the older fields where all mankind acknowledges his superiority. For the coffers of the empire are filling. A motley majority in the Reichstag not only accepts, but improves upon his protectionist demands. He has become the demigod of the bloated manufacturing, mining, and landlord interests throughout the country. He is now about to win the last of the great industries, and the one which withstood his blandishments the longest, viz., the trans-oceanic carrying trade. He is credited with having improved the state of certain trades, even by such as know perfectly well that, like the former depression, the present improvement in those has been universal. The whole country is becoming protectionist. All young men, even in Hamburg and Bremen, believe in protection as "the thing." The Prussian landlord, whose soul was steeped in free trade so long as Prussia was a grain-exporting country, cherishes protectionist convictions now that she must largely import cereals. The bureaucrat who had never sworn by other economic lawgivers than Adam Smith and his followers, now accepts Professor Adolphus Wagner's ever-changing sophisms. And as for the south and the west of Germany, why, they adore the man who had fulfilled that dream of protection in which they, as disciples of Friedrich List, had grown up. It is true that all large cities, even there, are protesting against the lately imposed and quite lately increased duties upon cereals; but then, "can any good thing come out of" large cities? Compared to the difficulties that impede the action of the free trade party in Germany, Mr. Bright's and Mr. Cobden's up-hill work sinks into insignificance.

Nothing, to a beginner in the study of Bismarck's character, would appear so utterly puzzling as his demeanor toward the communists, socialists, or, as they call themselves in Germany, Social Democrats. One of his most trusted secretaries is an old ally and correspondent of Herr Karl Marx, the high-priest of communism, who, toward the end of his London career, rode the whirlwind and directed the storm of German socialism. Bismarck himself confesses to having received in private audience Lassalle, one certainly of the most capable men of modern Germany, and to whom as its first author, a retrospective inquiry would trace back the present formidable, closely ruled organization of socialist operatives of Germany. The first minister of the Prussian crown was closeted once—people say more than once, but that does not matter—with the ablest subverter of the modern fabric of society. He found him "mighty pleasant to talk to." He liked his predilection for a powerful supreme authority overawing the organized masses, though "whether he did so in the interest of a dynasty of Lassalles or of Hohenzollerns" seemed to Herr von Bismarck an open question. After Lassalle's tragical death in 1864, we observe how the Prussian government, while watching with Argus-eyes every excess of speech among liberals, allowed his first successors, Schweizer and others, a vulgar set of demagogues, such license of bloody harangue as has of late years got Louise Michel into trouble in republican France. Then we hear of nothing as between Bismarck and the socialists for some years—the years I have described above as years of peace and concord in Germany—till suddenly, on the occasion of two attempts made in 1878, by Hödel and by Nobiling against the emperor's life, he came down upon that sect as with a sledge-hammer. His famous anti-socialist bill was at first rejected. It passed into law only after a dissolution, the electors having in their affectionate pity for the wounded emperor unequivocally given their verdict in favor of suppression. It has since been reaccepted three times by an unwilling house, and with exertions of the same man who had fostered and protected the beginnings of socialism, and who had the watchword given out at the last general elections in 1884, that "His Serene Highness the Chancellor would prefer the sight of ten Social-Democrats to that of one Liberal (Deutsch-Freisinige.)"

Now, what is the clew to this comedy of errors? No mere waywardness or perversity of character, but some powerful bias and a first-cousinship in principle must account for one of the strangest anomalies in modern history. Perhaps the following consideration will render both the "bias" and the "first-cousinship" at least intelligible. Prince Bismarck is a good hater. Now, if he has any one antipathy stronger than another, and that through life, it is that against the burgher class, the reverse of aristocrats, the born liberals, townsmen mostly yet not exclusively—the "bourgeois," as the French call them (although, if I err not, the exact counterpart to the "bourgeois" species is not found on German soil), a law-abiding set, independent of government, paying their taxes, and thoroughly happy. When they, through their representatives, bade him defiance in 1862 to 1865, and thwarted his measures of coercion, his inmost soul cried, *Acheronta movebo!* He sent for Lassalle, he paid his successors' debts, and generally assisted the sect. So much for the "bias." And now for the "first-cousinship."

No student of history will deny that despotism, whenever it has arisen, or been preserved in highly civilized communities, will extend more of a fatherly care to the masses than liberalism. This cannot be otherwise; for liberalism sets itself to educate the masses to self-responsibility, and each individual to thrift and self-reliance. The sight of an able-bodied beggar is, to a genuine liberal, a source of anger first, and only on further contemplation, of pity. He will exert all his energies to remove every obstacle from out of the way of his poorer brethren; he will preach wise economy, and facilitate it by personal sacrifices and legislative inducements; but he will not tempt the government of his country to act as a second providence for the operative classes. Quite the reverse is Bismarck's opinion. According to him, the state should exercise "practical Christianity." With Titanic resolution to drive out Satan through Beelzebub, he does not shrink from acknowledging and proclaiming the "right of labor." There is probably nothing left to say after your lips have spoken these unholy, blood-stained words. If there was, he would be the man to say it rather than allow himself to be outbid by mob-leaders of the socialistic feather. *Droit au travail*, forsooth! The phrase has cost thousands their lives in the Parisian carnage of June, 1848. In the mouth of Karl Marx and other outspoken champions of his cause, it means absorption by the state of all the *sources* of labor, such as land and factories, because by such absorption only can the state insure work for the unemployed. In the mouth of Bismarck it means a lesser thing, of course, in extent, but not in its essence. As chief minister of Prussia he has ably brought about the purchase of nearly all lines of railway within that monarchy. As chancellor of the empire he has tried his very best to obtain a monopoly on tobacco. All accident insurance companies have already been ruined and their place taken, so far as accidents to factory-hands, etc., are concerned, by an imperial office. His mighty hand is stretched out already to suppress and absorb all other insurances. The kingdom of the Incas, in ancient Peru, as described in Prescott's volumes, has probably not done more work for its subjects than Bismarck's ideal of a German empire would do for its inhabitants. With every species of occupation or enterprise managed directly by government, why should the ruler of an empire, or of a socialist republic, hesitate about proclaiming a right to labor? A critic might object that its proclamation by Bismarck, in 1884, was premature, inasmuch as he had failed in carrying his Monopoly bill, and could not be certain of success regarding other state encroachments. Granted. But a "first-cousinship" between his views on social reform and those of Messrs. Bebel and Liebknecht, is an actuality of modern Germany, and should be seen to by those who desire this central power of Europe to remain exempt from a social revolution. Cursory as this review of Bismarck's past life and present policy has of necessity been, some indulgent reader may perhaps bestow upon me—besides his thanks for having withstood the temptation to quote the pithy, and at times impassioned, utterances of the wittiest man in power of the present day—just enough of his confidence to believe that I have suppressed no trait of importance.

However, since there is one thing more important still than a great man, namely his country, let us not dismiss the interesting subject of this retrospect without inquiring what that country has gained and what lost through his agency. Germany possesses a federation, not constructed after any existing pattern, not made to please any theory, not the object of anybody's very passionate admiration, but accepted in order to alter as little as possible the accustomed territorial and political arrangements. In one sense it has no army, for the Prussian and the Bavarian armies, although the empire bears the cost, still exist. In one sense it possesses not the indirect taxation, for the individual states do the collecting of custom-house duties, etc. In one sense it has scarcely any organs of administration, for the whole internal government, the schools, courts of law, and police, all belong to the single states; and foreign affairs, the navy, the post-office, and railways in Alsace, are the only fields of imperial direct administration. Yet, what it has is valuable enough. The empire rules the army and can legislate over and control a prodigious amount of national subjects. Its foreign policy is one. The military command is one. Certain specified sources of revenue are the empire's. Patriotic aspirations are fulfilled. The individual sovereigns in Germany possess a guarantee of their status, the operative classes an opportunity for organization and improvement on a large scale. Monarchical feeling has gained in depth, both generally and with personal reference to the emperor and to the crown prince, both " representative men " in the best sense of the word, and the crown prince, the most lovable man of his day.

Another salutary constitutional reform—not of Bismarck's making, for he gave his consent unwillingly and not without first having marred its beauty, but yet an effect of his great deeds—is the Prussian " Kreis " and " Provinzial-Ordnung," first introduced in 1874. No more logical deduction was possible than this commencement of decentralization within the Prussian monarchy. Before that date provincial diets had existed for fifty years, and a kind of assembly had also managed certain affairs for the Kreis, an administrative unit smaller than an English county, and averaging about one hundred thousand inhabitants. In the same proportion as German unity made progress, it was believed that self-government ought to become more extensively introduced, and the " tendency of the blood toward the head " or capital, be obviated. The example of home rule presented by the " Kreis " and the provinces of Prussia since this reform, is not assuredly of a nature to frighten weak nerves. But much money is now usefully spent within and by the provinces independently of any decree from a central authority; and as regards willingness to work on provincial and (so to say) county boards, it is said to be beyond all praise. An English public man of high standing assured me, some years ago, that these Prussian beginnings of home rule had attracted the serious notice of Mr. Gladstone. I do not wonder at it.

Another permanent good for which Germany seems indebted to Bismarck, and the last I will mention, is of quite modern date—I mean his colonial policy. Individual Germans have, at all times and in immense numbers, found their way across the sea. On the Baltic and North Sea coast, German ports, though few in number, yet command a very large trade. Next to the English, German traders form the most numerous community in every place, however remote, where business of any kind can be transacted. But to convert the inland Philistines—that vast majority of Germans who have never sniffed sea-air—into enthusiasts for a colonial empire required all Bismarck's ability and prestige. No doubt he descried in the movement a chance for a diversion of the public mind from obnoxious topics. It was useful to him to produce an impression as if the export trade, stagnating as it must under the baneful effects of modern protection, could rally under the influence of colonial enterprise. These considerations would not, however, suffice to explain his long-considered, cautious proceedings in this matter. To comprehend his motives fully, it will be necessary to admit that his prescient mind would consider the time, apparently not very far distant, when what are now styled Great Powers will be dwindling fast by the side of such gigantic empires as seem intent upon dividing the earth's surface between them, like England with her colonial possessions, and Russia. The effect upon this country, its foreign policy, and the very character of its inhabitants, would be alike cramping, unless a way for expansion was opened for each. When the political schemes of a considerable man are subjects of speculation, it is wiser to guess at something exalted if you wish to come near the truth. So probably in this case. No doubt he, too, has foreseen the reaction which, at no very remote period of German history, will gain a mastery over people's minds, when failures and disappointments begin to crowd around each of the present equatorial enterprises. But he believes in his countrymen's capacity to overcome failure and disappointment without recourse to costly warlike expeditions, for which Germany is unfitted by her institution of universal and short military service.

CHARLES STEWART PARNELL

By Thomas Davidson

(1846–1891)

CHARLES STEWART PARNELL, the Irish politician, was born at Avondale, in County Wicklow, June 28, 1846. His father belonged to an old Cheshire family, which purchased an estate in Ireland under Charles II., and from which had sprung Thomas Parnell, the poet, and Sir Henry Brooke Parnell, created Baron Congleton in 1841. His great-grandfather was that Sir John Parnell who was long Chancellor of the Irish Exchequer, and an active supporter of Grattan in his struggle against the Union ; his grandfather, William Parnell, sat for County Wicklow, and published in 1819 a foolish political novel, anything but Irish in sentiment ; his mother, Delia Tudor Stewart, was daughter of Admiral Charles Stewart, of the United

States Navy. He was educated at Yeovil and elsewhere in England under private masters, and was for some time a member of Magdalene College, Cambridge, but took no degree. In 1874 he became High Sheriff of County Wicklow ; next year he contested County Dublin without success, but in April, 1875, was returned as an avowed Home Ruler for County Meath.

He attached himself to Joseph Biggar, the member for Cavan, who was the first to discover the value of deliberate obstruction in parliamentary tactics, and during 1877 and 1878 he gained great popularity in Ireland by his audacity in the use of the new engine. There were many scenes of violence and excitement, and the new horror of all-night sittings became familiar to the House of Commons. Throughout the struggle Parnell showed equal audacity and coolness, and acquired a masterly knowledge of parliamentary forms. Mr. Butt, the Irish leader, disapproved of this development of the *active* or obstructive policy, but his influence quickly gave way before Parnell's, and in May, 1879, he died. The year before, Parnell had been elected president of the English Home Rule Association. He now threw himself with energy into agrarian agitation, gave it its watchword : " Keep a firm grip of your homesteads," at Westport in June, and in October was elected president of the Irish National Land League, which had been founded by Michael Davitt.

Mr. Parnell next visited the United States to raise funds for the cause, was allowed, like Lafayette and Kossuth, to address Congress itself, and carried home £70,000. At the general election of 1880 he was returned for the counties of Meath and Mayo and for the city of Cork, and chose to sit for the last. He was now formally elected chairman of the Irish parliamentary party by twenty-three votes over eighteen for Mr. Shaw. Meantime the agrarian agitation grew, and in a speech at Ennis, September 19, 1880, he formulated the method of boycotting as an engine for punishing an unpopular individual. Mr. Gladstone's government now came to the conclusion that the objects of the Land League were contrary to the law, and in December put Parnell and several other members of the executive on trial, but the jury finally failed to agree. Next session the government brought in a Coercion Bill, which Mr. Parnell opposed vigorously. In the course of the struggle he was ejected from the House, after a stormy scene, together with thirty-four of his followers, February 3, 1881. Mr. Gladstone next carried his famous Land Bill, but this Parnell refused to accept as a final settlement until the result of certain test cases before the new Land Court was seen. On October 13th, Mr. Gladstone sent him to Kilmainham Jail, and there he lay till released on May 2, 1882, after some private negotiations with the government conducted through the medium of Captain O'Shea. Mr. Forster resigned the Irish secretaryship in consequence of the release, and next followed the terrible tragedy of Phœnix Park, of which Parnell, in his place in the House of Commons, expressed his detestation.

The Crimes Act was now hurried through Parliament in spite of the strenuous opposition of the Irish party. Already the Land League had been proclaimed as an illegal association after the issue of the " No Rent " manifesto, but

WALTER WILSON PINXIT.

PARNELL TESTIFYING AGAINST THE "TIMES."

early in 1884 the Nationalists succeeded in reviving it under the name of the National League, and Mr. Parnell was elected its president. The year before the sum of £35,000, mostly raised in America, had been presented to him by his admirers. After an unsuccessful attempt to make terms with the Conservatives, in the course of which he had a famous interview with Lord Carnarvon, the viceroy, Parnell flung his vote—now eighty-six strong since the lowering of the franchise—into the Liberal scale and so brought about the fall of the short-lived first Salisbury government. Mr. Parnell nominated the greater number of Nationalist candidates for the Irish constituencies, and the firm hand with which he controlled his party was seen in the promptitude with which he crushed a revolt of Healy and Biggar against his nomination of Captain O'Shea for Galway.

Mr. Gladstone's views on the question of Home Rule had by this time undergone a complete change, and accordingly he introduced a Home Rule Bill, which was defeated owing to the defection of a large number of Liberal members headed by Lord Hartington and Mr. Chamberlain. The consequent appeal to the country (July, 1886) gave Lord Salisbury a Unionist majority of over a hundred votes, and threw Parnell into a close alliance with Mr. Gladstone and the portion of the Liberal party that adhered to him. It was at this period that the *Times* newspaper published its series of articles entitled "Parnellism and Crime"—a tremendous indictment against the chief Nationalist leaders, the most startling point in which was a series of letters published in fac-simile, one, signed by Parnell, expressing approval of Mr. Burke's murder. After an elaborate trial (extending to one hundred and twenty-eight days), the most sensational event in which was the breakdown under cross-examination, and the flight and suicide at Madrid, of Pigott, the wretched Irishman who had imposed upon the *Times* with forgeries, Mr. Parnell was formally cleared of the charge of having been personally guilty of organizing outrages, but his party were declared to have been guilty of incitements to intimidation, out of which had grown crimes which they had failed to denounce. Parnell now began an action against the *Times*, which was quickly compromised by a payment of £5,000.

The "uncrowned king" of Ireland had now reached the summit of his power —the height of the wave was marked by the presentation of the freedom of Edinburgh, July 30, 1889, and the banquet given him on his forty-fourth birthday. But his fall in public esteem was quickly to follow. A few months later his frequent mysterious absences from his parliamentary duties were explained by his appearance, or rather his non-appearance, as co-respondent in a divorce case brought by Captain O'Shea against his wife. After formal evidence was given by the petitioner, the usual decree was granted with costs against Parnell (November 17, 1890).

The Gladstonian party in England now demanded his retirement from the leadership of the cause, and Mr. Gladstone informed the Irish members that they must make their choice between Parnell and himself. They met and reappointed him their chairman, expecting, as the majority explained later, that after this recognition of his past services he would voluntarily retire, at least for a time. But they had not calculated upon the characteristic obstinacy of his nature, and quickly found that their leader had no mind to efface himself. After some days of profitless and heated wrangling, the majority ended the discussion by leaving the room and electing Justin McCarthy as their chairman. Parnell, with the shattered remnants of his party, now carried the warfare into Ireland, where his condemnation by the Irish bishops and the emphatic defeat of his nominees for North Kilkenny and North Sligo showed that a large number of his fellow-countrymen shared the judgment of his conduct pronounced by Mr. Gladstone and the party in England. The career of the man who had forced the issue of Irish Home Rule upon the English people, and made it the great question of the day, was drawing rapidly to its close. He died October 6, 1891.

BENJAMIN HARRISON*

By Elbridge S. Brooks

(born 1833)

It is Francis Galton, the apostle of heredity, who makes the broad statement that a man's natural abilities are derived from inheritance, and that each generation of men has enormous power over the natural gifts of those that follow. Without entering upon a discussion of this theory, it may be said that there is no better example, in all Mr. Galton's long list of inheritors, than that of Benjamin Harrison, the twenty-third president of the United States. For, even if that genealogical record be not accepted that traces his line of ancestry back to two such notable progenitors as Thomas Harrison, of Staffordshire, most uncompromising of English patriots, falsely called "the regicide," and Ma-ta-oka, better known as Pocahontas, most famous of Indian women, the law of heredity is amply proven in the progression of acknowledged "forebears," in which occur two such notable Americans as Benjamin Harrison, of Virginia, signer of the Declaration of Independence, and William Henry Harrison, ninth President of the United States, forever famous under his popular sobriquet of "Tippecanoe."

Benjamin Harrison, great-grandson of Benjamin Harrison, "the signer," and grandson of William Henry Harrison, the president, was born in his grandfather's house at North Bend, in Hamilton County, O., on August 20, 1833. His father was John Scott Harrison; his mother was Elizabeth Irwin. John Scott Harrison was the third son of President William Henry Harrison, and, though unambitious of political honors and of public life, was twice elected to Congress, and, in 1861, declined the nomination for lieutenant-governor of Ohio. Elizabeth Irwin, his second wife and the mother of the future president, was a woman of gentle ways, firm principles, and unostentatious piety, a typical western "house-mother," as the Germans use the word, one of those self-sacrificing American women from whose homely firesides have sprung a race of American workers and leaders.

The Ohio farm to which Benjamin Harrison came as the second son in the year 1833, and on which he had his "bringing-up," was part of the great tract known as "the Symmes purchase," a reminder of pioneering days in " the Ohio country," when Judge John Cleve Symmes, the father-in-law of President William Henry Harrison, purchased a vast section of western land, embracing the five present counties of Southern Ohio and extending along the Ohio River, twenty miles above and twenty miles below the site of the city of Cincinnati, and comprising two million acres.

The Harrison farm was in the lower portion of the famous Symmes purchase; five miles below the town of North Bend and at the junction of the Miami and Ohio Rivers, lay the five hundred acres that John Scott Harrison received from his famous father. On this farm, known as "Point Farm," he lived and died, unambitious, save for his boys, and so ready to "accommodate" his friends that he was, before the close of life, brought to distress and debt by too frequent endorsement of unreliable "paper."

Benjamin Harrison received the education his father was determined he should have—no matter how pinching the times that came to that Ohio farm— first, in the old "cabin school" on the farm, and later at a preparatory "academy" known as Farmer's College, near Cincinnati, from which, when he was seventeen years of age, he entered the junior class of Miami University, in the village of Oxford, O. As a boy he was ambitious and studious, graduating from Miami University number four in a class of sixteen, and known to his associates as industrious and companionable, a ready and fluent speaker, an "unpretentious but courageous" student, excelling in history and political economy. He was prominent, too, in college sports and in the social life of the little university town, where his slight physique and almost girlish appearance were offset by a ready wit, a manly spirit, and those traits of character that make a young man attractive and popular.

He had been in college but a few months when he fell in love and, before he had entered the senior class, was engaged to marry Caroline Lavinia Scott, the daughter of the principal of the Academy for Young Ladies in that same village of Oxford.

Graduating from college in June, 1852, Benjamin Harrison found his father deeply embarrassed, and the original farm of five hundred acres largely reduced in extent and heavily mortgaged. The father had strained every nerve to educate the son, and now the boy was to make his own start in life, dependent upon his own unaided exertions. He wasted no time, and, as the first step, after determining upon the law as his profession and serving a short apprenticeship as law student in the Cincinnati office of Storer & Gwynne, he married Miss Scott in October, 1853, and speedily set up a home of his own. Mrs. Harrison proved herself a true helpmeet and a noble woman, and her death in 1892, after nearly forty years of married life, was a deep blow to her husband, but has left her name a gracious and enduring memory in American public life.

Upon his admission to the bar Benjamin Harrison removed to Indianapolis in March, 1854, and that enterprising western capital has ever since been his home. He had inherited from an aunt a small plot of ground in Cincinnati. Upon this, as security, he raised the sum of $800, and with this as capital the young husband and wife began life in Indianapolis.

Benjamin Harrison was, at this time, twenty-one—a pleasant-faced, light-haired, boyish-looking young man, poor but ambitious, modest but independent, ready in speech, methodical in manner, with a sympathetic voice and an aptitude for the details of his profession, that soon secured for him recognition and standing, not because he was a grandson of President William Henry Harrison, but because he was an able, promising, hard-working, and conscientious young lawyer—in fact, bound to "turn out," what is called in the vernacular of the West, "a swinge cat."

In 1855 he became law-partner with William Wallace, later clerk of Marion County, and in 1860 he joined the firm of Fishback & Harrison, which became, in 1865, Porter, Harrison & Fishback; in 1871, Porter, Harrison & Hines; and, in 1883, Harrison, Miller & Elam. Mr. Miller, upon the election of President Harrison, joined his cabinet as attorney-general.

Benjamin Harrison first entered public life in 1854, as crier of the Federal court at a salary of two dollars and a half a day. In 1860 he was elected reporter of the Supreme Court, for which post he had been nominated by the Republican State Convention. In 1876 he was defeated, by a small plurality, in the election for governor of Indiana; in 1878 he was chairman of the Republican State convention; in 1879 he was appointed by President Hayes as one of the Mississippi River commission; in 1880 he was one of the Indiana delegates to the National Republican Convention, and stood steadfast for the candidacy of Blaine to the end; in January, 1881, he was elected United States Senator for six years, and in 1888 he was elected President of the United States by a majority of sixty-five electoral votes.

It was while he was filling his first elective office as reporter of the Supreme Court of Indiana, that the Civil War broke out. Benjamin Harrison took decided ground on public matters and national questions. His father was a Democrat—but one who, when the test hour came, was, as he stated in declining the Democratic nomination for lieutenant-governor of Indiana in 1861, "for the Union before peace, for I know without union we can have no peace." But while John Scott Harrison was first a Jacksonian and then a war Democrat, Benjamin Harrison, his son, was from the first an ardent and emphatic Republican. As such he received his first public office at the hands of the people and, as such, when the critical moment came, he supported the Government unequivocally and with enthusiasm. When the call to arms came his zest for the daily routine was gone, he chafed under the restraint he placed upon himself, and, before long, as the logical consequence, he was in the army, following the flag.

The story of his enlistment is as dramatic as it is simple. It was after the battle of Pittsburgh Landing, in 1862, and the failure of the North to properly follow up the fruits of that great victory, that Mr. Harrison appeared in the office of Oliver P. Morton, Indiana's famous "War Governor." The governor was pacing his room gloomily and expressed himself as discouraged at the outlook. More troops were needed, and yet enlistments, he complained, were slow ; people followed their private interests and the country was in danger. "What can I do to arouse men to the necessity of the hour?" he asked. The question was direct, and Harrison's reply was equally direct. "Governor," he said, "if I can be of service I will go." And he did go. Leaving the governor's office, he purchased a "soldier cap," engaged a drummer and fifer, flung a flag out of his office window, and began recruiting for his new regiment. Recruits appeared speedily when it was known that "Ben Harrison" was to lead them. Harrison himself hired a Chicago drill-master to teach the regiment tactics, and worked night and day to fill up his ranks. In a month the ranks were filled ; and, in August, 1862, the newly raised Seventieth Regiment Indiana Volunteers, Colonel Benjamin Harrison commanding, was hurried to the front and faced the enemy before Nashville.

The colonel of the Seventieth was a fighter from the start. It was never "go ahead, men!" with him ; it was always "come on, boys!" and, as a result the "boys" all swore by "Little Ben," as they called their colonel, and followed wherever he led. It was thus that, at the head of the Seventieth Indiana, he charged the Confederate ranks at Resaca, was himself the first to scale the bloody parapet, and pluckily held the redoubt until relieved. It was thus that at Cassville and New Hope Church, at Gilgal Church, Kulps Hill, and Kenesaw, "the fight above the clouds," that he led the "boys" to battle, and, as part of Sherman's victorious army, in the Atlanta campaign, held the field so bravely against Hood's army, at Peach Tree Creek, that he won the day and his promotion, being brevetted for his gallantry, brigadier-general. "On every field," said General Joseph Hooker, in recommending this promotion, "when collision came, Colonel Harrison's command vindicated his wisdom as much as his valor."

26

The war over, General Harrison returned to his home and his law practice in Indianapolis, and speedily became one of the leaders in politics and public opinion, in his State. As a member of the National Republican Conventions of 1880 and 1884, his ability and good judgment were recognized by his fellow-Republicans, while his record as a senator was consistent and conservative, patriotic and strong. So it is not to be wondered at that, at the Chicago Convention of 1888, out of the fourteen candidates first ballotted for, Benjamin Harrison's name speedily came to the front, and on the eighth ballot he secured the nomination of the Republican party for President of the United States. In the presidential election in November following, Harrison was elected, carrying every Northern State, except New Jersey and Connecticut, and receiving 233 electoral votes against 168 for Grover Cleveland, his Democratic opponent.

President Harrison was inaugurated on Monday, March 4, 1889, with the usual civic display, and delivered his inaugural in the midst of a rain-storm, standing on the eastern portico of the Capitol. In his address he upheld the principles of protection for native industries and the reform of the civil service ; he approved of the augmentation of the navy, and suggested restriction of immigration, steamship subsidies, and a reform of the electoral laws. His administration was marked by no great measures, and was called to face no great crisis. It was able, patriotic, and American. Such, indeed, had been his record from his entrance into public life. He was, distinctively, an American and a believer in America's "manifest destiny." His devotion to this idea marks all his public utterances. "I am," he said, "a thorough believer in the American test of character. . . . He will not build high who does not build for himself. I believe in the American opportunity which puts the starry sky above every boy's head, and sets his foot upon a ladder which he may climb until his strength gives out." From youth he had been an ardent protectionist, and his favorite theory, "The American market for the American workman," secured him a wide popular following. The famous McKinley Bill of 1890, which decreed a new tariff schedule and stirred up wide-spread controversy, was at once the most notable political measure of his administration and, to a certain extent, the chief factor in his defeat at the polls in the presidential election of 1892.

During his term of office he visited the northern, southern, eastern, and western portions of the United States, his Pacific tour comprising the task of travelling ten thousand miles, and, within the limit of thirty days, delivering one hundred and forty impromptu addresses. His felicity and readiness as an impromptu speaker are indeed almost phenomenal. He is always ready, never labored, always interesting, versatile, patriotic, and tolerant. He seldom repeats himself, though speaking half a dozen times in a day, and he never talks over the heads of his hearers. It is as a practical and popular speech-maker that Benjamin Harrison has been enabled to exert a peculiar and lasting influence as an American executive and public man.

At the Republican National Convention of 1892, held at Minneapolis, on June 7th, Benjamin Harrison was renominated for the presidency, on the sev-

HARRISON RAISING THE AMERICAN COLORS ON THE "NEW YORK."

enth ballot. But at the presidential election in November following he was defeated by his former opponent, ex-President Grover Cleveland, by a majority of 132 in the electoral vote.

Benjamin Harrison's training and experience have all been legal, but, more than that, he is a natural lawyer, quick of comprehension and broad of judgment. He is a natural analyzer, too, and while always logical, is straightforward, simple, and easily understood. These natural gifts made him a careful, conservative, and wise executive, and his record as President of the United States is one which, as time softens the asperities of political dispute and the extravagance of political factions, every American will contemplate with satisfaction and point to with pride, as able, practical, statesmanlike, and American.

Elbridge S. Brooks

GROVER CLEVELAND *

By Clarence Cook

(born 1837)

THE history of our country discovers so many instances of men who have risen from humble beginnings to posts of honor and influence by their own energy, industry, and steadiness of purpose, that a fresh illustration, while always sure of sympathy, no longer causes surprise. But one element of interest always remains : the variety of character which makes each new arrival at the goal an illustration of human capacity different from all that have preceded it. As no two men are alike, and as the conditions of life are infinitely various, the outcome of character and disposition, as affected by circumstances, will also be infinitely varied ; and the discovery that every human experience puts the possibilities of life in a new light, makes, perhaps, the greatest charm of biography.

The life of Grover Cleveland is one that has appealed by its lessons to a large body of his countrymen, without distinction of party, for the plain reason that he is not removed from the mass of men by the possession of extraordinary faculties.   He has no genius, unless we accept Goethe's dictum that genius is only the capacity for hard work ; he has no ornamental accomplishments ; in social intercourse he does not shine by wit, nor charm by humor, and we have too often to regret that tact seems to have been wanting among his natal gifts.   In these respects he is himself one of the " plain people " in whom he seems always to be interested, and whose welfare he has always in view ; and as the plain peo-ple, fortunately, make up the bulk of the world, the example of one of our own number rising, unaided by friends or fortune, to so high a position, has in it a great encouragement.   In spite of political differences, which, after all, are largely fostered by politicians for their own advantage, the people at large are quick to recognize the sterling qualities of honesty, industry, and plain-dealing, and it is by these qualities that Mr. Cleveland's career has been determined.

Although we Americans have—rather ostentatiously, it must be confessed—declared our indifference to ancestry ; that

> " Our boast is not, that we deduce our birth
> From loins enthroned, and rulers of the earth ; "

yet we all have an innate conviction that there is something pleasant in know-ing that we come of good stock ; and indeed it would be strange if we valued that recommendation little for ourselves, as human beings, which we prize so much in the animals that serve us.   And so, although it has been left for others to make the discovery, the fact is not without interest that the American branch of the family to which the president belongs, runs back to 1635, when Moses Cleaveland came to Massachusetts from Ipswich, in Suffolk County, Eng-land.   The spelling Cleaveland is still retained by some of the collateral branches of the family on this side the water, but the form Cleveland was in common use in England, and it was so that John Cleveland, the Royalist poet, wrote the name.   It may be said, in passing, that it would not be without interest to dis-cover, if possible, if there were any connection between the family of John Cleveland and that of Grover Cleveland's English ancestors, for the resemblance between the characters of the two men is striking, and as honorable as it is strik-ing.   As we read John Cleveland's appeals to Cromwell for freedom and immu-nity after the death of the king, to whose cause the poet had so devotedly adhered until that cause was hopelessly lost, we seem to hear the prophecy of that bold-ness, that honesty fearless of consequences, that refusal to withdraw or apologize for sentiments honestly held and openly maintained, which are so characteristic of one who may easily be an offshoot of that vigorous stem.

The President's grandfather, William Cleveland, was a watchmaker doing busi-ness at Westfield, Mass., but on his marriage with Margaret Falley, of Norwich, Conn., he went there to live, and it was there that his son, Richard Falley Cleve-land, was born.   According to the old system, it was decided by his family to make a clergyman of Richard Cleveland, and accordingly after making his terms at Yale College, and studying divinity at Princeton, he entered the ministry ; and having made some preliminary trials, was finally settled in charge of the Presbyterian Church in the village of Caldwell, Essex County, N. J., and in this place his son, Stephen Grover Cleveland, was born, March 18, 1837. The name of Stephen Grover was given out of respect to the memory of a clergyman, Stephen Grover, who preceded his father in the charge of his new parish. When the boy was only four years of age, Richard Cleveland accepted a call to what was then almost the frontier-settlement of Fayetteville, Onondaga County, N. Y. Here the Cleveland family remained for eleven years making the most of life, and winning from the meagre salary of $600 earned by the father, a harvest of cheerful content, of homely comfort, and of unselfish mutual affection that might well be envied by many whose means are far greater. The children were blessed in their parents, and the parents were rewarded by the love and devotion of their children. Later in life, on the day of his election to the governorship of New York, in a letter to his elder brother, the Rev. William N. Cleveland, Grover Cleveland showed where his heart was, for his first words express a quiet regret that his mother's recent death had made it impossible to make her the recipient of his deepest feelings, of his hopes and fears on this important event in his life; and at the close of the letter he again recurs to the theme as if the memory of his mother were a part and parcel of his life.

In 1851, Richard Cleveland, with his wife and nine children, left Fayetteville, for Clinton, Oneida County, N. Y., where he was to act as the agent for the American Home Missionary Society, with a salary of $1,000 a year. But of more importance than this modest increase of pay, was the opportunity the new place offered for giving his children a better education than they had been able to get at Fayetteville. Grover did not leave Fayetteville with the rest of the family, because he had engaged himself for a year with the keeper of a grocery store in the village, where he was to receive the sum of $50 for the first year and $100 for the second. At the end of the first year, however, his father, ambitious for his boy's education, sent for him and placed him at the Academy in Clinton, where he was to be fitted to enter Hamilton College in due time. But this larger opportunity he was not to enjoy. His father received a call to take charge of a church at Holland Patent, a village near Utica, N. Y., and the whole family left their home in Clinton for this place; but only three weeks after their arrival the father died, October 1, 1853, and the wife, with so many of the children as still remained at home, were left to support life as their scanty means enabled them. The mother, evidently a woman of much force of character, remained on the rock where the waves of changing fortune last flung her, and by her own efforts and the willing hands of her children, kept the family together until, her loving duty done by all that remained to her, she died in 1882, living happily long enough to see the beginning of her high hope for her son Grover, fulfilled in his honorable career as Mayor of Buffalo.

Grover Cleveland was now to exchange for a short time the quiet life of a country village for the more stirring experience of life in a great city. His brother William, after leaving Hamilton College, had obtained employment as an instructor in the Institution for the Blind in New York City, where he was the principal of the male teachers.　After the death of his father, he secured for his brother Grover the place of book-keeper and assistant to the superintendent of the asylum.　The boy came to his new place, not only with the good character given him by his brother, then as now a man much respected by his associates, but with the good word of all with whom he had been connected, whether as school-boy or as work-boy.

Grover Cleveland left New York in the autumn of 1854, at the end of his year's engagement at the Institution for the Blind.　He returned to his mother's home for a brief visit, and then, with the hope of making a beginning in the profession of the law, which he for some time intended to take up, he visited some of the towns where his family was known, Syracuse and Utica, in the hope of finding employment ; but as no opening presented itself, he determined to visit Cleveland, a town named for one of his family.　He stopped on his way at Buffalo, to visit an uncle, Lewis F. Allen, a well-known farmer, who published each year a compilation made by himself : "The American Short-Horn Herd-Book." Pleased with his young relative, Mr. Allen persuaded him to remain in Buffalo and assist him in his work ; and thus it happened that Grover Cleveland found himself planted in a city with which in time his fortunes and his fame were to become closely associated ; while, on the other hand, the results of that connection to the city itself were to be far-reaching and of great importance.

By the recommendation of his uncle he obtained a place as office-boy in the office of Bowen & Rogers, one of the principal firms of lawyers in Western New York.　It was thus that he began his legal studies, reading hard in all his odd moments; and in his spare time after office-hours assisting his uncle, with whom at first he lived, in the compilation of the "Herd-Book."　Mr. Parker tells us that the first appearance in print of Grover Cleveland's name is in the "Herd-Book" for 1861, in which Mr. Allen expresses his acknowledgment of "the kindness, industry, and ability of his young friend and kinsman, in correcting and arranging the pedigrees for publication."　Prompt to seize every opportunity for increasing his knowledge of the world about him, and feeling, perhaps, that his uncle's farm in the outskirts of Buffalo was too much like the village he had left, he took rooms with an old schoolmate from Fayetteville in the old Southern Hotel in Buffalo, at that time a resort for drovers and farmers, where his knowledge of their business, obtained in his uncle's employ, brought him into closer acquaintance with at least one division of the "plain people" than could have been gained without that experience.

Grover Cleveland was admitted to the bar in 1859.　He did not at first begin the practice of the law on his own account, but remained for four years longer with his teachers, until he had gained the position of chief clerk.　In 1858, on coming of age, he cast his first vote, giving it to the Democratic party ; but not content with the mere performance of this part of the citizen's duty, "he took his place at the polls and throughout the day distributed ballots by the side of the veterans of his party."　"This habit," says Mr. Parker, "he kept up until his election as governor.　He was never a partisan, but he believed in working

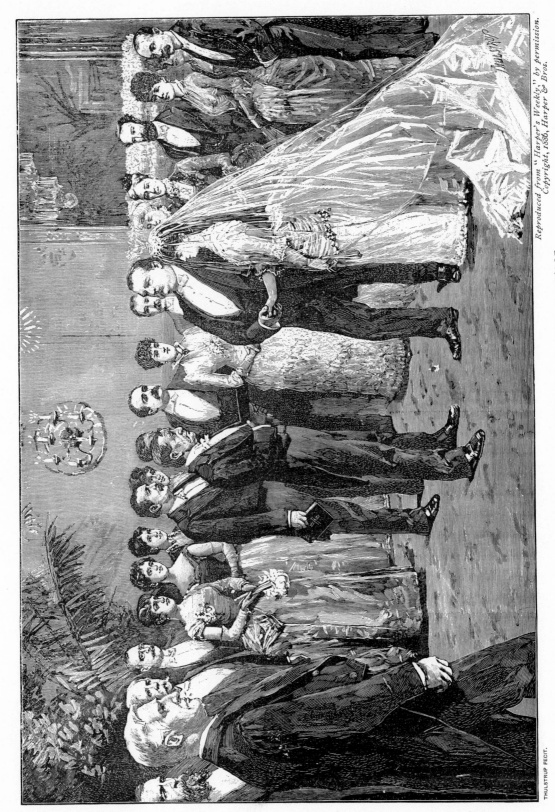

THULSTRUP FECIT.

THE CEREMONY AT GROVER CLEVELAND'S MARRIAGE.

for his party, and he not only worked for it at the polls, but he always marched in the procession whenever a great Democratic demonstration was made."

On January 1, 1863, Mr. Cleveland began his first independent work as a lawyer, and on leaving the office of the firm that had been his teachers and associates, he accepted the office of assistant district attorney of Erie County, to which he had been appointed. For this he gave up a salary of $1,000, and took one of $600, but he did this because he saw that the training and experience of such an office would be worth more to him than money. It was while he held this office that he was drafted into the army, and being convinced that he was more useful in his office than he could be as a soldier, he sent a substitute, borrowing the money for the bounty from his superior, the district attorney. This money, says Mr. Parker, he was not able to pay back until the close of his term as assistant district attorney, and until the war itself was over. Two of his brothers entered the army in 1861, and served through the war.

From this time Mr. Cleveland's rise was rapid, and made by great strides, each new position the result of the satisfactory way in which he had filled the one previously held. He was indeed defeated in his first contest, that for district attorney of Erie County. In 1870 he accepted the nomination of his party for the office of sheriff of Erie County. It was not usual for lawyers to accept this office, and Mr. Cleveland did not take it until after much deliberation and consultation with his party friends. He was finally moved to accept the nomination for the practical reasons that the place would give him leisure for much-needed study in his profession, and that it would also enable him to lay up a little money. He held the office for the full term, and returned to the practice of the law in 1874, becoming a member of the firm of Bass, Cleveland, & Bissell. Mr. Bass was the opponent who had defeated him in the contest for district attorney, and Mr. Bissell is now the Postmaster-General in the cabinet of his former law-partner.

In 1881, Mr. Cleveland was nominated for the office of Mayor of Buffalo, and was elected by a majority of thirty-five hundred, the largest which had ever been given in Buffalo for that office. It was a time of great excitement, for the government of the city had fallen into very bad hands, and in the election of Mr. Cleveland party lines were disregarded to an unusual degree. His fearless and energetic administration of this office ; his resolute refusal to give any support to those fictions of politicians and office-holders by which the citizens in all our great municipalities are robbed of their rights and their money ; his obstinate vetoing of one proposed law after another by which these people hoped to gain their ends—vetos for which he always gave his reasons in the plainest words, meant to be understood by the plainest people—his determination, in short, to be true to his principle declared on taking office, that the affairs of government were to be managed as a man would manage his private business—all this fixed the eyes of the people upon him as a man to be intrusted with still graver responsibilities.

In 1882, Mr. Cleveland was nominated for the high position of Governor of

New York, in opposition to Charles J. Folger, a man of high character, formerly chief justice of the Court of Appeals, and at the time of the contest, secretary of the treasury under President Arthur. For reasons into which we cannot enter here, but which, though purely political, gave good cause for public discontent, Mr. Folger's nomination roused the determined opposition of many of his own party, and this defection, added to the united enthusiasm of the Democracy, insured Mr. Cleveland's election by one hundred and ninety-two thousand eight hundred and fifty-four votes more than were cast for Mr. Folger.

Mr. Cleveland administered the office of governor in such a way as greatly to strengthen the admiration of his party, especially of the better portion of it, in spite of the fact that partisan advantages were often lost by Mr. Cleveland's independent and patriotic action. Nor can it be doubted that his election to the presidency, which followed, was the fruit of the experience the people had had of his character while in the governor's chair. That campaign was one of the most interesting, and we may say, one of the most valuable morally, that has been waged in our day in this country. So far as mere votes were concerned, it was not such a victory as that for the governorship, but in its political meaning, and its influence on the course of our history, it was of the first importance.

At the close of his first term of office as president, Mr. Cleveland was again nominated, but was defeated by his opponent, Mr. Harrison; yet when the time for choosing a successor to Mr. Harrison came round, Mr. Cleveland was again nominated, and was elected, defeating Mr. Harrison in his turn. The vote on this last occasion was so overwhelmingly in favor of the Democratic party as to have amounted virtually to a political revolution; but the limitation and character of this sketch do not permit us to go into a discussion of it. Our purpose has been to show the elements of character that have gone to make the truly extraordinary success that has marked Mr. Cleveland's political life. That success has not been due to genius, nor to social or personal advantages. It has been due to nobler causes; it is the result of sterling and well-tried honesty, of hard and unremitting labor applied to the understanding of every question coming before him for decision, and of a resolute independence; his fixed belief that

> "Because right is right to follow right
> Were wisdom in the scorn of consequence."

Clarence Cook